WOOD FURNITURE

Finishing, Refinishing, Repairing

by James E. Brumbaugh
revised and edited by John Leeke

An Audel® Book

Macmillan Publishing Company
New York

Maxwell Macmillan Canada
Toronto

Maxwell Macmillan International
New York   Oxford   Singapore   Sydney

THIRD EDITION

Macmillan Publishing Company   Maxwell Macmillan Canada, Inc.
866 Third Avenue   1200 Eglinton Avenue East, Suite 200
New York, NY 10022   Don Mills, Ontario M3C 3N1

Macmillan Publishing Company is part of the Maxwell Communication
Group of Companies.

Library of Congress Cataloging-in-Publication Data

Brumbaugh, James E.
    Wood furniture : finishing, refinishing, repairing / by James E.
Brumbaugh. — 3rd ed. / revised by John Leeke.
        p.   cm.
    "An Audel book."
    Includes index.
    ISBN 0-02-517871-7
    1. Furniture finishing. 2. Furniture—Repairing. I. Leeke, John. II. Title.
TT199.4.B76 1992
684.1'043—dc20   91-13108
                                                   CIP

Production services by the Walsh Group, Yarmouth, ME.

Macmillan books are available at special discounts for bulk
purchases for sales promotions, premiums, fund-raising, or
educational use. For details, contact:

> Special Sales Director
> Macmillan Publishing Company
> 866 Third Avenue
> New York, NY 10022

10 9 8 7 6 5 4 3 2 1
Printed in the United States of America

Contents

Foreword

The goal of this bok is to help you expand your knowledge of finishing. Knowledge is made up of two parts: information and experience. This Audel book gives you a foundation of information. As you work at finishing, you gain the experience that builds your knowledge of the trade.

The recent popular recognition of safety and environmental issues demands that even the amateur take a professional approach when it comes to health and safety issues. Throughout the text safety warnings refer to a new chapter on safety. This chapter on fire, health, and environmental safety covers the purchase, use, cleanup, storage, and disposal of finishing materials. Specific methods and lists of guidelines cover the handling of hazardous materials and safety precautions.

Another new chapter on stripping finishes details descriptions of the different types of chemical strippers, how to recognize each by looking at the container, how each type works, and how to use it. This chapter also contains tips for successful stripping, problems, and solutions. Safety and assessing the risks of using these hazardous materials are covered.

The paint and finish industry is going through a period of rapid change due to the new public interest in health and safety issues. Products, product lines, and whole companies are going through major alterations to meet the new regulations that address these issues. Finishers can keep abreast of new developments through the new reference section that lists manufacturers and suppliers, schools and training programs to learn more on refinishing, books and periodicals.

This new edition will be most useful for the amateur or do-it-yourself reader. Professional woodworkers or painters new to furniture finishing and refinishing can use the book as a broad overview of furniture finishing, but will want to move on to other sources of information. Those sources are listed in the new reference section.

The editor for this revision, John Leeke, is an experienced writer as well as a practicing tradesman and contractor. His practical experience ranges from traditional woodworking and furniture building skills to modern workshop practice. His main focus is the preservation of historic architecture, which includes solving many paint and finish problems. Leeke has written many articles on restoration and finishes and is a contributing editor for professional journals and books. This broad experience, coupled with that of other professionals, provides a wide range of top-notch resources, many of which are referenced at the end of this book.

A Note from the Revisions Editor

While working on this revision I talked with and visited the shops of several professional finishers. One phrase kept coming up in these discussions. As they showed me their methods they would often say, "Now here's the trick," of this or that finish. As if it took "magic" to be successful at finishing. Well, it does and it doesn't. Magic is what you don't truly understand about how something works.

You can learn a lot (perhaps half) of what you need to know about finishing from books. If you stop there, you probably do not know enough to do successful finishing. To progress you have to dig in and try your hand at it. After considerable experience learning from your mistakes you will know more. Most of your finishes will be successful. You will notice that some things work and you can call them the tricks. But you don't really know why they work.

You can pick up more tips and tricks from magazines and videotapes, but you will have to really study finishing to learn how and why finishes work. That's why I've included the chapter on finish technology, the reference section at the end of the book, and suggestions to use the library. This type of fundamental knowledge will help you move beyond dependence on magic to a more professional understanding of what you're doing. As your skills grow you will depend less on the tricks and more on your knowledge.

To gain the subtle nuances of finishing expertise, you will want to work with people who know more than you do and who are willing to share. The reference section at the end of this book lists several workshop and educational opportunities.

New products and the variability of wood and old finishes assure that no one ever knows everything about finishing. Successful finishers continue to study and learn.

Please feel free to write to me if you have any comment on this current edition. Your ideas and remarks will be used as the next revision is developed.

John Leeke
RR1 Box 2947
Sanford, Maine 04073

Acknowledgments

The knowledge of the following professionals who helped with this revision is matched only by their willingness to share what they have learned through costly research and diligent effort.

Thanks to David Winslow, furniture conservator of Jorgensen Antiques, Wells, Maine, for his review of the previous edition. Thanks to Bob Flexner, furniture restorer, of The Workbench, Norman, Oklahoma, for his knowledgeable and practical approach to furniture restoration and refinishing.

Pat Hardy and Susan Amons of Fancy Painters, Inc., Biddeford, Maine, provided photos of their painted furniture. Marie Locke and Liz Moberg of Ralff & Sons, Portland, Maine, demonstrated marbleizing.

Special thanks to Jody Marx, research assistant, in Tucson, Arizona.

CHAPTER I

Introduction to Wood Finishing

Furniture is a cultural product and its quality and design have long been related to the ascendancy or decline of a civilization. In this respect it is similar to styles of dress, types of pottery, architecture, and other elements of the material world with which people surround themselves. To an archaeologist or historian, these are clear indicators of cultural change and serve to supplement and verify historical data. In the absence of historical data, these cultural products may be the only means by which the development of a civilization can be charted.

There are many very excellent examples of furniture dating from the earliest historical periods. Some pieces have been obtained intact from tombs or reconstructed from remains discovered at archaeological sites. Other designs are known to us because some unknown artist saw fit to include them in a fresco or painting or in the design on a piece of pottery. All of our records, whether historical or archaeological, indicate that the development of furniture designs has been uneven, and is closely related to the level of civilization.

A high level of civilization is often paralleled by innovation and experimentation in furniture design. This is particularly true during periods of economic affluence. The histories of the Roman,

Chinese, and Egyptian civilizations provide us with ample evidence of the periodic fluctuations in the quality of furniture design. Western civilization presents us with more recent examples of this close parallel between the quality of furniture craftsmanship and the ascendancy of a civilization. The period extending from the seventeenth to the nineteenth centuries in England, France, and other countries of Europe witnessed not only the development of vast colonial empires and rapid economic growth, but also a tremendously varied development in furniture design. Some of our finest furniture styles go back to this period in European history.

Along with the developments in the structural design of furniture, one can also trace changes in the way furniture has been finished and decorated. Sometimes the finish and structural design will complement each other; at other times they will strongly conflict and produce a piece of furniture that is absolutely abominable.

An example of the way structural design, finish, and decorative effect can complement one another and result in an especially fine piece of furniture is a well-executed chair of the Regency style (1793–1830) (Fig. 1–1). Much of this furniture was lacquered, frequently in black, and trimmed with gilding. Unfortunately, this black and gold combination became so popular with the public that it was used too extensively. The result was that it spoiled the overall appearance of furniture that was otherwise well designed.

It is always essential that a proper balance be maintained between the finish, including any decorative effect, and the structural design. One should not overwhelm the other. This is an important

Fig. 1-1. Regency chair (1793-1830). *(Courtesy Reliance Universal, Inc.)*

point to remember, because there is a strong tendency for the beginner to become overly enthusiastic, particularly when decorating a piece of furniture. Too much gilding or striping, or the use of stencils that are too large or elaborate, will ruin the effect one is trying to create.

Wood Finishing

Wood finishing can be either the most satisfying or the most frustrating of experiences for the beginner. It is both an art and a skill, the latter being acquired largely through experience and practice. However, with careful attention to detail and an understanding of the basic fundamentals of wood finishing, the beginner will achieve considerable success.

Placing some sort of finish on the wood surfaces of furniture dates from the earliest periods of history. Whether these first wood finishes were intended primarily as decoration or as a means of preserving the wood is unknown. The early Egyptian varnishes and Oriental lacquers probably combined both functions. On the other hand, the hand-rubbed sweat finishes prevalent in Europe prior to the seventeenth century provided little more than a decorative effect for the wood.

Modern wood finishes are designed to be both protective and decorative. The nature or extent of the protection provided by the finish depends upon the type used, which is usually, but not always, determined by the intended service usage of the piece of furniture. A shellac finish, for example, does not provide the toughness and durability of varnish, enamel, or lacquer. It is therefore not advisable to use shellac on table and desk tops, children's furniture, chair arms, and other surfaces subject to hard wear. On the other hand, shellac finishes are much easier for the beginner to apply, and are often used for this reason. It should be apparent at this point that the selection of a finish is determined by a number of interrelated factors. Since some of these factors, such as ease of application and the degree of toughness, may be conflicting in nature, the worker must choose among the best possible combinations when selecting the most suitable finish to use.

Some of the factors in selecting a wood finish include the following:

1. Ease of application,
2. Cost,
3. Intended service conditions,
4. Appearance desired.

Ease of Application

This factor is generally of primary consideration to the beginner. The experienced worker will be familiar with the problems involved when working with various finishes, and will approach each accordingly. The beginner should be cautioned against placing too much importance on the ease of application. Although much has been said about the difficulty of working with such finishes as varnish or lacquer, these techniques can be learned with a relatively short practice period.

Cost

Although the better-quality finishing materials are not always the higher priced, you will generally discover that the better ones cost more. It is quite discouraging to find that the finish you bought at a bargain has resulted in a curiosity you prefer to keep hidden in the attic. On the other hand, do not rush to purchase the most expensive item in stock at your nearest retail supplier. If you are acquainted with the people working there, ask their advice. They will usually be quite honest with you and try to supply you with the finishing materials that will best fill your needs.

Intended Service Conditions

How is the piece of furniture to be used? In other words, to what specific service conditions will the wood surface be subjected? These are very important questions, for they bear heavily upon your ultimate selection. Furniture that will be subjected to rough use should be well-protected by a tough finish.

Appearance Desired

As a general rule, clear finishes (e.g., lacquer, varnish, shellac, etc.) are used over wood surfaces that have a particularly attractive grain pattern and/or color. The finish is designed not only to protect and preserve the wood, but also to enhance it. The opaque and semi-opaque finishes are usually applied to surfaces with unattractive grain patterns, poor colors, or various defects that would detract from the overall appearance. Their purpose is to obscure or conceal these surfaces.

Sometimes another, more expensive type of wood can be imitated by applying finish that will give this appearance. For example, white pine can be finished to imitate walnut; basswood or gum to imitate cherry, and so on. Special decorative effects can be obtained through antiquing, gilding, inlaying, and other special finishing and decorating techniques. Determine the type of appearance you desire within the limitations of the wood with which you are working, and proceed from there.

Furniture Kits, Plans, and Cabinet Woods

Furniture kits are available from a number of mail-order houses whose advertisements are regularly found in periodicals devoted to the home craftsperson and home workshop. These furniture kits are primarily reproductions of pieces from the American Colonial period. Examples range in complexity from the rather simple canopied cradle to the more complex corner chair, dropleaf table, or settee. These furniture kits consist of parts made from higher-quality woods (that is to say, cabinet woods) than the common variety of assembled unfinished furniture sold in many retail outlets. They assemble without great difficulty and present an excellent appearance when finished.

Furniture plans are also available at a modest price from the same mail-order houses. These are often full-size plans that do not require enlargement from a smaller size. As a result, the possibility of making an error in the pattern is practically eliminated. The better plans will include a perspective sketch indicating how the parts are to be assembled, as well as a complete list of materials and hardware.

Constructing a piece of furniture from a plan requires not only considerable woodworking skill, but also a source for fine cabinet woods. Many of the same mail-order houses that sell furniture kits and plans also offer a wide variety of cabinet woods and veneers. Moreover, a complete line of furniture hardware and trim in both contemporary and period styles can also be purchased (Fig. 1–2).

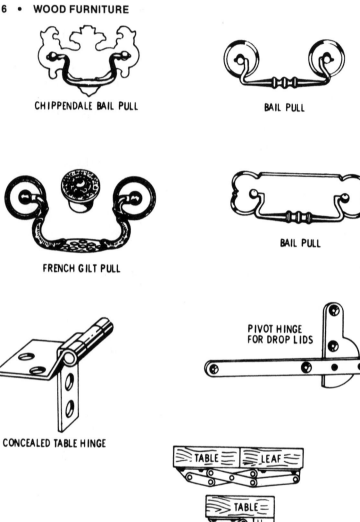

CHIPPENDALE BAIL PULL

BAIL PULL

FRENCH GILT PULL

BAIL PULL

CONCEALED TABLE HINGE

PIVOT HINGE
FOR DROP LIDS

TABLE LEAF

TABLE

LEAF

DROP LEAF TABLE LAZY TONG HINGE

Fig. 1-2. Various types of furniture hardware.

Finally, a number of different styles of furniture legs are available to the home craftsperson. These are generally made from fine hardwoods in sizes ranging from 4 to 28 inches. Most are mounted by means of top plates or hanger bolts (Fig. 1–3).

As was previously mentioned, furniture assembled from kits is generally made from fine hardwoods. The quality of the wood is such that knots and other surface imperfections are relatively rare

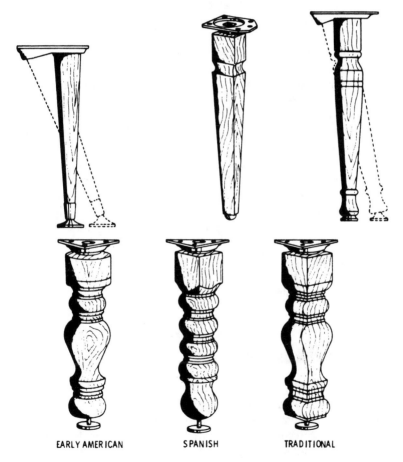

EARLY AMERICAN   SPANISH   TRADITIONAL

Fig. 1-3. Examples of furniture legs available from mail-order houses.

when compared to the woods used in the cheaper pieces of assembled unfinished furniture. This results in a much better appearance when a finish is applied. Furthermore, the opportunity to use transparent finishes is both increased and encouraged.

Assembled Unfinished Furniture

There are two general categories of assembled unfinished furniture. One category consists of pieces that are usually made from pine (Fig. 1–4). The wood is cheap, commonly contains knotholes and other surface imperfections, and finishing nails are used in the construction. It is this type of assembled unfinished furniture that is so easily obtainable in paint stores, hobby stores, and other retail outlets that are geared to the needs of the home craftsperson.

The second category of assembled unfinished furniture is obtained from individual cabinetmakers and small furniture factories that specialize in a specific period or piece of furniture (e.g. Windsor chairs). These are of a higher quality than the cheaper pine furniture, and will be somewhat more expensive. The higher expense is generally offset by the fact that applying a finish is easier in the long run because the wood will have far fewer surface imperfections to correct. The major problem in obtaining these better-quality pieces is locating a cabinetmaker or some other source that produces them. These sources usually do not advertise and will require some effort to locate. Inquiries can be made at furniture stores that sell the better-quality lines, and at local cabinet shops.

Antiques and Reproductions

It is probably the dream of many amateurs eventually to obtain and refinish a genuine antique. If you are fortunate enough to obtain one of them, I would strongly recommend placing it in the hands of a professional finisher. A furniture store or department store that handles the higher-quality, more expensive furniture lines generally sends any pieces it wants finished to a professional who specializes in this kind of work. Since these professionals are

Fig. 1-4. Examples of unfinished furniture.

independent craftspeople who are employed on a contractual basis, the store will usually give their names and addresses.

Actually, finding an antique that needs refinishing is much more difficult than one would imagine. Antique dealers frequently do their own refinishing, so they are not a very promising source, and the piece certainly will not be a bargain. It would probably be more profitable to look for antiques at used furniture stores, Goodwill stores, Salvation Army stores, or junk dealers. Auctions and tax sales occasionally provide good antique pieces.

Locating antiques that require refinishing is difficult, due not only to their scarcity, but also to the problem of identifying them. The word "antique" can mean many different things to different people. For example, the average person who does not possess an extensive knowledge of furniture will probably use the term very loosely, and identify any old piece of furniture as an antique. The antique dealer, on the other hand, is more selective when applying the term. Moreover, the dealer recognizes that antiques will vary in quality and value even when they come from the same period. A good genuine antique is a period piece that dates from about the middle of the nineteenth century or before, and is generally an original made by a noted cabinetmaker of a particular period. It will also be somewhat rare, well-built (though it may be in a state of disrepair when you obtain it), and aesthetically pleasing. This is an admittedly very loose definition of "antique," and I have no doubt that some will take issue with one or more aspects of it. In any event, it will have to serve our purpose here.

Unless you have a fairly extensive knowledge of antiques, you will be confronted with the problem of distinguishing them from restorations, imitations, and reproductions. A genuine antique should have all, or nearly all, of its original parts. This includes not only the wood portions but also the hardware. A missing leg, chair slat, drawer knob, or other item may be replaced without the particular piece of furniture losing its status as an antique if the replacements are kept to a minimum and are of the same material and style as the original. Extensive restoration results in a piece of furniture that is greatly reduced in value, because the extent of its restoration has produced a copy or reproduction of the original. In other words, not enough of the original antique remains to justify identifying it as such.

Age is frequently accepted as a basic criterion for identifying a piece of furniture as an antique. However, this is only one of several factors. Recognition as an original of a particular cabinetmaker is also extremely important. Every furniture style has had its imitators, many of them contemporaries of the better-known cabinetmakers. Sometimes their imitations were of very poor quality; sometimes quite excellent.

The fact that a piece of furniture is an imitation, even a poor one, does not necessarily mean that it is not an antique. It is certainly not as valuable as an original, nor is it particularly sought after by the sophisticated collector. However, the older the imitation, the greater the possibility that it is a handcrafted item. This in itself lends some value to it and distinguishes the piece from later, factory-produced furniture.

Reproductions and imitations are not exactly the same thing, although they may result in two pieces of furniture that are identical. It is probably a matter of ethics. An imitation is an attempt to copy another cabinetmaker's work and pass it off as theirs and thereby gain financial reward if the deception is successful. A reproduction, on the other hand, is a reproduced copy of an original, with no attempt made to conceal this fact from the buyer. In fact, a reproduction is almost always advertised as such.

Second-Hand Furniture

There is a great deal of good second-hand furniture that is excellent for refinishing. These are not antiques and are not especially valuable, but many second-hand pieces of furniture are well-constructed and are made from good hardwoods. A few minor repairs and a new finish will often work wonders, and you will have added an interesting piece of furniture to your home. However, the value of such furniture is erratic and not easily predictable. The market value for certain pieces may increase with the passage of time. Predicting which ones will increase in value requires a good knowledge of furniture and the ability to foresee future demand.

Finishing Schedules

All through this book you will encounter the term "finishing schedule." Each schedule is a series of instructions given in the form of an ordered listing of the steps to be followed in applying a specific finish.

Follow these steps in the order established by the schedule. As you gain experience, you will probably change certain portions of a schedule you are using because you will find that some procedures work better than others. This is a perfectly acceptable practice. Never feel bound by a finishing schedule to a form of blind obedience. Learn through experimentation. Alter your finishing schedules in accordance with what you learn. Keep written notes on your experiments and develop your own finishing schedules.

There are hundreds of finishing schedules available to the wood finisher. Entire books have been written on the subject. Those finishing schedules included in this book are offered simply as examples for the beginner. As you gain experience in wood finishing, I would suggest keeping a card file of those finishing schedules that have proven most successful.

Types of Finishes

All wood finishes can be grouped within one of three major categories:

1. Transparent finishes,
2. Opaque finishes,
3. Semiopaque finishes.

A *transparent finish* (also referred to as a *clear* or *natural finish*) is one that reveals the grain, and is usually the natural color of the wood. It is added to the surface to protect and enhance the beauty of the wood, not obscure or conceal it. Examples of transparent finishes include: (1) shellac, (2) varnish, (3) lacquer, (4) wax, (5) penetrating oil stain, and (6) boiled linseed oil.

An *opaque finish* is designed to obscure the wood surface completely, usually because the wood is particularly unattractive. Examples of opaque finishes include: (1) pigmented shellac, (2) pigmented lacquer, (3) enamel, and (4) paint.

A *semiopaque finish* gives the appearance of being transparent, but really is not. In almost every case, the wood surface is either partially or completely obscured. Examples include: (1) a clear finish mixed with pigment, or (2) a pigmented wiping stain.

Testing

Always test a finishing or refinishing procedure on a small area before proceeding with the whole job. The purpose of this testing is to determine if the products you intend to use will do what you expect, and to develop your skills in using them. Once you have considerable experience using particular products on certain types of furniture, you may be able to proceed without testing, depending on your knowledge gained from past projects.

Testing is particularly easy when finishing new furniture. Just use a sample board of the same wood the furniture was made of.

For refinishing old furniture, use an inconspicuous spot or area. Some furniture, like tables, may have one type of finish on the top and a different one on the legs. You will want to test each, although it is difficult to find an inconspicuous spot on the top of a table. Do table tops and other important work after you have had enough experience to judge the results before you begin. It is fun to learn from small mistakes and frustrating, or worse, to learn from big ones.

Compatibility

Various products are used to build up a complete finish. The products used in each layer must be compatible with each other. If they are not compatible, the finish may fail immediately, by not hardening, for example. Or failure may not occur until months or years later, by cracking or peeling, for example. When in doubt about compatibility, stick with one manufacturer's products for that project, and always follow the manufacturer's recommendations.

CHAPTER 2

Finishing Tools and Supplies

The tools and materials used in wood finishing can be as limited in scope as a retail finishing kit purchased for a specific job, or as varied as a completely equipped shop will require to do satisfactorily any number of different jobs. The purpose of this chapter is to give as complete a description as possible of the many different types of tools and materials available to the wood finisher. It will be your task to select among them those items required for your specific needs. Only you can properly make this selection.

The Work Area

Ideally, the work area should be free from dust, low in humidity, and have a room temperature ranging from 65° to 75°F. Temperatures extending beyond this range tend to affect adversely the application of the finish. In houses, basements often provide the best work areas but hazardous fumes can find their way to the living space upstairs. Garages are safer, but frequently suffer from fluctuating humidity and temperature, and from dust in the air.

The work area should always be kept well ventilated. Many finishing materials and supplies give off strong fumes that can be quite unpleasant and even harmful, if inhaled too long.

You should also provide yourself with enough space to work comfortably. The work area should be sufficiently isolated to prevent other activities from interfering with your project. Ideally, a finishing work area will be a separate room. The door to the room can then be shut and wet finishes allowed to dry for the required period of time without fear of accidental marring. This is particularly true where children are present.

If it is impossible for you to locate your work area in a separate room, try to separate it from other areas either by partitions or by about three to four feet of space. Once again, the prime consideration is to establish a work area that will remain undisturbed by other activities. The worst situation is one in which you must constantly put away your tools, materials, and the piece you are working on.

Some finishing books recommend applying certain types of finishes, bleaches, and other coatings outdoors. The principal concern here, of course, is adequate ventilation for materials that are harmful when inhaled. However, you should take into consideration the fact that you will run the risk of dust and dirt blowing onto the wet surface before it has had a chance to dry. One factor should be weighed against the other. If your indoors work area has adequate ventilation, I would recommend working there.

Adequate storage facilities for the finishing tools, materials, and supplies are also extremely important. These storage facilities should be within easy reach of the work area. They should also be a safe distance from heat sources. Remember that many finishing materials and supplies are extremely flammable.

See the chapter on safety for more on work area and storage.

Protective Clothing

Always wear protective clothing when stripping or applying finishes. Old clothing is a must. No matter how careful you try to be, you will eventually, perhaps inevitably, spill or drop something on your clothes, or carelessly wipe a sleeve or another part of your clothing across a wet surface.

Some people have skin that is extremely sensitive to the various finishing supplies. Selecting a comfortable pair of rubber gloves

VINYL-COATED GLOVES

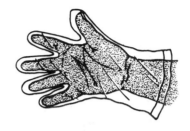

DISPOSABLE POLYETHYLENE GLOVE

Fig. 2-1. Examples of protective gloves. *(Courtesy Singer Safety Products)*

(Fig. 2-1) will often eliminate skin irritations and discomfort. These can be purchased in most hardware or paint supply stores. Filter masks (Figs. 2-2 and 2-3) are strongly recommended, especially when spraying surfaces with paint or other finishes. Inhaling these fumes can make a person ill. In some cases, the fumes are so toxic they can prove extremely dangerous. This is particularly true in the case of oxalic acid (used in bleaching wood).

Fig. 2-2. Respirator-type mask recommended for spraying. *(Courtesy Dockson Company)*

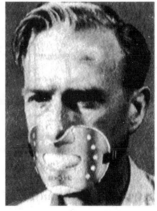

Fig. 2-3. A protective face mask equipped with cotton pad filters. *(Courtesy Dockson Company)*

See the chapter on safety for more on protecting your person.

Health and Safety Measures

As already mentioned, many finishing materials are potentially dangerous to the user's health or safety, since they contain substances that are flammable and that can cause severe irritation or even damage to the skin, eyes and lung tissues. It is therefore necessary to take every precaution to protect yourself from these harmful effects. *Always* read the manufacturer's health and safety warnings on the container and *follow them to the letter*.

Bleaches can be particularly dangerous when not used correctly. Bleach in an undiluted solution will not only attack and destroy clothing fibers, but will also severely irritate the skin. Wearing old clothing and gloves is therefore especially important when working with a bleach. Some kind of eye protection should also be used because bleaches sometimes splatter. If the bleach comes in contact with the skin, wash it off *immediately* with water. Finally, bleach should be applied to bare wood *only*. When a bleach is applied over a finish (especially shellac, varnish, or lacquer), a chemical reaction resulting in spontaneous combustion may occur.

From time to time you will find it necessary to heat a finishing solution in order to prepare it for use—for example, boiled linseed oil. This is usually mixed on a one-to-one basis with a flammable solvent (e.g., turpentine) and then heated to a predetermined temperature. *Always* do any of this type of heating in a double boiler. *Never* attempt to heat a finishing solution in a single container over an open flame or electric heating coil. The can containing the finishing material should be inserted into the container containing the boiling water (Fig. 2–4). Any spatter from the heated finishing material will then drop into the boiling water and not onto the heating coils or flame.

See the chapter on safety for more on health and safety measures.

Tack Rags and Cloths

Soft, clean, lint-free cloths are used at every stage in the finishing schedule to dust the surface lightly after each coat has thor-

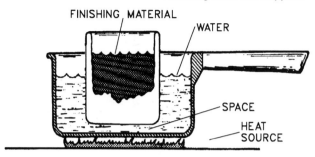

Fig. 2-4. Heating finishing materials.

oughly dried. Cheesecloth, muslin, and lint-free cotton cloths are the most widely used in finishing.

Cheesecloth is frequently used to make tack rags, although other types of cloth can be substituted. The purpose of a tack rag is to pick up any dust or sanding particles that might fall on the surface. Dust, lint, and other particles trapped in a finish will result in a very unsightly and unprofessional appearance. This is a major problem encountered by the finisher, especially when working with varnish. If the problem becomes too severe, the surface will have to be stripped and refinished. The tack rag thus is a very useful tool to the finisher.

Tack rags can be purchased in most paint and hardware stores, or can easily be made from a piece of cheesecloth (Fig. 2–5). If you decide to make your own tack rags, be sure that the cloth is clean. Store your rags in a tightly closed glass jar. The lid of the storage container must be tight enough to keep the tack rag moist. Never allow the tack rag to dry out, or it will be useless. When it appears to be drying, use the steps illustrated in Fig. 2–5 to remoisten it. Tack rags purchased from paint and hardware stores (or mail-order houses such as Minnesota Woodworkers of Minneapolis) are chemically treated so that they will always remain soft and tacky; at least, this is the manufacturer's claim.

Burlap is frequently used to remove excess filler by rubbing across the grain of the wood (Fig. 2–6). The burlap should be clean, dry, and folded into a pad about the size of the hand.

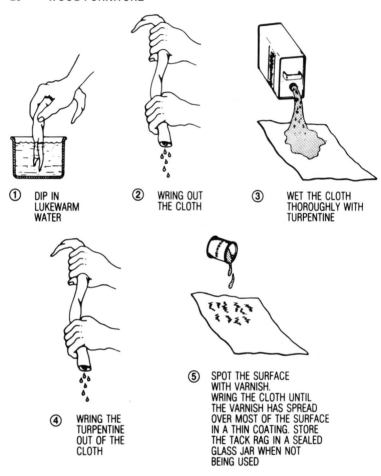

① DIP IN LUKEWARM WATER

② WRING OUT THE CLOTH

③ WET THE CLOTH THOROUGHLY WITH TURPENTINE

④ WRING THE TURPENTINE OUT OF THE CLOTH

⑤ SPOT THE SURFACE WITH VARNISH. WRING THE CLOTH UNTIL THE VARNISH HAS SPREAD OVER MOST OF THE SURFACE IN A THIN COATING. STORE THE TACK RAG IN A SEALED GLASS JAR WHEN NOT BEING USED

Fig. 2–5. A process used in making a tack rag.

Sandpaper

Sandpaper is a coated abrasive available in a number of different types, sizes, and grits (Fig. 2–7). There is a sandpaper to meet the requirements of almost every type of sanding application.

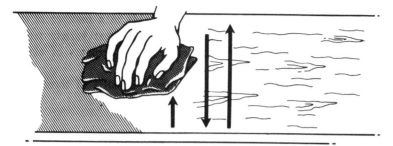

Fig. 2-6. Removing excess filler with burlap.

Fig. 2-7. Examples of three grades of sandpaper. *(Courtesy Minnesota Mining and Mfg. Co.)*

A coated abrasive such as sandpaper consists of three principal parts:

1. The abrasive mineral,
2. The adhesive (bonding agent),
3. The backing.

The abrasive mineral acts as the cutting agent. It may be of natural origin (flint, garnet, or emery) or artificially produced (aluminum oxide or silicon carbide). Garnet paper is recommended for use in furniture finishing, although other types may also be used. Table 2–1 lists the various abrasive minerals and gives some of their major characteristics.

The mineral grains used in the manufacture of sandpaper are obtained by reducing rock-size chunks under great pressure to the small particles that are bonded to the backing. Most mineral grains are separated according to size by passing them over a series of screens, each having different-sized holes. This process produces the very coarse to very fine grades. A water sedimentation or air-flotation process is used to produce the extra fine and super fine

Table 2-1. Comparative Qualities of Abrasive Materials

Type of Mineral	Color	Cutting Power	Durability	Uses
Flint	Grayish-White to Tan	Poor to Fair	Short	Removing Paint, Minor Sanding Operations
Garnet	Red to Reddish-Brown	Good	Long	All Types of Woodworking and Wood Finishing
Emery	Black	Poor	Short	Woodworking, Wood Finishing, Metal Finishing
Aluminum Oxide	Reddish-Brown or White	Good to Excellent	Long	Woodworking, Metal Finishing
Silicon Carbide	Bluish-Black	Good to Excellent	Long	Woodworking, Metal Finishing

grades. The *grit size* of each grade of sandpaper is the basis for its identification.

Grit sizes can be expressed by the older, arbitrarily assigned numbering system (0, 2/0, 3/0, 4/0, etc.), by the modern two- and three-digit system based on the mesh number (60, 80, 100, etc.), or by descriptive terms (fine, very fine, extra fine, etc.). A comparison of these three systems is shown in Table 2–2.

Paper or cloth are the two most common types of backing used for sandpaper. Fiber backing and two types of combination back-

Table 2-2. Comparison of Sandpaper Grit Sizes

Grit Sizes		General Use
Ultra Fine	2000 1500 1200 1000 600 500		Sanding Finishes, Touch up, and Matching Gloss
Extra Fine	400 360 320 280	10/0 9/0 8/0	 Sanding Finishes
Very Fine	240 220 180	7/0 6/0 5/0	Sanding Finishes Sanding Finishes Sanding Finishes
Fine	150 120 100	4/0 3/0 2/0	Sanding Finishes, Intermediate Coats Sanding Finishes, Intermediate Coats Sanding Finishes, Intermediate Coats
Medium	80 60	1/0 1/2	Intermediate Coats, Rough Sanding Intermediate Coats, Rough Sanding
Coarse	50 40 36	1 1 1/2 2	Rough Sanding Rough Sanding Rough Sanding
Very Coarse	30 24 20	2 1/2 3 3 1/2	Rough Sanding
Extra Coarse	16 12	4 4 1/2	

ings (paper and cloth, fiber and cloth) are also used. Paper backing is available in four different weights: A-weight, C-weight, D-weight, and E-weight. A-weight backing paper is used to make fine-grade grit sandpaper. It is also the lightest and most pliable grade of sandpaper.

Cloth backing is available in two weights, J-weight and X-weight, the former having a lightness and flexibility similar to A-weight paper backing.

Some backings are waterproof, so that the paper can be used in either dry or wet (with oil, water, etc.) sanding operations. These will be so marked by the manufacturer.

Sanding Blocks

Sanding blocks used to hold the sandpaper are available commercially, or can be made in the home workshop. The commercial variety (Fig. 2–8) are usually made of hard rubber, plastic, or metal. However, it is often preferable to make your own

Fig. 2–8. Examples of commercially available sanding blocks.

sanding block, because then you can design it to fit your specific needs.

A sanding block can be made from a piece of hardwood cut to the size you require, a piece of rubber, or a felt pad. The last two are excellent backings for sanding curved surfaces because they are flexible and will bend to conform to the surface curvature. If hardwood is used for the sanding block, a piece of felt should be inserted between the sandpaper and the wood block (Fig. 2–9). Otherwise, you will run the risk of scratching and marring the wood surface with the hard edge of the sanding block.

Electric Sanders

A portable electric sander (Fig. 2–10) can be very useful for sanding long frame pieces and for removing paint or other finishes. These machine sanders are available in a number of sizes. Smaller-size machines are recommended for finishing work.

Sanders can also be classified according to their method of operation. The principal methods of operation are:

1. Rotating band or belt,
2. A rotating disk,
3. An oscillating surface which may be either orbital or in-line.

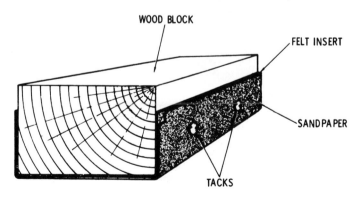

WOOD BLOCK

FELT INSERT

SANDPAPER

TACKS

Fig. 2–9. Sanding block with felt insert.

A

B

C

Fig. 2-10. Portable electric sanders. Belt sander (A) removes material quickly. Random orbital sander (B) will not leave circular scratches. Foam pad (C) allows sanding of curved surfaces. *(Courtesy Porter Cable)*

The random orbital is the most desirable for finishing work because it seldom leaves marks on the surface.

Steel Wool

Steel wool is available in seven different grades, ranging from coarse to super fine (Table 2–3). As an abrasive, it offers certain advantages over sandpaper. For example, it has much less tendency to scratch the surface, it is easier to clean, it can always be used wet, it will produce a finer and smoother surface, and it is so flexible that it can reach into corners, cracks, and carvings where sandpaper cannot. A principal disadvantage of using steel wool is that it sheds fine metal particles during the rubbing operation. These particles must be completely removed before proceeding with the next step in the finishing schedule. Unfortunately, they are harder to detect than the wood particles left by sanding.

Steel wool can be used either wet or dry, although it is usually the latter. The No. 3, No. 0, No. 000, and No. 0000 grades are used for dry rubbing in wood finishing. Both the No. 3 and No. 0 grades are used for preliminary smoothing operations in which the wood surface is prepared for the finishes. The No. 000 grade is commonly used between the various steps in the finishing schedule. No. 0000 (super fine) is used in the last step in the finishing schedule *before* the final finishing coat is applied. It also has other special uses, such

Table 2-3. Steel Wool Grades

Grade	Quality	Approximately Strand Size
No. 3	Coarse	.003″
No. 2	Medium Coarse	.0015″
No. 1	Medium	.001″
No. 0	Fine	.0008″
No. 00	Very Fine	.0005″
No. 000	Extra Fine	.0003″
No. 0000	Super Fine	.0002″

as producing a dull sheen on a lacquer finish or buffing a waxed surface.

No. 0 grade steel wool can be used wet (soaked in paint remover) to remove paint or varnish. The No. 0000 (super fine) grade is excellent with linseed oil or mineral spirits for adding special touches to finishes.

Common steel wool has oil added to it to prevent rust. This oil can contaminate some finishes. Oil-free steel wools are available to eliminate the problem.

Cabinet Scrapers and Hand Scrapers

Some finishers use a cabinet scraper and hand scraper to prepare a flat wood surface *prior* to the sanding operation. Scrapers are planelike tools used in wood preparation when large amounts of material have to be removed from the surface, particularly when this cannot be accomplished satisfactorily with a plane (e.g., on a hard, cross-grained wood). The cabinet scraper (Fig. 2–11) is

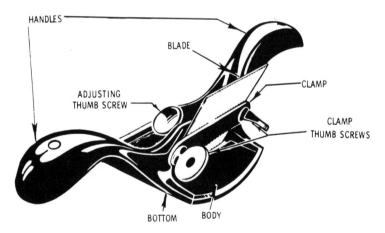

Fig. 2–11. A typical cabinet scraper. In operation, the blade springs backward, thereby opening the mouth and allowing the shavings to pass through. As soon as the working pressure is released, the blade springs back to its normal position.

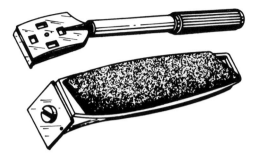

Fig. 2–12. Commercially-available hand scrapers.

used initially for the coarser work, and is followed by the hand scraper, which is designed to produce an even smoother surface.

Hand scrapers (Fig. 2–12) are designed to provide a number of different blade adjustments for cutting. Some cabinet scrapers are provided with reversible blades, one end for fast scraping and the other for smooth finishing. Because there are a number of different designs on the market, you will have to base your selection on your own particular needs. Remember: The cabinet scraper will not work well on soft woods, because it will shave the wood too deeply. Both cabinet scrapers and hand scrapers work most effectively on the moderately hard to hard woods. Do not confuse the term "hard wood" with "hardwood." They do not mean the same thing. See Chapter 3, *Types of Wood.*

Sharpening Scrapers

The unmounted hand scraper is simply a rectangular steel blade, whose cutting edges are formed by a surface at right angles to the sides. (Fig. 2–13 and 2–14) Quicker cutting is secured by having the cutting edge more acute, but more labor is required to keep it sharp. The cutting edge is sharpened by filing or grinding. For smooth work the roughness of the edge may be removed by an oil stone but the rougher edge will cut faster. In cutting, the scraper is inclined slightly forward.

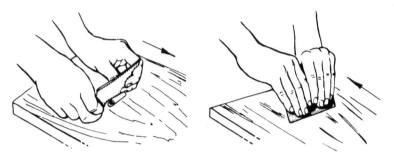

Fig. 2-13. A hand scraper and its method of use. In operation, the hand scraper is pushed or pulled, thus removing surface irregularities in the work; when properly used, it provides the work with a smooth and glossy finish.

To Sharpen Scraper Blade for Heavy Work—A good method of sharpening the scraper so as to avoid too frequent use of the oil stone is as follows:

1. File cutter to a keen edge, removing wire edge with a coarse, medium oil stone.

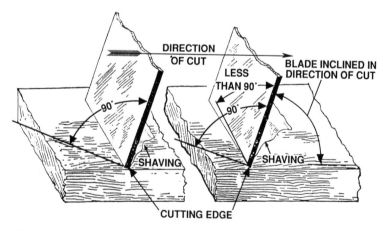

Fig. 2-14. Scraper with normal (90°) cutting edge and acute (less than 90°) cutting edge, showing position of scraper in cutting.

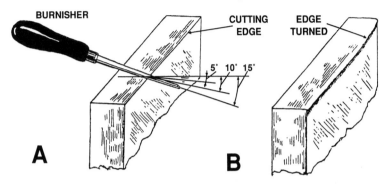

Fig. 2-15. Application of burnisher in turning the edge of a scraper after filing and honing. (A) shows angles at which burnisher should be held. The edge is usually turned in two or three strokes with burnisher at 5°, 10° and finally and at 15° as shown. (B) shows appearance of turned edge (greatly enlarged).

2. Holding burnisher in both hands, turn the edge (Fig. 2–15).
3. Begin with light pressure and hold the steel at nearly the same angle as the file was held in filing.
4. Bear down harder for each successive stroke, and let the tool come a little nearer level each time, finishing with tool at angle of about 60° from the face of the blade.
5. Be sure that the steel never comes down squarely on the fine edge, for that will ruin it.
6. Keep the edge a little ahead of the face of the cutter. The object is to get a hook edge that is sharp.

Pumice Stone

Pumice stone is a white powder used for polishing and buffing a surface after the last sanding of the final finishing coat. The grades are based on the size of the particles and range from a No. 7, which is extremely coarse, to the super fine No. FFFF grade. Grade No. FF (fine) and grade No. FFF (very fine) are generally used for operations that require fine rubbing. Sometimes coarser

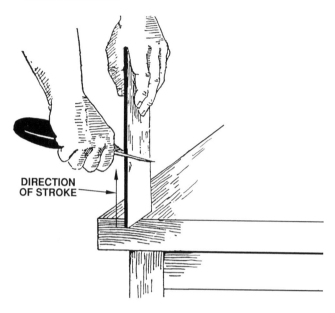

DIRECTION OF STROKE →

Fig. 2-16. Turning edge with burnisher. Note angle at which the tool is held. The stroke is made from bottom up as indicated by the arrow. Slightly lubricate burnisher to assist it in sliding over the edge of the scraper without scratching.

grades (e.g., No. 1 or 1½) are used for work that requires coarser rubbing.

Powdered abrasives such as pumice stone and rottenstone are more difficult to use than other types of abrasives. It is often recommended that pumice be sifted through some sort of screening device before use in order to remove lumps and impurities. The screen must be of a design that will allow the fine pumice powder to penetrate into a pan underneath, while at the same time blocking the passage of lumps and other impurities. Cheesecloth is frequently recommended for this purpose.

Pumice stone is coarser than rottenstone, and therefore faster cutting. It should be used only on surfaces that are absolutely flat, or the powder will fall away from the surface and reduce the overall efficiency of the rubbing operation.

A felt pad or a clean, lint-free cloth is recommended when rubbing with pumice stone. Paraffin oil, a light motor oil, sewing machine oil, raw linseed oil, boiled linseed oil, and others have all been used with varying degrees of success as the lubricant with pumice stone. Paraffin oil and the two types of linseed oil are recommended over the others. Mail-order houses sell a rubbing oil especially designed for use with both pumice stone and rottenstone.

Rottenstone

Rottenstone is another powdered abrasive similar to pumice stone, but its particles are much finer. Rottenstone is therefore commonly used after the pumice stone to obtain an extra-high polish. It is used with many of the same lubricants as pumice stone.

Brushes and Brush Care

Brushes should be selected with as much care as the finish. It is to your advantage to purchase the most expensive brush that you can afford. It will last longer (if it is properly cleaned and stored), and it will produce a better finish.

A typical brush with the basic parts labeled is illustrated in Fig. 2–17. The *ferrule* is a metal (sometimes leather) band wrapped around the brush and fastened to the handle. A good brush will have a tightly-fastened ferrule. In a cheaper brush, the ferrule will not be as tight and the bristles can be easily pulled out. This frequently occurs while you are applying a finish, and is true even with brand-new brushes. For this reason, I do not recommend purchasing a cheap brush with the idea of using it only once.

Brush bristles are made from either natural animal hair, usually hog bristle, or a synthetic material (such as nylon), and are available in flat, round, or oval shapes. Open any mail-order catalog from a firm that sells finishing supplies or go to any local retail outlet that stocks them, and you will find that many different kinds

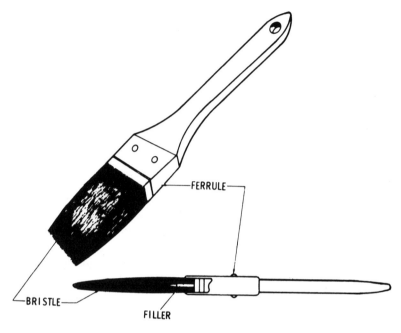

Fig. 2-17. Brush components.

of brushes are available for this type of work (Fig. 2–18). Among them you will find artist's brushes, fitch brushes, glue brushes, ox-hair brushes, varnish brushes, and filler brushes. Some are named according to their composition (e.g., oxhair, red sable brushes, etc.); others receive their name from the function they perform (e.g., varnish brushes, glue brushes, etc.). You will have to select your brush on the basis of what works best for you. My recommendation is that you purchase a suitable brush for each type of finishing operation, and *label* it as such. Your work area might have a collection of brushes as extensive as the following:

1. Scrub brush,
2. Dusting brush,
3. Varnish brush,
4. Enamel brush,

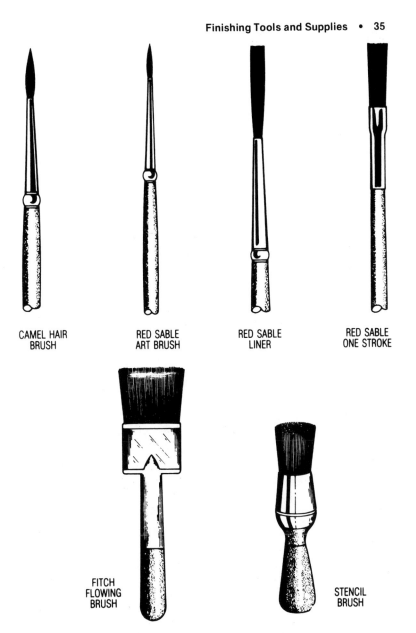

CAMEL HAIR
BRUSH

RED SABLE
ART BRUSH

RED SABLE
LINER

RED SABLE
ONE STROKE

FITCH
FLOWING
BRUSH

STENCIL
BRUSH

Fig. 2–18.   Examples of brushes used in finishing.

5. Lacquer brush,
6. Shellac brush,
7. Stain brush,
8. Paint brush,
9. Paint and varnish remover brush,
10. Striping brush,
11. Filler brush,
12. Picking brush,
13. Glue brush.

Your own experience and the advice you receive from store clerks will help you in matching the most suitable brush with each of the above finishing operations.

A good-quality brush will have the following characteristics:

1. The tip edge of the bristles will be cut to form a wedge or chisel shape. A blunt edge is usually an indication of a cheap brush.
2. The tip of the bristles will taper to a fine, narrow, almost invisible edge.
3. The bristles will be securely fastened to the handle, and will not come loose while the finish is being applied.
4. The bristles will have a good flex (that is, they will be firm without being stiff, and flexible without being excessively loose or floppy).

Carefully clean your brushes after you use them. Clean them in the solvent recommended for the finish or a commercial brush cleaner, and then wash them in soap and water.

Brushes should be stored so that the bristles retain a flat, tapered shape. This can be accomplished by wrapping them in paper and laying them flat, or by hanging them by the handle so that the bristles do not touch any surface (Fig. 2–19). Brush storage containers can be purchased in paint or hardware stores.

Most professional finishers recommend preconditioning the brush before using it. The most common technique is to wrap the brush in paper and suspend it in a container of linseed oil for 18 to 20 hours. The brush is then removed and the linseed oil is pressed out of the bristles. Clean the bristles with turpentine and press dry a second time. Shape the bristles with a comb and hang the brush

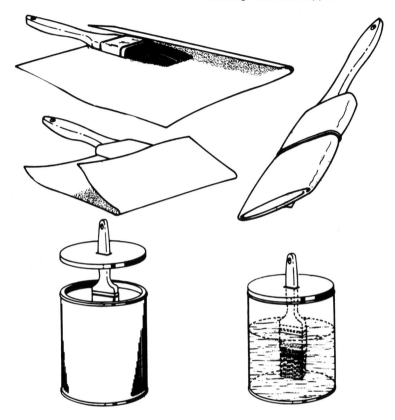

Fig. 2-19. Brush storage methods.

up to dry. Before using it on a surface, dip it in the finish and brush it several times across a piece of scrap wood. This method of conditioning will soften the bristles and lessen their tendency to stiffen after frequent use.

Spray Guns and Compressors

Spraying a finish onto a surface has a number of advantages over brushing. Not only is spraying much faster, it dries more quickly and generally produces a more uniform coat. Moreover, spraying a finish will enable the worker to reach areas that are difficult to cover with a brush.

A portable spraying outfit generally consists of a spray gun, a compressor, and air hoses (Fig. 2–20). The compressor supplies air to the spray gun at approximately 30 lbs. or more of pressure. Spray guns are available in a number of different types and designs. However, it should be pointed out that not every spray gun is suitable for every type of compressor. The CFM rating (cubic feet per minute) of the spray gun should match the CFM rating of the compressor. Otherwise, you may find that your compressor is supplying more air to the spray gun than it can adequately handle.

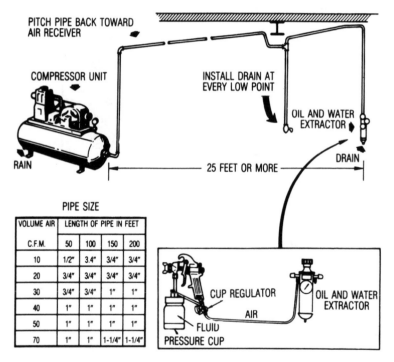

PITCH PIPE BACK TOWARD AIR RECEIVER

COMPRESSOR UNIT

INSTALL DRAIN AT EVERY LOW POINT

OIL AND WATER EXTRACTOR

RAIN

25 FEET OR MORE

DRAIN

PIPE SIZE

VOLUME AIR	LENGTH OF PIPE IN FEET			
C.F.M.	50	100	150	200
10	1/2"	3.4"	3/4"	3/4"
20	3/4"	3/4"	3/4"	3/4"
30	3/4"	3/4"	1"	1"
40	1"	1"	1"	1"
50	1"	1"	1"	1"
70	1"	1"	1-1/4"	1-1/4"

CUP REGULATOR

OIL AND WATER EXTRACTOR

AIR

FLUID PRESSURE CUP

Fig. 2–20. Compressor with pressure-feed hookup. (*Courtesy Reliance Universal, Inc.*)

There are basically three types of compressors:

1. Diaphragm-type compressors,
2. Piston-type compressors,
3. Turbine-type compressors.

The diaphragm-type compressors are less expensive, and cannot supply as much air pressure (only about 30-45 psi) as the piston-type compressors. The diaphragm-type compressor consists of an electric motor with an eccentric drive crankshaft. The latter moves a connecting rod against the center of a flexible diaphragm. The diaphragm moves up and down in an enclosed space, compressing the air above it.

The piston-type compressor is also driven by an electric motor, but in this case the motor drives a piston within a cylinder. Because the compressed air is produced within the cylinder, special precautions must be taken to prevent the oil required to lubricate the piston from mixing with the compressed air. A filter system is necessary for this purpose. Diaphragm-type compressors do not have this problem because the chamber in which the compressed air is formed is separated from the motor and connecting rod by the diaphragm. Piston-type compressors are capable of producing air pressure in excess of 40 psi.

Turbine systems compress air with a high-speed turbine impeller and are known as High Volume Low Pressure (HVLP) systems. Diaphragm and piston systems operate with Low Volume High Pressure (LVHP). HVLP systems provide a large supply of air, 50 to 100 cubic feet per minute, at a relatively low pressure of up to 10 psi.

The high-speed impeller heats the air by rotational friction. As the air warms up and expands, the relative humidity of the air drops, resulting in dry oil-free air. The warm air aids the application of some finish materials.

Many turbine units clean the air with a pre-filter. Some systems have superchargers or boosters that work with a venturi effect and increase free flow pressure at the spray gun two to three times. This may be needed for low VOC finish materials that have higher viscosity. Pressure-feed external-mix spray guns with large air passages and rated for HVLP use are used with these systems.

Turbine spray systems produce less overspray, thus making the work environment safer. Some systems can provide breathable air to an air-supplied respirator if the turbine and booster are located in an uncontaminated area.

Spray guns (Fig. 2–21) can be classified into two basic types, depending on how the finishing liquid is fed to the nozzle. These two types are:

1. The pressure-feed type,
2. The suction-feed type.

The *pressure-feed* type of gun (Fig. 2–22) uses a portion of the air pressure to force the finishing liquid from its container up into

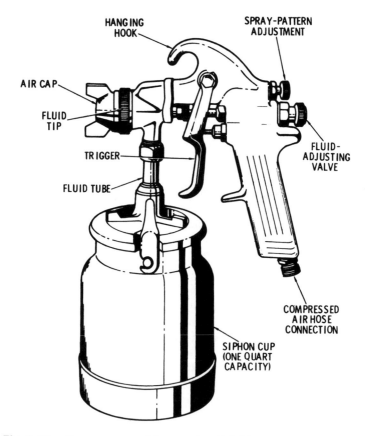

HANGING HOOK

SPRAY-PATTERN ADJUSTMENT

AIR CAP

FLUID TIP

TRIGGER

FLUID TUBE

FLUID-ADJUSTING VALVE

COMPRESSED AIR HOSE CONNECTION

SIPHON CUP (ONE QUART CAPACITY)

Fig. 2-21. Spray gun used in spraying finishing materials.

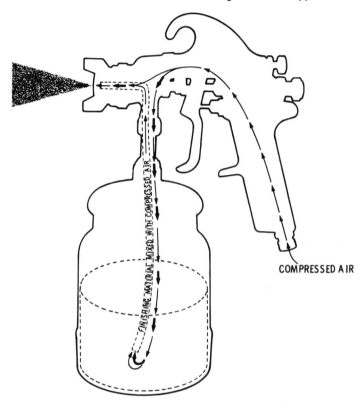

COMPRESSED AIR

Fig. 2–22. The pressure-feed spray gun.

the nozzle. Because the pressure is so strong in this type of gun, faster spraying with heavier liquids is possible.

The *suction-feed* type of gun (Fig. 2–23) uses a vacuum and the siphon principle to bring the finishing liquid to the nozzle. The vacuum is created by passing the air over the feeder tube at a high rate of speed. The vacuum causes the finishing liquid to be sucked up into the nozzle.

Spray guns can also be classified as bleeder-type or non-bleeder-type. Bleeder-type spray guns allow the air to pass through continuously. There is no device on the gun to shut off or control the air pressure. The finishing liquid, however, is controlled by the gun trigger, flowing through the gun only as longer as the trigger

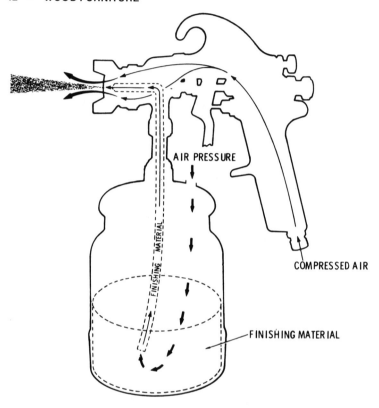

AIR PRESSURE

COMPRESSED AIR

FINISHING MATERIAL

FINISHING MATERIAL

Fig. 2–23. The suction-feed spray gun.

remains in the pulled position. Bleeder-type spray guns can only be used with compressors, because they would soon exhaust a limited air supply.

Non-bleeder-type spray guns control both the finishing liquid and the air supply with the trigger mechanism. As a result, they can be used with limited air supplies, such as in tanks or other types of containers.

Spray guns can also be equipped with either internal-mix or external-mix nozzles. Internal-mix nozzles (Fig. 2–24) mix the finishing liquids and compressed air before they leave the opening. These are found only on pressure-feed spray guns. External-mix nozzles (Fig. 2–25) are found on both pressure-feed and suction-

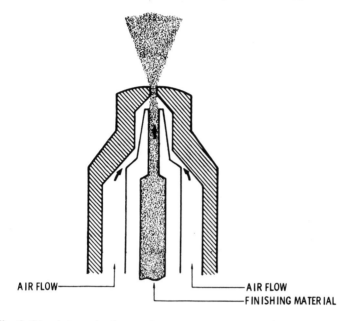

Fig. 2-24. Internal mix nozzle.

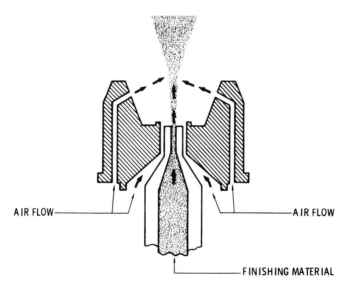

Fig. 2-25. External mix nozzle.

SPRAY WIDTH ADJUSTMENT. TURN RIGHT FOR ROUND, LEFT FOR FAN.

FLUID CONTROL SCREW. TURN RIGHT TO DECREASE FLOW, LEFT TO INCREASE.

Fig. 2–26. Spray gun adjustment controls. *(Courtesy Reliance Universal, Inc.)*

feed spray guns. In this type of nozzle, the air is mixed with the finishing liquid after the latter leaves the opening.

The controls (Fig. 2–26) adjust the spray width and the rate of fluid flow. Spray width is adjustable to a variety of patterns, ranging from round to flat (Fig. 2–27). Fig. 2–28 illustrates a number of faulty spraying patterns and the methods used to correct them. Poor spraying results can also be caused by not holding or moving the spray gun correctly (Fig. 2–29).

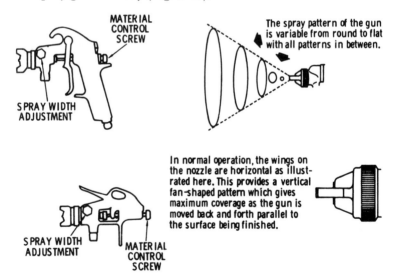

MATERIAL CONTROL SCREW

SPRAY WIDTH ADJUSTMENT

The spray pattern of the gun is variable from round to flat with all patterns in between.

In normal operation, the wings on the nozzle are horizontal as illustrated here. This provides a vertical fan-shaped pattern which gives maximum coverage as the gun is moved back and forth parallel to the surface being finished.

SPRAY WIDTH ADJUSTMENT

MATERIAL CONTROL SCREW

Fig. 2–27. Gun with adjustments. *(Courtesy Reliance Universal, Inc.)*

PATTERN	CAUSE	CORRECTION
	Dried material in side-port "A" restricts passage of air through it. Results: Full pressure of air from clean side-port forces fan pattern in direction of clogged side. **A**	Dissolve material in side-port with thinner. Do not poke in any of the openings with metal instruments.
	Dried material around the outside of the fluid nozzle tip at position "B" restricts the passage of atomizing air at one point through the center opening of air nozzle and results in pattern shown. This pattern can also be caused by loose air nozzle. **B**	If dried material is causing the trouble, remove air nozzle and wipe off fluid tip, using rag wet with thinner. Tighten air nozzle.
	A split spray or one that is heavy on each end of a fan pattern and weak in the middle is usually caused by (1) too high an atomization air pressure, or (2) by attempting to get too wide a spray with thin material.	Reducing air pressure will correct cause (1) To correct cause (2) open material control to full position by turning to left. At the same time turn spray width adjustment to right. This will reduce width of spray but will correct split spray pattern.
SPITTING	(1) Dried out packing around material needle valve permits air to get into fluid passageway. This results in spitting. (2) Dirt between fluid nozzle seat and body or a loosely installed fluid nozzle will make gun spit. (3) A loose or defective swivel nut on siphon cup or material hose can cause spitting.	To correct cause (1) back up knurled nut (E), place two drops of machine oil on packing, replace nut and tighten with fingers only. In aggravated cases, replace packing. To correct cause (2), remove fluid nozzle (F), clean back of nozzle and nozzle seat in gun body using rag wet with thinner, replace nozzle and draw up tightly against body. To correct cause (3) tighten or replace swivel nut (G).

Fig. 2-28. Faulty spray patterns and methods used in correcting them. *(Courtesy Reliance Universal, Inc.)*

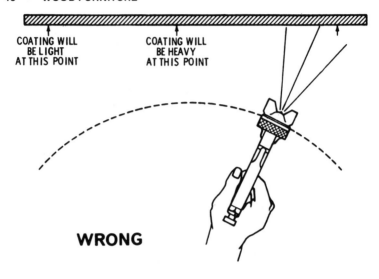

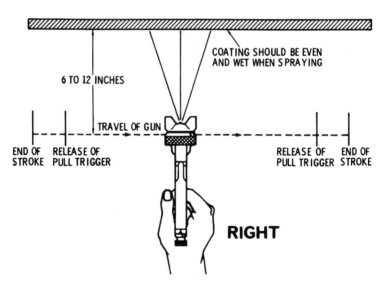

Fig. 2–29. Correct and incorrect spraying techniques.

Aerosol Spray Cans

A number of finishes (stains, enamels, lacquers, paints, etc.) are available in disposable aerosol spray cans. These cans usually contain about 16 ounces of fluid. They are inexpensive, easy to use, and require no thinning. Aerosol spray cans are very convenient for spraying small areas or small pieces of furniture (e.g., stools, end tables, or bookcases). For larger pieces, spray guns and compressors are recommended.

Always shake the can well before using. As you shake it you will hear what sounds like small steel balls rattling in the can. This is exactly what they are; they are inserted in the can to aid in stirring the fluid. Test the spray on a piece of cardboard or paper. If it looks too thin, it probably needs more shaking.

Spray cans are also manufactured with different types of nozzles. Some produce a conical spray; others, a fan spray. Some nozzles are fixed, whereas others rotate. No spray can nozzle will give a spray as wide as that produced by a spray gun, and this is a major limitation.

Some spray cans are of the refillable type. The compressed air propellants are replaceable, and the finishing material must be thinned for effective use.

Correct and incorrect techniques for using aeroso l spray cans are shown in Fig. 2–30. *Read* the manufacturer's instructions on the can before using it. Never store these cans near a heat source or use them near a flame. Proper ventilation is just as important when using spray cans as with finishes in any other form.

Tools for Veneering and Inlaying

The tools for veneering and inlaying are largely specific to those two methods of decorating the wood surface. They are described in detail in Chapter 5, *Veneering*, and Chapter 6, *Inlaying*. For purposes of reference, veneering and inlaying tools include the following:

1. Veneer saw,
2. Veneer roller,

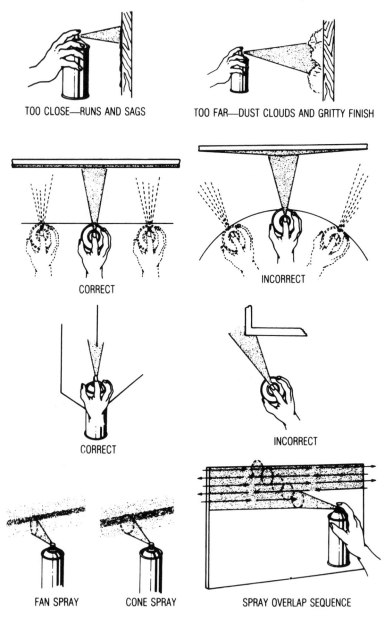

TOO CLOSE—RUNS AND SAGS

TOO FAR—DUST CLOUDS AND GRITTY FINISH

CORRECT

INCORRECT

CORRECT

INCORRECT

FAN SPRAY

CONE SPRAY

SPRAY OVERLAP SEQUENCE

Fig. 2-30. Correct and incorrect techniques for using aerosol spray cans.

3. Veneer edge trimmer,
4. Veneer groove cutter,
5. Veneer strip and border cutter,
6. Veneer press frame,
7. Small hand router,
8. Machine router,
9. Veneer repair tool,
10. Veneer tape.

Paint and Finish Lifters

Lifters are tools used to scrape off paint or finishing material once it has been softened by a solvent. Typical examples of paint and finish lifters are:

1. Putty knives,
2. Scrapers,
3. Picking sticks,
4. Steel brushes,
5. Toothbrushes,
6. Pocket knives.

A putty knife is very useful for removing paint remover sludge after the old finish has been softened (Fig. 2–31). It should be used carefully, however, to avoid nicking, scratching, or gouging the

Fig. 2-31.   Putty knife used to remove paint removal sludge.

wood. To reduce the possibility of damaging the surface, some finishers prefer to use a scraper made of hardwood.

A picking stick can be made from a sharpened dowel. With its tip wrapped in cloth, a picking stick can probe into the recesses of carvings and other difficult-to-reach areas. Toothbrushes are also useful for this purpose. Steel brushes, on the other hand, are useful for removing paint and other finishes from large surfaces. Once again, you run the risk of scratching the surface, because the bristles are made of steel.

There are a number of other finishing tools and materials that are very useful.

Masking tape (or a masking liquid) is used when spraying furniture or when any decorative painting is being done in which two or more colors are used. It is placed as protection over those areas you do not intend to paint at the moment.

Mason jars with screw-on lids make very good mixing containers for finishing materials. Old drinking glasses can also be used for mixing finishes or solvents.

CHAPTER 3

Types of Wood

The ability to identify the different types of wood used in furniture construction is very important in wood finishing. This knowledge should include not only the ability to recognize a particular wood, but also an understanding of how it reacts to different types of finishes. This requires a more sophisticated knowledge than simple recognition. For example, the worker must be able to distinguish between an open-grained and a close-grained wood, because the former requires a filler in order to produce a smooth surface for finishing. Some knowledge of grain and texture is also necessary, as these characteristics of the wood are important considerations in veneering, inlaying, and other aspects of wood finishing. As you can see, wood finishing requires a certain basic knowledge of the various types of wood used in furniture construction. It is the purpose of this chapter to identify some of these woods and their characteristics.

Hardwood and Softwood

Hardwood and softwood are the two most common terms of reference, and the two that probably cause the most confusion. The term *hardwood* does not necessarily mean that the surface of the wood is hard. Although many hardwoods do have hard surfaces (hickory, for example), there are hardwoods with soft wood surfaces (butternut, yellow poplar, etc.) *Hardwood* (like *softwood*) refers to the type of tree. A hardwood is a deciduous tree. These are the relatively broad-leaved trees that shed their leaves during certain seasons of the year. Examples of deciduous trees are the maple, oak, and chestnut. A softwood, on the other hand, is a coniferous tree. These are the needle-bearing or cone-bearing trees, of which Douglas fir, white fir, redwood, and ponderosa pines are examples.

Color

A tree contains both *heartwood* and *sapwood*. The heartwood extends from the center of the tree to the edge of the sapwood. This portion of the tree no longer contains living cells. It is usually filled with resins, gums or other materials (e.g., tyloses) that contribute to the coloring. When we speak of the color of a wood, we almost always mean the color of the heartwood. The sapwood is found near the outside of the trunk and branches of the tree. This layer contains living cells. Its principal function is the storage of food and the conduction of sap. It should not be confused with the *cambrium* layer. The cambrium layer is located between the sapwood and the bark, and its cells are continually subdividing to produce new layers of both bark and wood. Almost all sapwoods are light in color, or virtually white. Any coloring is usually a discoloration from fungus or chemical stains (Fig. 3–1).

Grain, Texture, and Figure

Grain, texture, and figure are all terms describing the surface appearance of the wood. Unfortunately, they are used rather loosely and tend to overlap in meaning, which causes a certain amount of confusion.

Grain is often used in reference to the fibers of the wood, their arrangement, their prominence, the direction in which they run, or to the annual growth rings and the spacing between them. Painters

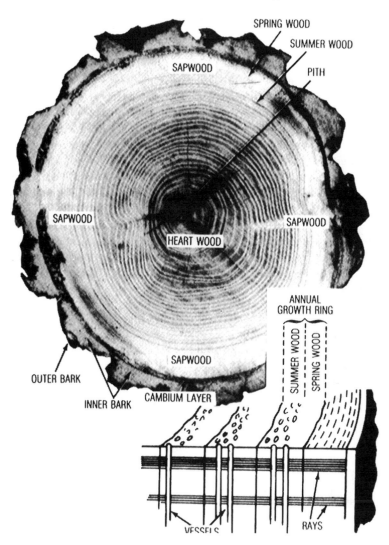

Fig. 3-1. A cross section of a tree trunk.

frequently refer to woods as *open-grained* or *close-grained*, meaning by this the size of the pore openings. To add to this confusion, *fine-grained* is used synonymously with close-grained, and *coarse-grained* with open-grained.

Fine-grained woods are characterized by narrow, inconspicuous annual growth rings. Coarse-grained woods, on the other hand, have wide, conspicuous annual growth rings. Open-grained woods have large pores. None of the softwoods and only some of the hardwoods (black walnut, butternut, white ash, etc.) are open-grained. Close-grained woods have small pores.

The terms open-grained and close-grained would be more appropriate in reference to texture. Since *texture* is also a term of overlapping and confusing meanings, we will use it here to refer specifically to the size and distribution of the individual cells (pores) on the surface of the wood. This could range anywhere from extremely fine (more frequently a characteristic of the softwoods) to extremely coarse. Table 3–1 illustrates how the meanings of these terms overlap.

Both grain and texture are aspects of *figure*, a term that more generally describes the wood surface. Basically, figure is any distinctive pattern or marking appearing on the surface of the wood. Annual growth rings, knots, irregularities in coloring, rays, and deviations in grain patterns, all singularly or in combination produce the distinctive markings known as figure. Some of the confusion in these overlapping terms may be explained in Table 3–1.

The remainder of this chapter contains a brief description of a number of hardwoods and softwoods used in furniture construction. They have been grouped according to whether they are hard-

Table 3-1. Wood Terms

Grain		Texture	
Wide, conspicuous annual growth rings	Narrow, inconspicuous, annual growth rings	Larges pores	Small pores
Coarse-grained	Fine-grained	Open-grained or Coarse-grained	Fine-grained or Close-grained

woods or softwoods. As you will notice, the hardwoods are by far the larger of the two groups.

Hardwoods

Red Alder   (*Alnus rubra*). This wood is grown all along the Pacific coast from California to Alaska. The color of its wood ranges from an off-white to a pale pinkish brown. It is about average in weight, average in strength, and low in shock resistance. Red alder has a tendency to shrink, so it must be properly seasoned before being used. It is used principally in the manufacture of furniture, and can be stained to resemble maple, cherry, and other more expensive woods.

Apple   (*Malus pumila*). A hardwood originally imported from Europe, the apple is now found throughout the United States. The color of apple wood ranges from a cream or offwhite to a very light, almost pale brown. This is very heavy wood, weighing on the average 48 pounds per cubic foot. Not infrequently a pattern of thin brown lines runs at random across the surface of the wood. The grain is very fine, the pores extremely small.

Years ago, along the eastern seaboard, apple wood was used quite extensively in furniture. It is still used today for chair legs. It does not split easily, turns well, but is difficult to carve. Apple wood takes a stain well (a light-colored stain is recommended so that the natural color is not obscured). A filler is not necessary.

Black ash   (*Fraxinus nigra*, brown ash, northern brown ash, and swamp ash). This tree is found primarily in the eastern United States, but only in the northern sections. Its range of growth does not extend any further south than Tennessee and Virginia. It has little or no figure and a straight, uninteresting grain. The color of black ash ranges from medium brown to dark brown. It has an average workability with hand tools. Its tendency to split is about average, as are its strength, resistance to decay, and ability to take a clear finish.

White ash   (*Fraxinus americana*) (Fig. 3–2). White ash is found throughout the eastern United States except in the coastal plain

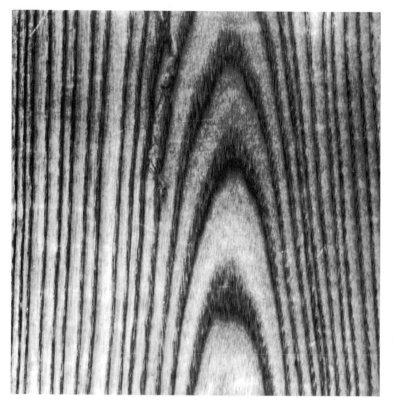

Fig. 3-2. White ash. *(Courtesy Fine Hardwood Veneer Association)*

areas. The color of the wood is a brown to grayish brown, with occasional examples of a cream or off-white variety. There is frequently a reddish tint in the coloring. Like black ash, it possesses little or no figure. White ash is a fairly heavy wood, weighing about 42 pounds per cubic foot. It has a straight grain, which is not brought out appreciably by staining (stains seem merely to color it), and a texture similar to oak. The pores are large and visible to the eye. White ash, for the most part, works well with hand tools, except that it tends to split easily. The wood is strong, stiff, and hard, and has good resistance to shock. It is frequently used in furniture construction. White ash bleaches well, and may be finished with or without a filler, depending upon the effect desired.

Aspen (*Populus tremuloides*, quaking aspen, popple, poplar, cottonwood). Aspen is found throughout most of the northeastern and western United States, with the greatest concentration in the lake states and the New England area. The color of aspen wood ranges from a white to a light brown. It is light in weight, averaging 26 pounds per cubic foot. The pores on the surface are small and generally not visible, but a filler should be used with most finishes. It reacts well to bleaching. Aspen wood ranks very low in hardness, somewhat higher in shock resistance, and low in strength. These poorer characteristics are offset by very little tendency to split and a very low rate of shrinkage after proper seasoning. Aspen also works well with either hand tools or machine tools. This wood glues easily and reacts well to paint. Aspen is frequently used in the manufacture of high-grade excelsior. It can also be found in veneers.

Avodire (*Turraeanthus africana*). This is a wood grown in West Africa and imported to the United States for use in fine furniture. Avodire wood has a pale yellow to golden coloring; some varieties appear almost white. Avodire possesses an open grain with an average capacity for taking a stain. A filler should be used with most finishes. Avodire reacts favorably to bleaching. This wood is about average in weight, possesses an average workability with hand tools, and shows about the same tendency to split. Avodire has a relatively low strength.

American basswood (*Tilia americana*, bass, linden) (Fig. 3–3 and Color Plate 1). This hardwood is grown throughout the eastern United States, particularly in the region around the Great Lakes. The wood has a creamy white to creamy brown coloring, with one particularly attractive variety tending toward a rather light, yellowish brown. The wood is sometimes highlighted with streaks of a slightly deeper color. American basswood is lightweight (26 pounds per cubic foot), with a straight, even grain. Because of the evenness of the grain, stains take very well. This wood is frequently stained to resemble other woods (e.g., cherry, mahogany, or walnut) that are more expensive or difficult to obtain. The pores are

Fig. 3-3. American basswood. *(Courtesy Fine Hardwood Veneer Association)*

quite small, with extremely faint growth rings. American basswood is easy to work with hand tools, and does not split easily. It is not a strong wood, and has a low shock resistance. It is used as a core material in high-quality furniture veneers (usually overlaid with walnut or mahogany). It is also frequently used as a wood for furniture legs and stained to resemble the rest of the piece.

American beech (*Fagus grandifolia*) (Fig. 3–4). A hardwood found growing primarily in the eastern United States, and as far west as Texas and Missouri. The coloring of the wood ranges from a reddish white to a reddish brown. It is heavy (45 pounds per

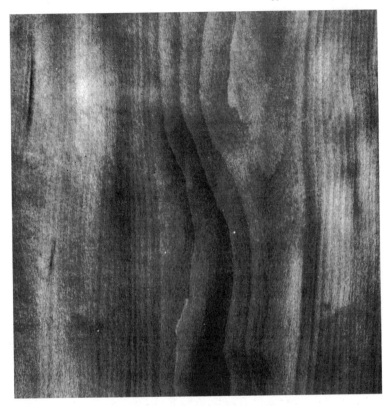

Fig. 3-4. American beech. *(Courtesy Fine Hardwood Veneer Association)*

cubic foot), strong, and hard. The grain is even. The pores are so small that they are not visible to the naked eye, but the rays are prominent and cover the surface. A water-based stain works well on this grain, without raising it. American beech is frequently stained to resemble more expensive woods. This wood strongly resembles sugar maple, except that the coloring of the wood is darker, the grain coarser, the weight lighter, and the general strength somewhat less. This wood is difficult to work with hand tools. It splits easily, and nails are difficult to remove. However, it does machine well, giving a smooth surface. American beech is used in table legs, chair legs, and veneers.

Yellow birch (*Betula allegheniensis*, gray birch) (Fig. 3–5 and Color Plate 2). This wood is grown in the northern United States and in the Appalachian Mountains as far south as southern Georgia. The wood of the yellow birch is a light reddish brown. It has a fine, close grain, with pores not readily visible. Because the grain is so uniform (it takes a stain very well), yellow birch is used for furniture wood and veneer. Yellow birch is not easily worked with hand tools, but it machines well. This is a heavy wood, weighing almost 45 pounds per cubic foot. It is hard, strong, and stiff. It has both a high shock resistance and a high nail-withdrawal resistance. Yellow birch shows a strong tendency to shrink, and should be properly seasoned before using.

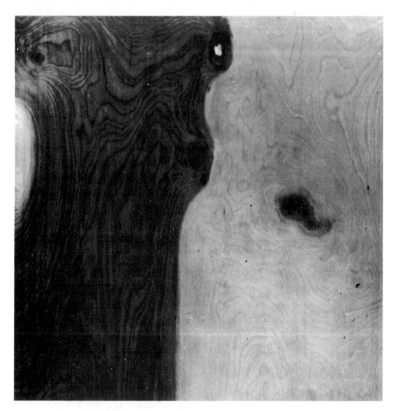

Fig. 3–5. Birch. *(Courtesy Fine Hardwood Veneer Association)*

Butternut (*Juglans cinerea*, white walnut). Butternut is found growing throughout the northern half of the eastern United States. Its southernmost limits appear to be northern Mississippi, Alabama, and Georgia. The color of the wood is a light brown with traces of red. Its texture is coarse, its pores open and large. This is a lightweight wood, weighing on the average 27 pounds per cubic foot. Butternut is easy to work with hand tools and machine tools. It takes stains well, and is often stained to resemble walnut.

Black cherry (*Prunus serotina*, cherry, wild cherry, chokecherry, American mahogany) (Figs. 3–6, 3–7 and Color Plate 3). This is

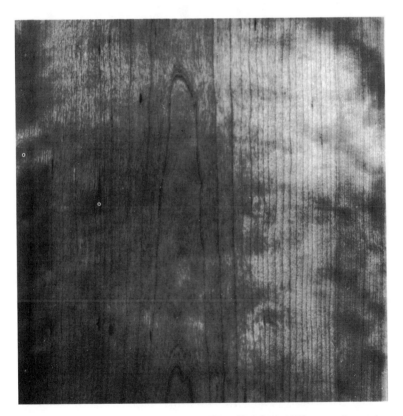

Fig. 3-6. Black cherry. *(Courtesy Fine Hardwood Veneer Association)*

Fig. 3-7. Black cherry, figured. *(Courtesy Fine Hardwood Veneer Association)*

another hardwood grown primarily in the eastern United States. The color of the wood is a light to dark reddish brown. Black cherry weighs, on the average, about 36 pounds per cubic foot, which places it in the average to slightly above average weight category. This wood has a fine, close grain that takes a stain well. A filler is not required. Cherry reacts very poorly to bleach. There is a distinctive flake pattern of the rays on quartersawed surfaces. Black cherry is often referred to as "American mahogany," although it is stronger and harder than any of the varieties of mahogany. It is also stronger than walnut, but lacks the strength of maple. This wood is stiff, strong, and has a high resistance to shock. Since black cherry has a strong tendency to shrink, it must be carefully seasoned before use. This wood is difficult to work with hand tools, but machines easily. Black cherry is considered one of the finest furniture woods.

Chestnut (*Castanea dentata*, American chestnut, sweet chestnut). This tree was formerly found in the northern half of the eastern United States. Unfortunately, it has almost been killed off by a blight. The color of the wood ranges from grayish to reddish brown. The widespread prevalence of blight has left only a "wormy chestnut" grade available for commercial uses. This is an open-grained wood with a coarse texture. Because of its large pores, it resembles oak or walnut (chestnut has been used to imitate both these woods). It is very easy to work with hand tools, cutting more easily than oak, and with less tendency to splinter. Because of its durability and resistance to warp, it is particularly sought after for use in the construction of furniture drawers and veneer cores.

Cottonwood (*Populus deltoides*, eastern cottonwood, Carolina poplar, yellow cottonwood). This variety of cottonwood grows throughout the eastern United States. The color of the heartwood ranges from grayish white to grayish brown. The pores of the wood are very small, the texture is uniform, and it is generally straight-grained. The weight is average to light, weighing about 25 pounds per cubic foot on the average. The wood tends to be softer than most, and shows a lower than average resistance to shock. The hand-tool workability is about average. It does not split easily and is low in nail-withdrawal resistance. Cottonwood takes paint very well, and is not difficult to glue. It is used as a veneer core and as a furniture wood.

American elm (*Ulmus americana*, white elm, gray elm, water elm) (Color Plate 4). This hardwood is found throughout the eastern United States except in the Appalachian highlands and southern Florida. The color of the wood ranges from brown to dark brown with traces of red. The wood is of average weight (about 35 pounds per cubic foot), hardness, and stiffness. The texture is rather coarse, with large, open pores (except in the summerwood, where the pores cannot be seen). American elm wood offers a better than average shock resistance. It shows a strong tendency to shrink, and must be seasoned properly before use. American elm machines well, but is not easily worked with hand tools. It bends very easily, and for this reason is widely used in the bent parts of the wood furniture frame. American elm offers no difficulty in gluing.

Rock elm   (*Ulmus thomasii*, hickory elm, cork elm) (Color Plate 5). This wood is also grown in the eastern United States, but does not extend any further south than Tennessee. The color of rock elm wood resembles that of American elm. This is a heavy wood, weighing on the average 44 pounds per cubic foot. Only hickory and dogwood exceed it in hardness among the American hardwoods. It resembles American elm in shrinkage, hand-tool workability, and bending qualities. The grain patterns, pore sizes, and texture of the two are also very similar. Rock elm is used in furniture construction and veneers.

Slippery elm   (*Ulmus rubra*, red elm). Slippery elm occupies the same regions as the American elm, except for the coastal plain areas, where it is almost never found. This wood has all the characteristics of American elm. It too is used in the manufacture of furniture and veneers.

Goncalo alves   (*Astronium fraxinifolium*, zebrawood, kingwood). This is a wood found in the tropical jungles of eastern Brazil, and imported to this country for use in fine furniture and cabinets. The color of the wood ranges from a yellowish to pinkish to golden background, with darker stripes running across it. It has a straight grain with small, open pores. A filler is generally recommended, but bleaching is not. The texture varies. It is easy to work with hand tools.

Hackberry   (*Celtis occidentalis*). This wood grows throughout the eastern United States as far south as Tennessee. The color of the wood ranges from a pale yellow to a greenish or grayish yellow. It is about average in weight and strength (particularly the bending strength). Hackberry is above average in hardness, low in stiffness, and tends to shrink more than average unless seasoned properly. This wood is used primarily in the manufacture of furniture.

Hickory or true hickory can be divided into four classes: (1) shagbark hickory (*Carya ovata*); (2) pignut hickory (*Carya glabra*); (3) shellbark hickory (*Carya laciniosa*); and (4) mockernut hickory (*Carya tementosa*). Hickory grows throughout the eastern United States except for southern Florida, northern Maine, northern Vermont, and northern Michigan and Wisconsin. The color of the wood ranges from brown to dark brown, sometimes with a reddish tint. Hickory is a very heavy wood, averaging from 42 to 52 pounds per cubic foot. It is very hard, strong, and stiff, with a high resistance to shock. Hickory is difficult to work with hand tools, particularly in its tendency to splinter. The pores are not well defined. However, cutting along the grain produces pore channels that are distinctive to hickory. Hickory is used in lawn furniture, rockers, and Windsor chairs.

American holly (*Ilex opaca*, boxwood, white holly, evergreen holly). This tree is found along both the Gulf and Atlantic coasts, and throughout the Mississippi Valley. The color of the wood varies from white to off-white, and can easily be stained a variety of different colors. It also reacts well to bleaching. This is a heavy wood, and well above average in hardness. Its texture is uniform and compact. American holly is frequently used as a furniture inlay.

Imbuya (*Phoebe porosa*, imbuia, Brazilian walnut). This hardwood is found in Brazil and imported for use in the more expensive furnitures. The color of the wood ranges from a light (almost yellow) brown to a dark brown. Imbuya can be bleached with better than average results. It is a heavy wood, averaging 44 pounds per cubic foot in weight. Imbuya is open grained with a fine texture, and generally requires a filler. It is about average in hardness, and high in durability. Imbuya is easy to work with hand tools, and it machines well.

Kelobra (*Enterolobium cyclocarpum*, parota, guanacaste). This wood is grown in Mexico and northern Central America, and imported to the United States for use in fine furniture. Because of its beautiful grain pattern, it is also used extensively in high-grade veneers. It takes a stain well (generally dark brown), and requires a filler. Do not bleach.

Koa (*Acacia koa*). Koa is a hardwood grown in Hawaii and used in the manufacture of expensive, fine-quality furniture. The color ranges from a gold to a dark brown. Koa will respond well to bleaching. Some varieties have a darker stripe running across a light background. This is a fine, open-grained wood with a texture similar to that of walnut. It requires a filler.

Lacewood (*Cardwellia sublimis*, silky oak) (Fig. 3–8). This tree is found in both Australia and Europe. Because of its distinctive figure that resembles lace, this hardwood is used as a furniture overlay. The color ranges from a light red (almost pink) to a light red-

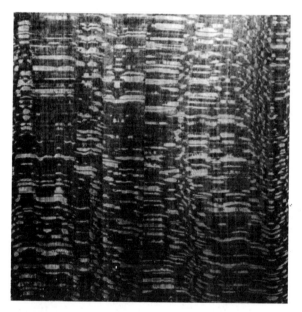

Fig. 3-8. Lacewood grain. *(Courtesy Fine Hardwood Veneer Association)*

dish brown. A filler is generally recommended. If necessary, it can be bleached with better than average results.

California laurel (*Umbellularia californica*, mountain laurel, pepperwood, myrtle). This variety of laurel is grown along the Pacific coast. The color of the wood ranges from green to brown, with mixtures of yellow that produce a variety of shades. It weighs about 38 pounds per cubic foot (kiln-dried weight), which places it in the same weight class as black cherry or mahogany. It produces beautiful distinctive figure patterns that make it highly valued as a decorative wood in fine furniture.

Magnolia (*Magnolia grandiflora*, southern magnolia, big laurel, evergreen magnolia). This hardwood is found in the southern United States from North Carolina to Texas. The color of the wood ranges from a light to a dark brown, with shadings of yellow or green. It weighs about 34 pounds per cubic foot. The wood is usually close grained, with a close, uniform texture. It is about average in hardness and stiffness, above average in shock resistance, and low in shrinkage. It very closely resembles yellow poplar. Magnolia wood is used in the manufacture of furniture and veneers.

Mahogany (*Swietenia mahogani*, American mahogany, true mahogany, West Indian mahogany). This excellent hardwood is found in the islands of the West Indies and in southern Florida. The color of the wood ranges from various shades of red (including a light pink) to a rich dark brown. Its grain has a fine texture and the surface of the wood frequently shows an attractive figure. True mahogany is a heavy wood with about average hardness. It is high in strength and shock resistance, and does not shrink appreciably. This variety of mahogany is easily worked with hand and machine tools. It is easy to glue, easy to fasten (with nails or screws), and takes both a stain and paint well. In short, this is one of the finest furniture and cabinet woods.

African mahogany (*Khaya ivorensis*, khaya, Benin mahogany). This wood is imported from West Africa and is used for the manufacture of furniture and veneers. Most of its characteristics resemble those of American mahogany. However, it has a heavier grain pattern and the texture is noticeably coarser.

Honduras mahogany (*Swietenia mahogani*, Central American mahogany). Honduras mahogany is found in the tropical regions throughout Latin America as far north as southern Mexico. Most of its characteristics resemble those of American mahogany. It is especially noted for its fine grain patterns and even texture. It is a strong, medium-hard wood, with a weight somewhat above average (about 32 pounds per cubic foot). It is used in the manufacture of furniture and veneers.

Philippine mahogany is a commercial trade name for a variety of hardwoods belonging mostly to the genus *Shorea* (red and white lauans) of the *Diptero-carpaceae* family. The color of the wood ranges from a light khaki or tan to a dark red. It is an open-grained, coarse-textured wood with an average hand tool workability. It machines well. It requires considerable sanding to produce a smooth surface. For this reason, it is used in cheaper grades of furniture than the other mahoganies.

Makori (*Mimusops heckelli*, African cherry, Makori cherry mahogany). This hardwood is grown in southern Africa and imported to the United States for use in furniture construction. Makori strongly resembles mahogany, but surpasses the latter in texture, weight, and hardness.

Maple (Color Plate 6) is a name given to a large genus (*Acer*) of trees, many of which have no value as a furniture wood. Two noted exceptions are the big-leaf maple (*Acer macro-phylum*) found along or near the Pacific coastal areas of North America, and hard maples, which include sugar maple (*Acer saccharum*) and black maple (*Acer nigrum*), both found primarily in the eastern United States.

The hard maples have a light reddish brown wood. Some varieties of hard maple have a distinctive figure with very small spots of curled grain resembling a bird's eye. For this reason, it is frequently referred to as bird's-eye maple. All three types of hard maples are used in the manufacture of quality furniture. Bird's-eye maple is particularly suitable for use in inlays and overlays.

Hard maples are heavy woods, averaging 44 pounds per cubic foot. This wood is generally straight-grained (the bird's-eye varieties being the exception), with a fine texture. It takes stain and wax well and can produce a high polish. It machines well, but is difficult to work with hand tools. This is a strong, stiff wood, with a high resistance to shock. The pores are not visible to the naked eye. It has a strong tendency to shrink and must be properly seasoned before use.

Narra (*Pterocarpus indicus*, amboyna, angsana). This wood is grown in the East Indies and imported to the United States, where it is used in the manufacture of expensive grades of furniture and fine veneers. The color of this hardwood ranges from red to rose to a yellowish brown. This is a heavy wood. It is not as durable as some and is relatively low in strength. Because of its hardness, it is difficult to work with hand tools. A filler is recommended for all finishes. Narra can be successfully bleached.

Oak (Fig. 3–9 and Color Plates 7, 8) is a name given to a large genus (*Quercus*) of trees found in the temperate zones primarily of the northern hemisphere. Three of the most common types used in furniture construction are: (1) the white oaks, which include (a) white oak (*Quercus alba*); (b) bur oak (*Quercus macrocarpa*); (c) chestnut oak (*Quercus prinus*); and (d) live oak (*Quercus virginiana*; (2) english oak (*Quercus robur*, brown oak); and (3) the red oaks, which include among others (a) southern red oak (*Quercus falcata*); (b) laurel oak (*Quercus laurifolia*); (c) northern red oak (*Quercus rubra*); (d) black oak (*Quercus velutina*).

Both white oak and red oak have a grayish brown wood. Red oak wood is distinguished by a reddish tinge. Oak is a heavy wood, ranging in weight from 45 to 47 pounds per cubic foot. The wood is hard, strong, and stiff, with a high resistance to shock. It is characterized by large, open pores. The pores of all white oaks (except chestnut oak) are filled with a hairlike growth called tyloses. Oak is difficult to work with hand tools, although it machines well. English oak shares most of the characteristics of the other oaks. However, its color tends to be a deeper brown with a distinctive grain pattern. It is widely used in fine grades of furniture. Quartered oak

Fig. 3-9. White oak, flat grain. *(Courtesy Fine Hardwood Veneer Association)*

is a method of cutting the wood so that the cuts are formed in a radial direction. This procedure produces very interesting grain patterns of flakes from the wood rays. It is used in the construction of furniture and veneers.

Pearwood *(Pyrus communis)*. A hardwood found in both the United States and Europe. The color of the wood ranges from a pink to a white. It reacts well to bleaching. This close-grained wood with a fine texture, but a filler is generally recommended. It has a grain pattern that is distinguished by a mottled figure. Pearwood is used in high-quality furniture and veneers.

Yellow poplar (*Liriodendron tulipifera,* American Tulip Wood) (Color Plate 9). The yellow poplar is a hardwood found in the eastern United States. The wood is a brownish yellow with tinges of green. The grain and figure are not particularly distinctive. Because the texture is even, it takes a stain very well. Yellow poplar is frequently stained to imitate other, more expensive woods. The wood is on the light side (averaging about 30 pounds per cubic foot). It is average in hardness, stiffness, resistance to shock, and bending properties. It also rates average in its machining properties and its ability to take glues. It is easy to work with hand tools. Although its nail-withdrawal resistance is low, it does not split easily. Yellow poplar is used extensively in the lower grades of furniture.

Primavera (*Cybistax donnellsmithii*, golden mahogany, white mahogany) (Fig. 3–10). A hardwood imported from southern Mex-

Fig. 3-10. Primavera. *(Courtesy Fine Hardwood Association)*

ico and Central America for use as a furniture and cabinet wood. The color ranges from a light to golden yellow. Primavera reacts well to bleaching. The characteristics of this wood closely resemble those of American mahogany. The grain is straight, the texture coarse. Use a filler.

Sapele (*Entandrophragma cylindricum*, sapele mahogany, sapeli). A hardwood native to West Africa and imported to the United States for use in the manufacture of furniture, especially as a veneer. It has most of the characteristics of African mahogany, except that it is heavier and harder. Do not attempt to bleach this wood. A filler is recommended with all finishes.

Satinwood (*Chloroxylon swietenia*) (Fig. 3-11). A hardwood imported from the East Indies and used for inlays and marquetry in furniture construction. It ranges in color from a golden yellow to a

Fig. 3-11. Satinwood. *(Courtesy Fine Hardwood Veneer Association)*

yellowish brown. This is a strong, hard, heavy wood with a fine grain pattern. There is a West Indian variety of satinwood (*Zanthoxylum coriaceum*) that strongly resembles the East Indian wood. Its color, however, is more a pale orange. Do not attempt to bleach satinwood.

Sweetgum   (*Liquidambar styraciflua*, red gum) (Color Plate 10). Sweetgum is found throughout the eastern United States. The color of the wood is reddish brown. This is a close-grained wood with a strong figure in some varieties. A filler is not required. Sweetgum stains very well (a maple or walnut stain is recommended), and is frequently used in furniture construction in conjunction with more expensive woods. It is above average in weight (about 35 pounds per cubic foot), hard, strong, and moderately high in shock resistance. However, sweetgum machines poorly and has only an average hand-tool workability. Because sweetgum warps easily, great care must be taken in seasoning it. It does not split easily and it holds nails well.

American sycamore   (*Platanus occidentalis*, buttonwood) (Color Plate 11). A hardwood found in the eastern United States. The color of the wood ranges from reddish brown to flesh brown. It can be successfully bleached. It is a medium-heavy wood, averaging 34 pounds per cubic foot. It has a close, interlocking grain and a coarse texture. The pores are not visible to the naked eye, but are very prominent. Sycamore is about average in hardness and strength, and slightly above average in hand-tool workability. It tends to warp and shrink. Great care should be taken to season the wood properly before use. This wood is generally used in cheaper grades of furniture and veneers.

Tamo   (*Fraxinus mandschurica*, Japanese ash) (Fig. 3–12). Tamo is a hardwood imported from Japan and used in furniture frames and veneers. The wood has a light yellow color and a pronounced grain pattern resembling that of oak. A filler is generally required. It can be bleached with better than average results. It has many of the same characteristics (strength, stiffness, resistance to shock, etc.) as American ash.

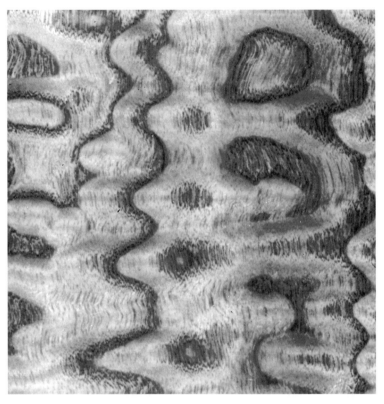

Fig. 3-12. **Tamo wood.** *(Courtesy Fine Hardwood Veneer Association)*

Teak (*Tectona grandis,* teakwood) (Fig. 3-13). A hardwood found in Burma, India, Thailand, and Java and imported to the United States for use in fine grades of furniture. The wood is a yellowish brown. A filler is recommended. It is strong, hard, and durable. In its other characteristics it strongly resembles walnut.

Black tupelo (*Nyssa sylvatica,* black gum, tupelo gum) (Color Plate 12). This is a hardwood found in the eastern United States, and particular in the southeastern region. The color of the wood ranges from a pale to a dark brownish gray. This is a fine-grained

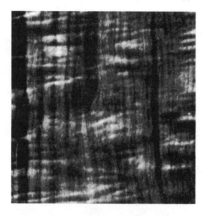

Fig. 3-13. Teak wood, wavy figure. *(Courtesy Fine Hardwood Veneer Association)*

wood with small pores. There is usually no pattern, although some varieties have black streaks with no discernible arrangement to them. Because it will take almost any kind of stain, it is used to imitate other woods. Unstained, the wood closely resembles poplar (the latter is distinguished by the green tinge to the heartwood). Its workability with hand tools ranges from average to above average. It carves well. Because of this and its excellent staining properties, it is used extensively in the manufacture of legs for veneered tables.

Black walnut *(Juglans nigra,* American walnut) (Fig. 3–14 and Color Plate 13). A hardwood found in the regions east of the Mississippi, and as far west as portions of Texas and Nebraska. The wood has a chocolate brown color with darker, occasionally purple streaks. This is a heavy wood, averaging 38 pounds per cubic foot. It has a striking grain pattern with large pores that take the form of dark streaks on the longitudinal surfaces. It is strong and stiff with good shock resistance. Black walnut is easily worked with hand tools and machines well. The wood takes a high polish, stains well, holds paint with no difficulty, and takes well to gluing. A filler may or may not be used, depending upon the finish desired. It is necessary, however, for a smooth finish. Black walnut's many excellent

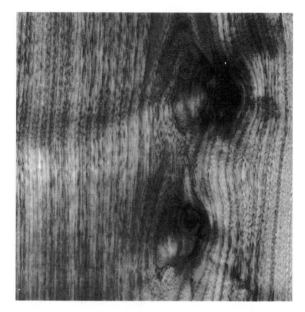

Fig. 3-14. Black walnut. *(Courtesy Fine Hardwood Veneer Association)*

attributes make it one of the woods most extensively used in furniture construction.

Black willow *(Salix nigra).* This is a hardwood found primarily in the Mississippi Valley. The wood is a grayish brown or light reddish brown with darker streaks. It has an interlocking grain pattern with a uniform texture. The wood is light, averaging 27 pounds per cubic foot. It is medium soft, rather low in strength, and moderately high in shock resistance. Black willow wood is used in inexpensive furniture.

Softwoods

Alaska cedar *(Chamaecyparis nootkarensis,* yellow cedar). This tree grows along the Pacific coast from Alaska to as far south as southern Oregon. The wood is a bright, clear yellow. It does not take a stain well. It weighs about 30 pounds per cubic foot. Alaska cedar rates about average in strength, stiffness, and hardness. It is somewhat higher than average in resistance to shock. This wood is frequently used in furniture construction.

Eastern red cedar (*Juniperus virginiana*, red cedar). This tree is found throughout much of the United States east of the Rockies. The wood ranges in color from red to a reddish brown. It weighs on the average 34 pounds per cubic foot. This is a close-grained, even-textured wood. An oily film on the surface of the wood makes it necessary to seal it (a shellac is often used) before completing the finish.

Incense cedar (*Libocedrus decurrens*). A softwood found in California and southwestern Oregon. The wood has a reddish color. This is a light wood, weighing on the average 26 pounds per cubic foot. It has a flat, straight grain. In appearance it closely resembles western red cedar. Incense cedar is a medium soft, rather weak wood, with a low shock resistance. It is easy to work with hand tools. It formerly enjoyed widespread use in the construction of cedar chests.

Western red cedar (*Thuja plicata*). This is a softwood that grows in the western United States. The wood has a reddish brown color. It is a lightweight wood, averaging 23 pounds per cubic foot. The wood is generally straight-grained, and the texture is coarse. It is soft, not very strong, and low in shock resistance. It is subject to only slight shrinkage. It is very easy to work with hand tools. Western red cedar does not hold nails well. It is easily glued, holds paints well, and will produce a good finish. It was used as a furniture wood in former times far more extensively than it is today.

Bald cypress (*Taxodium distichum*, southern cypress, white cypress, red cypress, yellow cypress, cypress). This softwood grows all along the coastal plains from Delaware to the Mexican border. The wood ranges in color from a light yellowish brown to a reddish brown. It is a close-grained, even-textured wood with little or no figure. Bald cypress is a medium-heavy wood, weighing on the average of 32 pounds per cubic foot. It is about average in strength and stiffness. Bald cypress reacts well to most stains, and is easy to work with hand tools.

Douglas fir (*Pseudotsuga menziesii*, red fir, yellow fir, Douglas spruce). This softwood is found west of the Rocky Mountains in the United States, southern Canada, and northern Mexico. The color of the wood ranges from orange red to red with tinges of yellow. It weighs about 33 pounds per cubic foot. It is average in hardness, strength, and resistance to shock. It is a little more difficult than some softwoods to work with hand tools. It has above average gluing properties.

Western hemlock (*Tsuga heterophylla*). Western hemlock grows on the Pacific coast and in the Rocky Mountains. The color of the wood is white with a purple tinge. It averages about 29 pounds per cubic foot in weight. The texture of the grain is not as coarse as that of eastern hemlock; consequently, it cuts more easily and produces smoother surfaces. This wood is about average in hardness, strength, and stiffness. Its shock resistance is low. Western hemlock is easy to work with both hand tools and machine tools. It is sometimes used in the construction of furniture.

Sugar pine (*Pinus lambertiana*) (Color Plate 14). Sugar pine grows from southern Oregon south through southern California and into Mexico. It is lightweight, averaging 25 pounds a cubic foot. The wood is moderately soft, limber, weak, and low in shock resistance. It is very easy to work with tools and does not split easily in nailing. Sugar pine is used for lumber in buildings, general millwork, and furniture.

Eastern white pine (*Pinus strobus*, white pine, northern white pine, soft pine). This wood is found growing in the northern sections of the eastern United States. It extends no further south than northern Georgia. The wood is a light brown color, frequently with a reddish tinge. It is a light wood, averaging about 24 pounds per cubic foot in weight. It is about average in hardness, but low in strength and resistance to shock. It has a uniform texture and a straight grain. No filler is required with this wood. Eastern white pine is extensively used in furniture construction.

Western white pine (*Pinus monticola*) (Color Plate 15) Western white pine grows from the Canadian border southward into Montana, Idaho, and California. Moderately light in weight, it averages 27 pounds a cubic foot. The wood is moderately soft and stiff. It works easily with tools and glues readily. It does not split easily in nailing. This pine is used in construction and millwork products including furniture.

Yellow pine (*Pinus echinata*, shortleaf pine, southern yellow pine). This softwood grows throughout the southeastern United States. The color ranges from yellow and orange to a light or reddish brown. A filler is not generally required. It weighs about 36 pounds per cubic foot. It is about average in hardness, strength, stiffness, and shock resistance. Yellow pine is sometimes used in the construction of furniture.

Redwood (*Sequoia sempervirens*). The redwoods grow along the California coast and into southern Oregon. The color of the wood is a deep reddish brown. It weighs about 28 pounds per cubic foot. Redwood is average in hardness, strength, and stiffness. It is slightly below average in shock resistance. The grain in redwood is generally straight. A filler is not required. It is generally easy to work with hand tools, although it does show a tendency to split. Redwood will take a paint well under normal circumstances. Care must be taken to seal the surface of redwood, or the sap will bleed through the paint. This wood is sometimes used in the construction of lawn furniture.

The color plates which follow show the grain pattern of each type of wood. Beginning at the top of each plate, end grain, edge grain, and flat grain are displayed. This is done because certain identifying characteristics show up best on each surface. All photos are courtesy of Forest Products Laboratory.

CHAPTER 4

Introduction to Finish Technology

An understanding of how finishes work can help you choose the correct product, use it in the right way, and solve some of the problems that arise in its use. To understand these materials, we will look at them very closely to find out just what happens as they are used. There are three ways to think about finish coatings: superficially, microscopically, and chemically.

Superficial The first is the most common one that we all know. You open a can of paint, dip in a brush, and spread it on the surface. At first the paint is wet and then it dries. The result is a surface that is a different color or is more shiny than before. When the coating fails the surface looks cracked or is peeling. (Fig. 4–1)

Microscopic The second way is to consider that the liquid paint or varnish is a mixture of various materials that have combined physically into the dried film. By looking at the film very closely, with a microscope for instance, you can see it has a definite thickness. The different parts of the film are visible. You can tell exactly how the coating is cracked or peeling. (Fig. 4–2) The scale mark shows the film is a little less than three-thousandths of an inch (0.003″) thick—about the same thickness of the paper this page is printed on.

You can see the film is made up of two layers. The bottom

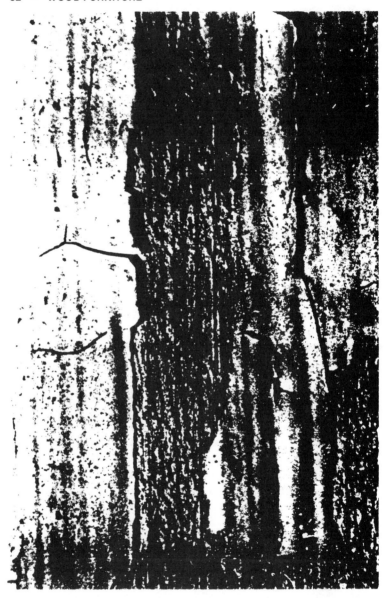

Fig. 4-1. Peeling paint film. *(Courtesy Forest Products Laboratory)*

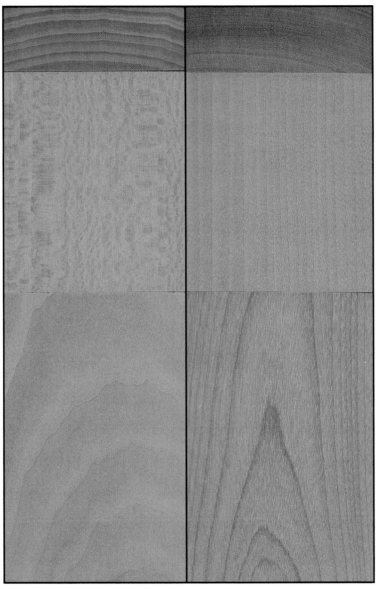

1. American Basswood   2. Yellow Birch

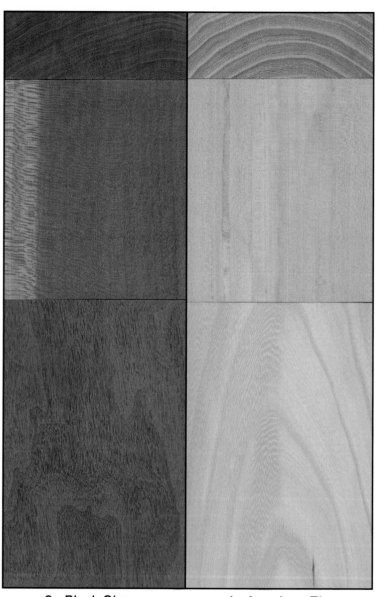

3. Black Cherry 4. American Elm

5. Rock Elm   6. Sugar Maple

7. Red Oak   8. White Oak

(Courtesy Forest Products Laboratory)

9. Yellow Poplar   10. Sweetgum

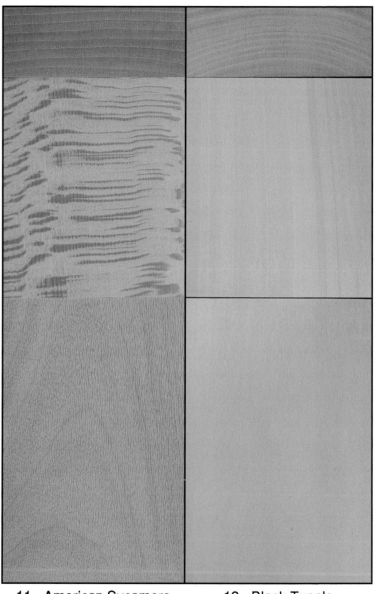

11. American Sycamore   12. Black Tupelo

13. Black Walnut 14. Sugar Pine

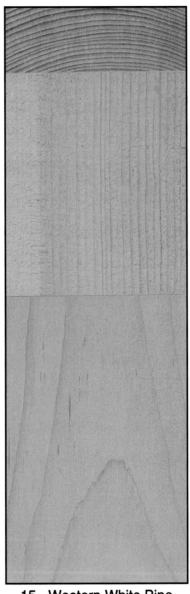

15. Western White Pine

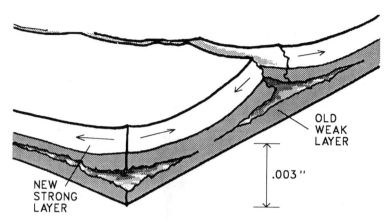

Fig. 4-2. Microscopic view of peeling paint film. *(Courtesy Practical Restoration Reports)*

layer is an old weak oil paint. The top layer is a new coat of stronger alkyd paint. The continued curing of the stronger alkyd film causes shrinkage that can eventually pull the lower, weaker layer apart. The result is cracking and peeling.

Chemical The third way to think about coatings takes place on a much smaller scale. You cannot see it, even with a microscope. The liquid materials are made up of basic building blocks called *molecules* which are bonded, or linked together, to form larger molecular structures called *compounds.* Compounds can divide and recombine to form new compounds. These changes are called *chemical reactions.* As the reaction takes place, the outward physical characteristics of the material change. For example, as liquid varnish cures, the compounds in the varnish combine with each other. This new compound with larger molecular structures has the physical characteristics of a solid forming the dry varnish film (Fig. 4-3).

The Finish System

Finishes can be divided into two broad categories, those that penetrate the surface of the wood, and those that form a film or coating on

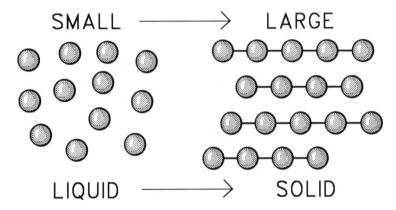

Fig. 4-3. Chemical Reaction. The smaller molecules of a liquid link to form the larger molecules of a solid. *(Courtesy Practical Restoration Reports)*

top of the surface. A complete coating system is usually made up of two or more coats, or layers, often of different materials.

Paint, varnishes, and other finish products must meet a wide range of requirements. They should not be too costly to make and must remain in a liquid, usable condition until bought and used. They should spread easily onto a surface and flow into a flat layer, and stop flowing just when they are smooth. And finally, they need to harden into a tough durable film that is easy to renew when it wears out. These three steps in film formation are called *application*, *fixation*, and *cure*. Exactly how the film forms depends on the materials of which the finish is made.

Liquid paint, for example, is made of three very different materials. The *pigment* gives color to the paint and is mixed in the vehicle, or liquid part of the paint. The vehicle is made of two parts. The *binder* cements the pigment particles together and sticks it to the surface being painted. The *solvent* thins the binder so the paint can be easily spread. Sometimes the binder is thin enough that solvent is not needed. Clear finishes like lacquer and varnishes are simply binder and solvent without pigment. All three parts work together as a system to make the final film possible. (Fig. 4–4)

Solventborne Systems

Common oil-based paints and varnishes are solventborne systems. Solvent, binder, and pigment are mixed to make the liquid as you see it in the can. When you spread the paint, its surface area exposed to the air is increased. The solvent begins to evaporate, the film feels tacky, and then dry to the touch. Even though the film feels dry, it may not reach its full strength until after some days or weeks of curing. (Fig. 4–4)

Waterborne Systems

Waterborne finishes work on a very different principle than solvent systems. The vehicle is water and the binder is a thick liquid distributed in the water as fine droplets. This is called an *emulsion*, or suspension of fine droplets of one liquid dispersed in another liquid. This emulsion is a brushable mixture that has the pigments mixed in. Pigments are the same as those used in solvent paints. Latex paints are well known waterborne systems, and waterborne varnishes are becoming more common. (Fig. 4–5)

As soon as the finish is spread on a surface, the water begins to evaporate. After a few hours, the water is mostly gone and the individual droplets of resin begin to merge, or coalesce, into the final film, trapping the particles of pigment. At this point the film feels dry, but the droplets will continue to fuse together for a day or so. The binder will continue to cure and gain full strength within a few days or weeks.

A waterborne system allows the use of resins that are much thicker in consistency than those used in solvent coatings, while letting the finish as a whole remain spreadable. The binder can be made of much larger molecules that are more resistant to the chemical attacks that break down a finish film. Less solvent is

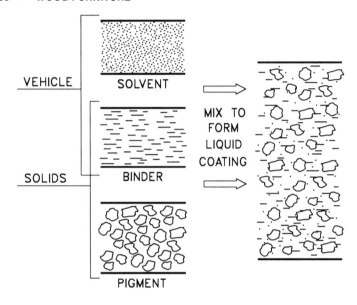

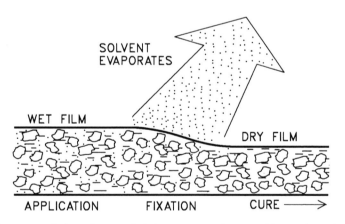

Fig. 4-4. Solventborne finish system. Composition of typical solventborne paint system (top). After the liquid paint is applied (bottom), film formation begins. As time passes, the solvent evaporates into the air and fixation occurs. During evaporation and fixation, cure begins. *(Courtesy Practical Restoration Reports)*

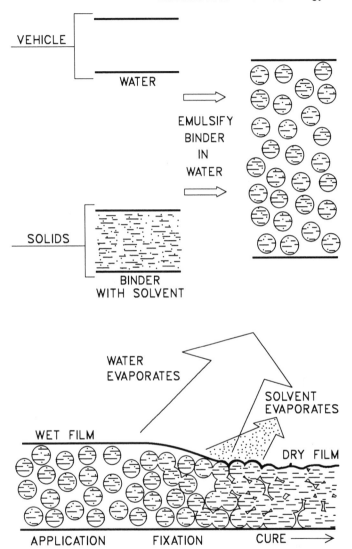

Fig. 4-5. Waterborne finish system. Composition of typical waterborne system (top). Film formation (bottom) begins with application. As water evaporates, the droplets of binder move closer together. The droplets begin to merge, or coalesce. Pigment is left out for clarity. *(Courtesy Practical Restoration Reports)*

needed since the binder is not a part of the vehicle. This makes the application of waterborne systems much safer for the environment and your health.

Cure

The binders in a finish cure in two very different ways, by evaporation of a solvent or by a chemical reaction. The type of cure depends on the type of binder.

Evaporative The binder in shellac and lacquer finishes cures when the solvent in the finish evaporates. Alcohol is the solvent for shellac and acetone is a solvent for lacquer. After application, the solvent evaporates from the surface of the wet film. As this happens, the resin molecules compact closer and closer together. When evaporation is complete, the resin forms a hard dry film. (Fig. 4–6) The molecules of resin are in close contact with each other but they are not strongly bonded. The original solvent used in the finish can easily dissolve or loosen the resins, putting them back into solution. You would not use shellac to finish a table top because the alcohol in a mixed drink would easily dissolve it.

Reactive The oils and resins commonly used as binders in paints and varnishes cure by a chemical reaction. After application the larger surface area of the wet film is exposed to the air. Oxygen from the air bonds with oil molecules, initiating a chemical reaction. The oil molecules begin to bond with each other, forming larger compounds that become the dry film. Alkyd resins form much larger molecules as they cure, making them more resistant to chemical attack. Adding a solvent like mineral spirits to the surface of cured alkyd varnish will have little effect on it.

Polyurethane resins commonly used in varnish begin curing by oxidizing with the air. But then the molecules form *cross-linked* or three-dimensional networks like tinkertoys on a molecular scale. (Fig. 4–6) This reaction is called *polymerization* and produces a dry film that is highly resistant to chemical attack. Ordinary household chemicals like vinegar and alcohol cannot loosen the bonds between the molecules and so have no effect on the cured film.

EVAPORATIVE

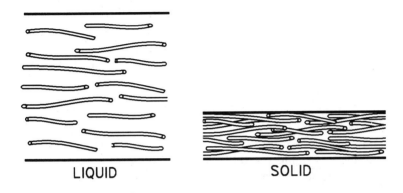

LIQUID   SOLID

REACTIVE

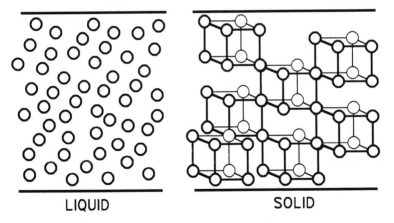

LIQUID   SOLID

Fig. 4-6. Curing of binders. Shellac and lacquer cure by physical compaction as the solvent evaporates (top). Oils and resins cure by a chemical reaction that joins the binder molecules to each other (bottom).

Materials

Binders

Binders are made of naturally-occurring substances such as vegetable oils, gums, and resins, and also from synthetically-manufactured resins. To be useful in a coating system, these materials must be able to change, within a reasonable period of time, from a liquid to a solid when spread in a thin film. This outward physical change is the result of chemical reactions combining the molecules of the binder.

Drying Oils   The binders of oil finishes and pigmented oil paints are made of liquid vegetable oils. Linseed and tung oil are well known for their use in penetrating finishes on furniture. Safflower and soya oils are also used. When spread in a thin film, the molecules that make up these oils combine with oxygen from the air and begin to dry. As this drying by oxidation occurs, the oil molecules are linking together into larger molecules, making the film more solid. The initial small size and long drying time of the liquid molecules allows them to penetrate further into the pores of the surface being coated. To take advantage of this, oil finishes and paints should be rubbed or brushed well into the pores of the surface. After the initial cure an oil paint film is flexible, yet tough and durable. But, because oxygen is always available, polymerization continues, making the film harder, until in a few years, it becomes brittle and begins to fail. This continued curing is the reason penetrating oil finish needs to be renewed and why some varnishes with high oil content become dry and powdery with age.

Raw linseed oil has small molecules and penetrates the pores of a wood surface easily, but takes a long time to dry. *Boiled linseed oil* has been treated so that it is partly polymerized. This means it has larger molecules and will dry faster, but will not penetrate as well as raw oil. Boiled linseed oil usually has metallic salt driers (Japan drier) added to further shorten cure time.

Tung oil dries harder and is more resistant to moisture than linseed oil. It lends these properties to paints and varnishes that contain it. Tung oil makes an excellent penetrating finish used alone or mixed with mineral spirits as a thinner. Japan drier can be added for a shorter recoating time.

Oleoresins The durability of oils can be improved by combining them with natural or synthetic resins that become a part of the binder and increase its hardness and resistance to chemical attack. Binders with more resin will be the most resistant but may be too hard and brittle for some uses. The balance between oil and resin is based on the intended final use of the coating. A binder that is mostly oil, called *long oil* binder, will be flexible and tough. Spar varnish is this type of finish, and when made with tung oil it is especially resistant to water. A *medium oil* binder with more resin is harder and has shorter drying time, both valuable characteristics for a floor varnish or enamel.

Short oil binders used in furniture and piano varnishes are fast drying and somewhat brittle. They are useful indoors where wood is expanding and shrinking less and requires less flexibility in the finish. Their brittleness is an advantage when sanding between coats since the sandpaper does not fill with particles of finish. Zinc stearate pigment may be added to aid sanding by acting as a lubricant. *Sanding sealers* have this type of formulation.

Varnishes used to be made with natural resins from pine trees or fossil resins such as amber, copal, and kauri, petrified tree saps dug from the earth. Now manufactured resins are used. These resins are altered chemically to improve their characteristics and then cooked in large kettles with a drying oil. The resulting binder dries in the usual way for oil but has greater resistance to chemical attack and abrasion due to the resins. Partial polymerization may also take place during cooking, which means these binders will not penetrate especially well but will dry and cure faster than oil. Oleoresin undercoats, enamels and varnishes apply fairly easily and dry rapidly with a hard, semigloss, or gloss finish for interior use. In the past, varnishes and pigmented enamels using only oleoresins as binders were more common. Now these resins are most often used as supplements to improve properties such as hardness in finishes that depend mainly on synthetic resins.

Alkyd Resins Paints and finishes had remained largely the same throughout the nineteenth and early twentieth century. But by the 1950's, many synthetic and highly-processed natural materials were being used by the coatings industry.

The *alkyd resins* have become particularly important, since they appear in most of the common types of coatings. They are made from glycerin, acids, and drying oils. As they are cooked in a large kettle, ingredients are varied to control the properties of the resin produced. These resins are not as thick and viscous as natural resins, so less oil is needed to make a spreadable binder. The binder dries by oxidation and polymerization of the oil portion of the molecules. Because there is less oil in proportion to resin, it dries in less time. The short drying time and the large size of the molecules allows only limited penetration, but the resin is highly adhesive and the film bonds well with the surface being coated. This makes alkyd coatings very good for new work, where adhesion and film strength are important, but it can cause problems in recoating old paint films that may be fairly weak (Fig. 4–2).

Primers and undercoats made with alkyd binders seal the surface and *hold out*, or do not penetrate. They are useful in covering surfaces that vary in porosity, such as furniture made of different types of wood. On this kind of surface, oil paints would soak in at different rates and there would be unsightly differences in the surface sheen.

Interior white or light-colored top coats made with alkyds are less likely to yellow with age than oil paints. They are most resistant to this discoloring when made with safflower, soya, or refined tall oil.

Alkyd resins react unfavorably with alkali. Residues from caustic paint strippers must be completely neutralized to avoid adhesion problems with finishes containing alkyd resins.

Urethane Resins—*Urethane resins*, or *isocyanates*, are used in films that are highly resistant to chemical and mechanical damage. They are sometimes used as binders in pigmented enamels, but are better known for their use in clear varnishes. The resin is usually modified with a drying oil. The molecules of these resins are already mostly polymerized and are quite large. Their size does not allow them to penetrate into the surface being coated. Trying to rub or brush this type of coating into the pores of a surface will only trap air in the liquid finish, forming bubbles and pinholes in the final film (Fig. 4–7). This type of coating should be laid on the surface with full, even brush strokes. When urethanes are applied to a surface, the solvent evaporates and the resin oxidizes, leaving a film that is tack-free in a fairly short time. However, it may take some days or weeks for a full cure. The final film gets its strength and

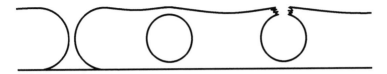

Fig. 4-7. Pinholes and bubbles. Overbrushing polyurethane varnish can create pinholes and bubbles that penetrate the film.

durability from the complex three-dimensional network of molecules formed during this final cure. It is important to allow enough time for the final cure. For instance, if the finish is waxed before the cure is complete, the wax could react with the urethane, forming a sticky mess that might never dry.

Manufacturers' instructions for recoating should be followed closely. After a certain point in the curing, the film may not react with a second coat to form a bond between the two films. *Intercoat peeling* could result.

Initial preparation of the surface is particularly important with urethane finishes. The very large molecules will not penetrate the surface, and the limited number of reactive sites provides little adhesion. This is usually not a problem when coating fresh wood surfaces, but old finishes should be roughed up with sandpaper or steel wool and then thoroughly washed with a solvent to remove any traces of oil or grease. Often these contaminants come from unexpected sources such as hydrocarbon emissions from auto exhaust, which, mixed with the air, will find their way indoors to wood surfaces. Alkyds are sometimes added to urethane products to improve adhesion.

The oils and resins discussed so far are used in clear varnishes, enamels, and pigmented paints. Sunlight tends to deteriorate these coatings. The pigments in enamel and paint protect the binder by absorbing or reflecting the light. The surface beneath is shaded by the pigments. All clear varnishes, on the other hand, are limited in their ability to withstand sunlight. Furniture can be exposed to sunlight through windows or when it is used outdoors. Sunlight can stimulate urethane to continue polymerizing, causing the film to embrittle and crack. Ultraviolet light that reaches wood beneath the film will decompose the surface fibers, releasing the film and allowing it to peel or flake away. *UV absorbers* can be added, but even they break down within a year or two. *Tung oil-phenolic resin* varnish probably gets its good outdoor durability from its dark color, which limits the amount of light that can penetrate.

Solvents

Solvents are thin liquids that evaporate easily at room temperatures. Some come from plant materials. Alcohol is distilled from grain and turpentine from pine sap. Others are derived from coal tar and petroleum. During finish manufacture, the binder may be too thick to mix with the pigment. A solvent is added to thin the mixture so less energy will be used in mixing. Solvents work by keeping the molecules of binder separated. As the solvent leaves the finish film, the binder molecules move together and combine to become a solid. The solvents used by finish manufacturers are much more powerful than ordinary paint thinners, which only *dilute* the paint allowing easier application.

In the wet paint film, solvent migrates to the outer surface as a liquid where it vaporizes to form a thin layer of vapor-laden air just over the surface. If this layer is disturbed by high winds outdoors, or strong drafts indoors, evaporation is increased and the film may skin over, limiting further evaporation. This can weaken the final film and lessen its useful life.

Everyone knows the cooling effect of moisture evaporating from skin, and the same effect occurs on the drying film. With evaporation that is too rapid, the surface can become cool enough for moisture to condense, causing a white *bloom* to appear on dark colors or cloudiness to appear in clear finishes. This is most likely to happen when the relative humidity is high with wind or strong drafts. The unfortunate result may be only temporary, but it can also be permanent.

Manufacturers use powerful *aromatic solvents* like *benzene* (Benzol), *toluene* (Toluol), and *xylene* (Xylol), which vaporize easily and are noted for their odor. Benzene is particularly hazardous and products containing a lot of it, like some varnishes and paint strippers, should not be used in or around the house. Its vapors are toxic even before they can be smelled. Somewhat less toxic are the *aliphatic solvents*, mineral spirits, naphtha, and benzine that are found in common paint thinner.

Pigments

Pigments are very small particles of insoluble materials suspended throughout the finish. Some pigments are mined from the earth and ground to a fine powder, but most are altered or produced chemically. They are added to thicken the paint, resulting in a thicker film that will also be harder and less porous. And, of course, pigments give the finish color.

White pigments are made from materials that are actually translucent. They appear white because they are so finely divided that the light striking them is passed back out (Fig. 4–8). A ray of light is bent, or refracted, when it passes into a particle of pigment, and is refracted again as it leaves the particle. Each particle in the film helps to keep the light from getting through the film. Most of the light that enters a film of white paint is passed back out. If most of the light made it all the way to the bottom of the film and came back out, as one of the rays does, the surface below would be seen and the paint would not be doing a very good job of hiding it. Some decorative glazing techniques require this translucent effect in the paint film. This could also happen if there is not enough pigment to keep the light from the lower surface. The paint may be spread too thin or may not have enough pigment to begin with. The film will be the right thickness if you follow the manufacturers' directions for *square feet of area covered.* The pigments *Titanium Dioxide* and *Zinc Sulfide* bend the light a lot and are called *active* or *hiding* pigments. Choose a paint that has more of these pigments if hiding the old surface is important, as when changing from dark to light colors.

Most of the light that strikes a film of white paint is reflected or passed back out, but colored pigments stop some of the light as it passes through the film. When you see red paint, the pigment in it stops all but the red light which leaves the film to reach your eyes.

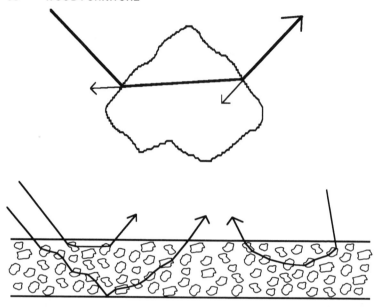

Fig. 4-8. Pigment and light. A ray of light bends as it passes through the surface of a translucent particle of pigment (top). A certain amount of light is also reflected. Light rays enter the paint film and can be refracted and reflected back out (bottom). *(Courtesy Practical Restoration Reports)*

The darker colors absorb more of the light. Black lets almost no light escape. Dark paint applied in direct sunlight will be more likely to blister and peel than lighter colors. The light changes into chemical and heat energy within the film. The film skins over, trapping solvent, which is then vaporized by the heat, forming blisters. During the first few hours after application, the film is very sensitive so you should always dark apply dark-colored paint indoors or in the shade if working outdoors.

Supplemental pigments are used that do not have good hiding power, but serve other purposes. *Calcium Carbonate*, or chalk, helps keep the active pigments suspended in the liquid paint, which helps to promote the greatest hiding power and even color. Talc is sometimes added because its particles have a fibrous shape that help tie the film together. Talc, like the other *silicate pigments*, costs less and paints of lower quality will contain more of them.

The amount and type of pigment has an important effect on the strength, gloss, flexibility, moisture resistance, and washability of the final film. A mixture containing less pigment in relation to binder will level out to a flat smooth glossy surface and reflect light like a mirror (Fig. 4–9). Mixtures containing more pigment will result in a surface that is irregular, reflecting light in many directions, giving a *flat* or matte finish. The smooth, glossy surface will be easier to wash and keep clean because it does not have the crevices of a matte surface that can hold dirt.

In manufacture, the pigment is mixed, or *ground* into the vehicle, which must completely coat each particle of pigment. As the solvent evaporates from the liquid film, the binder hardens, trapping each particle of pigment. Insufficient grinding in cheap paints can cause poor film formation and uneven color, when the particles lump together with no binder in between.

Reading Labels

How can you find out what materials are in the finish product you want to use? By reading the label. Generally the directions on product labels are reliable and should be followed very carefully. Particular attention should be paid to manufacturer's recommendations for coating one product over another. Some finishes are incompatible and there will be problems if they are used in the wrong combinations.

By using another set of information provided on most labels, you can find out more about the product you are about to use. This is an analysis by percentage of weight of the materials used to make the product. It is usually just about the smallest print you ever saw, but is the only way you can know what is inside the can. This information will help you make a judgment of your own about the product's suitability for your intended use. The materials may be described in only a general or semi-specific way. At times the listing is quite specific.

The analysis first divides the finish material into two parts, the

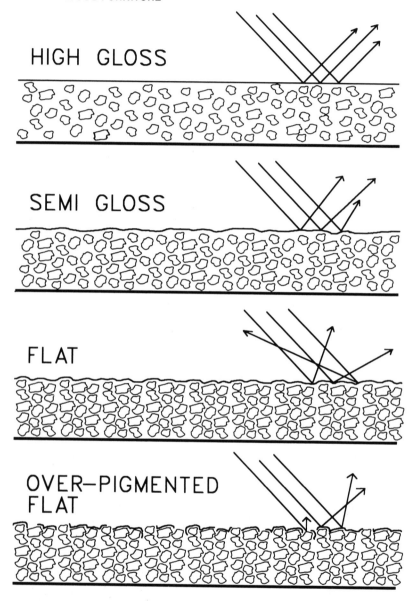

Fig. 4-9. Pigment and gloss. The amount of pigment in a paint film controls gloss.

pigment and the vehicle, with a percentage for each. Then each is further divided into the separate ingredients. These figures show how much of each ingredient is in either the vehicle or pigment, but not in the whole paint. To find the percentage of an ingredient in the whole paint multiply its percentage times the figure for the vehicle or pigment, whichever it is under. An example:

PRODUCT ANALYSIS OF WHOLE PAINT	MATH	PERCENT OF WHOLE PAINT (rounded to nearest %)
Pigment - 36% Titanium Dioxide 40% Silicates 60%	$.40 \times .36 = .14$ $.60 \times .36 = .22$	14% 22%
Vehicle - 64% Acrylic Resin 20% Water 80%	$.20 \times .64 = .13$ $.80 \times .64 = .51$	13% 51%

This is rather involved, but the results give you a clearer idea of what the paint is made of. Some manufacturers are listing ingredients in percentages of the whole product. A few do not list ingredients at all.

Another way to find out about products is to contact the manufacturer. Most manufacturers freely offer technical support in how to best use their products, but they are often reluctant to give specific information about the formulation of their products. They consider this proprietary (secret) information. You can sometimes get the information you need by asking for the general type of material in their product rather than the specifics. Often material safety data sheets list the ingredients of a product. These are readily available from the manufacturer. Another source of product information is medical toxicology literature. Often manufacturers list ingredients in toxicology handbooks. Ask your reference librarian for help.

CHAPTER 5

Veneering

Contrary to popular opinion, veneering will produce a stronger and more durable piece of furniture than one constructed from a solid piece of wood. Solid wood is subject to warping, cracking, shrinkage, and other defects resulting from such conditions as moisture loss and the effects of heat. A veneer construction, on the other hand, combines three to five layers of wood glued together to form a single piece. A typical example of veneer construction is illustrated by the piece of furniture in Fig. 5–1. It should be pointed out that gluing a face veneer to a solid base (such as a furniture table top) is not a true veneer construction, but rather a way of dressing up the appearance of the surface.

It is incorrect to view a veneer as simply the gluing of a thin layer of expensive wood over the surface of a cheaper and less desirable one. Veneering is an extremely old process that requires considerable skill, and the final composition of the veneer is more complex than one would initially suspect.

The term *veneer* can refer either to a face veneer or to each of the several layers (ply) used in the construction of a sheet of plywood or a wood panel. The primary purpose of the face veneer is to provide an attractive surface. These face veneer sheets are either glued directly to a solid base (e.g., a table top) or to the outer sur-

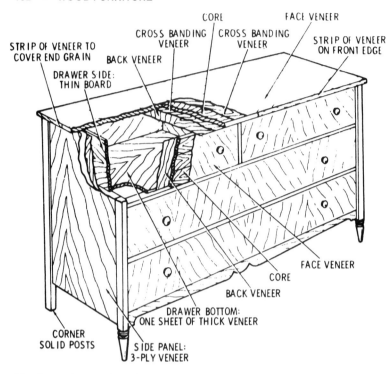

Fig. 5-1. Examples of veneer construction. *(Courtesy U.S. Department of Agriculture)*

face of a wood panel. The wood panels are usually constructed from three sheets (three-ply) or five sheets (five-ply) veneer. The three-ply panels can have either a veneer core or a lumber core, the latter providing a thicker and stronger panel (Fig. 5–2).

A *face veneer* is a very thin sheet (generally sold in $\frac{1}{28}$ inch thicknesses) of high-quality wood selected for its particularly attractive figure (the distinctive marking or design created on the wood surface by grain patterns, annual growth rings, coloring, the method of cutting, and other factors) (Table 5–1).

Some woods with attractive figure patterns tend to be very expensive, and furniture constructed entirely from them would in most cases be beyond the financial reach of the average person. Other woods with equally attractive figure patterns may be too

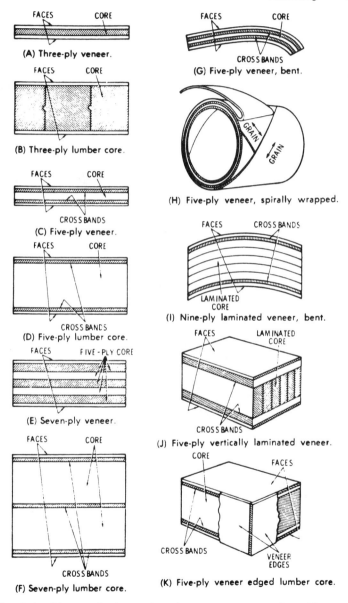

FACES   CORE

(A) Three-ply veneer.

FACES   CORE

(B) Three-ply lumber core.

FACES   CORE

CROSSBANDS
(C) Five-ply veneer.

FACES   CORE

CROSSBANDS
(D) Five-ply lumber core.

FACES   FIVE-PLY CORE

(E) Seven-ply veneer.

FACES   CORE

CROSSBANDS
(F) Seven-ply lumber core.

FACES   CORE

CROSSBANDS
(G) Five-ply veneer, bent.

GRAIN   GRAIN

(H) Five-ply veneer, spirally wrapped.

FACES   CROSSBANDS

LAMINATED
CORE
(I) Nine-ply laminated veneer, bent.

FACES   LAMINATED
CORE

CROSSBANDS
(J) Five-ply vertically laminated veneer.

CORE   FACES

CROSSBANDS   VENEER
EDGES
(K) Five-ply veneer edged lumber core.

Fig. 5-2. Types of plywood and veneer construction. *(Courtesy U.S. Department of Agriculture)*

Table 5-1. Veneer Thicknesses

Thickness of veneer is expressed in fractions of an inch, or how many pieces of veneer are required, when placed one on top of another, to make an inch. When the woodworker speaks of 1/24th veneer, he means it is 1/24 of an inch in thickness, or that 24 thicknesses are required to make an inch. The most common veneer thickness and their principal uses are listed below:

5/16 inch 1/4 inch 3/16 inch 1/6 inch 1/7 inch 1/8 inch 1/9 inch 1/10 inch 1/12 inch 1/16 inch	SPECIAL COMMERCIAL USES Usually rotary cut, although sometimes sawed or sliced. Mostly "plain" figured wood. Used for boxes; architectural products, such as doors, panels, etc.; cross banding; and the familiar commercial uses for veneer; other than face veneers for furniture.
1/20 inch 1/24 inch 1/28 inch 1/30 inch 1/32 inch	FURNITURE, CABINETS, ETC. Usually rotary cut or sliced, although sometimes sawed, such as "quarter-sawed" oak. Used for face veneers on furniture, pianos, theater seats and similar articles. Fancy figured crotches, burls, etc., are usually sliced. Plainer figures are rotary cut.
1/50 inch 1/60 inch 1/72 inch 1/80 inch 1/100 inch	CIGAR BOXES, WALLPAPER, ETC. Usually rotary cut or sliced. Used for special purposes, such as airplane construction, covering or linings for cigar boxes, etc. Frequently mounted on paper or cardboard backing to give greater strength and to prevent damage in handling.

weak or too heavy. Veneering is a method of overcoming these problems. The attractive veneer sheet is glued to a core of very strong, lightweight, inexpensive wood.

Unfortunately, veneering is still associated with products of cheap quality. It gained this reputation largely in the last half of the nineteenth century. During the 1860s, veneers were introduced in furniture construction for the first time on a widespread commercial basis. The quality was extremely disappointing. Consequently, veneering quickly became associated with poor-quality furniture. This is no longer true of veneering. New methods of cutting or slicing the veneer sheets, better construction, and a wider selection of face veneers have improved both quality and strength.

Do not confuse veneers with plastic laminates. Veneers are thin sheets of natural wood. Plastic laminates (Formica is a common brand name) are composition materials that are sometimes used to imitate wood. This is not to imply that one is inferior to the other. They are simply two entirely different materials. Plastic laminates are described in greater detail in a section at the end of this chapter.

Wood Figure

Sometimes the term *figure* is used synonymously with *grain*. This is incorrect, or at best only partially correct. Grain is only one aspect of figure. As was pointed out above, the term figure is correctly applied to the distinctive wood surface markings or designs created by such surface factors as grain patterns, annual growth rings, coloring, and texture in combination with the method of cutting or slicing the wood. A particular figure may thus have a natural origin (that is, it may be characteristic of a certain wood or woods), or it may depend more on the way in which the wood was cut (for example, the flake figure in black cherry produced by quartersawing the wood). Some figure patterns are found in only one or two types of wood (for example, the lace pattern in lacewood), whereas others (for example, the stripe or ribbon effect) are found with slight variations in a number of woods.

The veneer suppliers offer sample sets of real veneer for a small fee. You get a variety of veneer types. Use such samples for study to get familiar with the sight, smell, and feel of the different woods. The samples can also be used for testing different finish effects and for small repairs.

There are many types of figure patterns and as many names for them. Some of these names describe the pattern (e.g., bird's-eye, ribbon, mottle), while others refer to the origin of the cut (e.g., crotch). The portion of the tree from which the cut is made will frequently determine the figure (Fig. 5–3).

The *crotch figure* (Fig. 5–4) is created by cutting below the

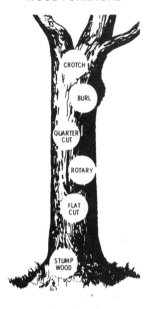

Fig. 5-3. Areas of a tree trunk from which different cuts are taken. *(Courtesy Fine Hardwood Veneer Association)*

Fig. 5-4. Mahogany wood, crotch cut. *(Courtesy Fine Hardwood Veneer Association)*

point where a fork in the trunk (or large branch) begins. The figure has a splash or swirl pattern caused by the distortion of the fibers during the formation of the fork. A *feather crotch figure* is characterized by a featherlike spread of the fibers. A *swirl figure* (Fig. 5–5) originates in the same general area, but on the outside edge of the crotch.

A *plain-stripe figure* (Fig. 5–6), or *ribbon figure* or *ribbon-stripe figure*, is obtained from quartersawed cuts (cuts at a right angle to the annual growth rings). The annual growth rings form the stripes. The grain is generally interlocking. A *rope figure* (Fig. 5–7), often found in avodire, is one characterized by broken stripes, with the breaks in the stripes all running in the same direction. This pattern results from interlocking grains coming together with wavy grains. A *broken stripe figure* (Fig. 5–8), as its name suggests, is characterized by broken stripes. It differs from a rope figure in that the breaks are irregular.

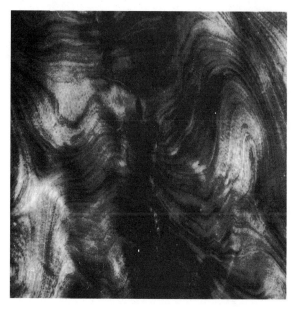

Fig. 5–5. Mahogany wood, swirl cut. *(Courtesy Fine Hardwood Veneer Association)*

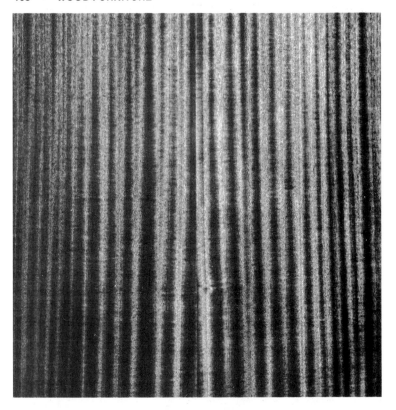

Fig. 5-6. Sapele, striped figure. *(Courtesy Fine Hardwood Veneer Association)*

The *blister figure* shows uneven annual growth rings that are produced through plain sawing. A *quilted figure* is similar in appearance to the blister figure, but usually covers a wider area. As with the butt figure, these are produced through compression of the grain. However, in the quilted figure this occurs higher on the trunk, generally beneath a large branch.

A *butt* or *stump figure* (Fig. 5-9) is obtained from the stump or base of the tree. As the tree grows, the wood at the base is compressed. The compression creates the waves and ripples known as butt figure. Walnut is the usual source for this interesting pattern.

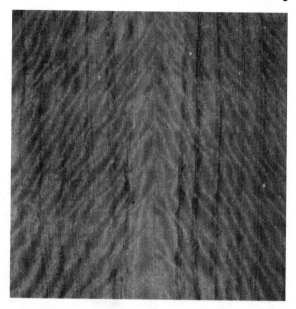

Fig. 5-7. Avodire, rope figure. *(Courtesy Fine Hardwood Veneer Association)*

A *burl figure* (Fig. 5-10) results from a strong distortion of the grain pattern caused by the protrusion of a thick, twisted growth of wood that extends from the trunk or a branch. The burl usually results from temporary cell division caused by an injury to this area of the tree. A figure closely resembling a burl is the *snail figure.* This is produced by a compression of the fibers in the trunk. Like the butt figure, it is usually found in walnut.

The *bird's-eye figure* (Fig. 5-11) receives its name from the many small circular patterns caused by the indentation of the fibers.

A *curly figure* results from the grain fibers being twisted during growth. This produces a curly or wavy pattern that usually follows the contours of a knot or some other defect.

A *wavy figure* is characterized by a parallel wave in the grain. The *fiddleback figure* (Fig. 5-12, 5-13), found in some types of mahogany, is also characterized by a wavy grain pat-

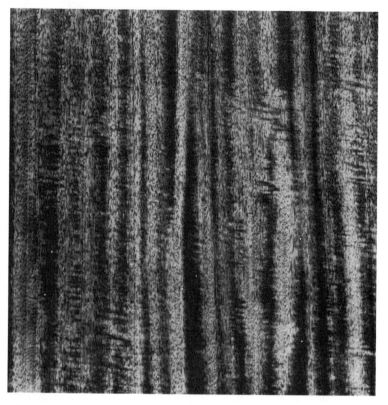

Fig. 5-8. Mahogany, broken stripe figure. *(Courtesy Fine Hardwood Veneer Association)*

tern. This wave pattern results from an irregular fiber arrangement. The fiddleback waves are more broken than those in the wavy figure.

Cutting through the medullary waves of the wood with a quartersaw cut will produce a *silver grain figure* (usually found in sycamore and oak) or a *flake figure* (black cherry). Another figure produced by quartersawing is the *mottle figure* (Fig. 5-14) found in narra and teak. The grain is either twisted or interwoven, with the fibers arranged in short, wavelike configurations. Grain waves also appear around tiny knots (Fig. 5-15).

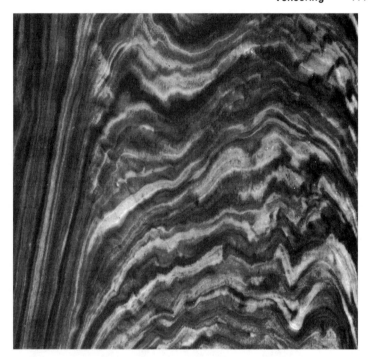

Fig. 5-9. Walnut butt figure. *(Courtesy Fine Hardwood Veneer Association)*

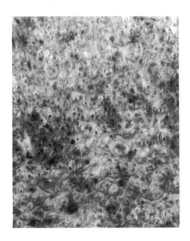

Fig. 5-10. Carpathian elm, burl figure. *(Courtesy Fine Hardwood Veneer Association)*

Fig. 5-11. Maple tree, bird's-eye figure. *(Courtesy Fine Hardwood Veneer Association)*

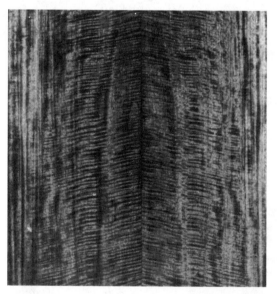

Fig. 5-12. Mahogany, fiddleback figure. *(Courtesy Fine Hardvood Veneer Association)*

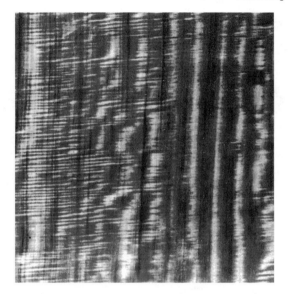

Fig. 5-13. African mahogany, mottled and fiddleback figure. *(Courtesy Fine Hardwood Veneer Association)*

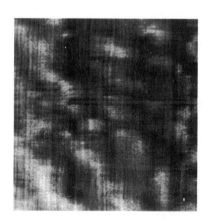

Fig. 5-14. Makori, mottled figure. *(Courtesy Fine Hardwood Veneer Association)*

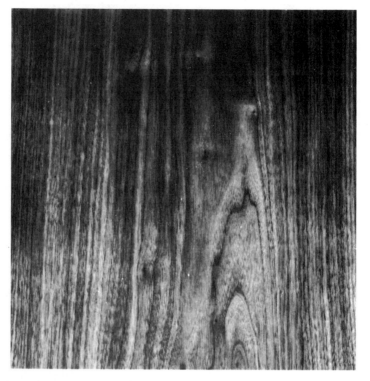

Fig. 5-15. Walnut, pin-knotty. *(Courtesy Fine Hardwood Veneer Association)*

Veneering Woods, Tools, and Materials

Many of the fine woods used in veneering were described in the last chapter (Chapter 3, *Types of Wood*). Almost every type of wood color and figure is available to the home craftsman for veneering. It is a problem of selection, not supply.

The tools and materials used in veneering are largely specific to this type of finishing operation. For veneering, an adequately equipped workshop should include the following:

1. Veneer saw,
2. Veneer roller,
3. Veneer edge trimmer,

4. Veneer groove cutter,
5. Veneer strip and border cutter,
6. Veneer press frame,
7. Veneer repair tool,
8. Veneer tape,
9. Nonflammable contact cement.

A veneer saw (Fig. 5–16) is a double-edge cutting device used for trimming the edges of a veneer sheet, or for creating tight-fitting joints between two or more veneer sheets. The cut should be guided with a straightedge.

The veneer roller (Fig. 5–17) consists of a free-turning, hardwood wheel used for rolling veneer joints and for pressing veneer sheets to core panels. Using a veneer roller greatly reduces or eliminates the possibility of burnishing the veneer.

Sometimes you will find it necessary to make smooth and even cuts on edges of glued veneers. A veneer edge trimmer (Fig. 5–18)

Fig. 5–16.   A veneer saw.

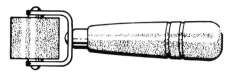

Fig. 5–17.   A veneer roller.

Fig. 5–18.   A veneer edge trimmer.

Fig. 5-19.   A veneer groove cutter.

is recommended for this purpose. This tool is designed to cut the veneer with both a forward and backward movement, thereby eliminating the usual chips or splits at the ends of the veneer.

A veneer groove cutter (Fig. 5-19) will enable you to cut straight, curved, and circular grooves in a single operation. The grooves can be of various depths and widths, depending upon the adjustment.

The veneer groove cutter is generally used in conjunction with a veneer strip and border cutter (Fig. 5-20). This tool contains a

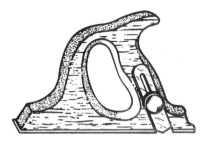

Fig. 5-20.   A veneer strip and border cutter. *(Courtesy Home-craft Veneer)*

single retractable knife on one side and a set of two knives with spacers on the other. It is used for cutting and trimming wide borders, or for cutting strips of veneer to a number of different widths.

A veneer press frame (Fig. 5–21) is recommended for applying the pressure required when gluing veneer sheets to a core with a glue other than contact cement. This tool is constructed from adjustable press screws and two or more frames. The frame should be made from a strong, hard wood (e.g., maple, oak, or yellow pine), and all joints should be strongly bolted together.

The veneer repair tool (Fig. 5–22) is designed for cutting out and replacing by insertion small damaged areas or defects on the surface of a veneer. It uses a spring ejector for both removal and insertion. The cuts are made in irregular shapes so that the patch is less obvious.

The most suitable glue for veneering is a nonflammable contact cement (Fig. 5–23). Use of this glue requires that both the core

Fig. 5–21.   A veneer press frame. *(Courtesy Adjustable Clamp Co.)*

Fig. 5-22. A veneer repair tool. *(Courtesy Homecraft Veneer)*

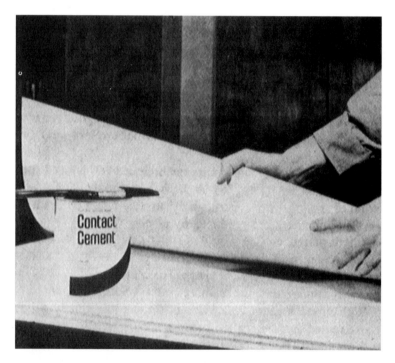

Fig. 5-23. Using contact cement to glue a face veneer to a core.

surface and the bottom of the veneer be coated and allowed to dry thoroughly before being brought into contact. Elmer's white glue is recommended for joining the edges of matching pieces of veneer. A veneer tape (or masking tape) is used to hold veneer sheets together temporarily and in the desired position while the glue is drying or the edges are being trimmed.

Tools not specifically designed for veneering may also be used for this type of work. For example, an X-acto knife (Fig. 5–24), a straight-edged razor, or a jack plane can be used for trimming. Feel free to substitute any type of tool that will help you do your work better.

Fig. 5–24.   An X-acto knife. *(Courtesy Franklin Glue Co.)*

Cutting the Veneer

The three basic methods for cutting a veneer sheet from the log are:

1. Sawing,
2. Slicing,
3. A number of rotary-cut processes—the straight rotary cut, the half-round rotary cut, and the back rotary cut (Fig. 5–25).

In both the sawing and slicing methods, a flitch is used rather than the whole log (Fig. 5–26). A *flitch* is a squared longitudinal section of the log with a particularly striking figure or grain pattern. Sawed veneers are produced by placing the flitch on a movable carriage and cutting with a circular saw. Sliced veneers are produced by placing the flitch on a carriage or platform that raises and lowers before the cutting blade. The blade is a stationary one. The flitch is presoaked in steaming water before being sliced.

With sawed veneers, both sides of the cut are equally suitable as an exposed surface. In the case of sliced veneers, the side toward the knife (this is called the *open* or *loose* side) suffers imperfections

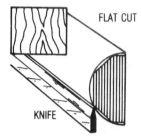

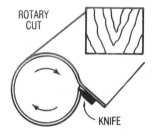

FLAT CUT: half log is moved up and down against the knife. Slicing is parallel to the center line. Veneer sheets are log length, vary in width. Pattern curvaceous at center to ripple striped edges.

ROTARY CUT: whole log revolves against blade, peeling off continuous sheet, wide as log length. Standard size sheets cut from it; pattern quite bold.

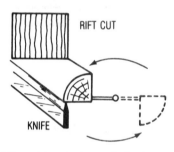

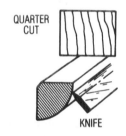

RIFT CUT: used for oak, shows striped grain pattern. Quartered log is swung in arc against blade.

QUARTER CUT: quartered log moves against blade at right angles to growth rings. Produces striped veneer pattern; some species pencil-lined, others wavy, often flakes.

Fig. 5–25. Various veneer cutting methods. (Courtesy Fine Hardwood Veneer Association)

from the knife as a result of the cutting process. This is the side to which the glue is applied.

Sawed veneers can be either quartersawed or plain sawed. Quartersawed wood (Fig. 5–27) has a grain that runs parallel to the length of the wood. This type of grain is sometimes referred to as *vertical grain* and results from the cut being made to form a radius to the annual growth rings. In plain-sawed wood (Fig. 5–28), the grain runs along the width of the wood because the cut was made more or less parallel to the annual growth rings.

Fig. 5-26. Preparation of walnut flitch. *(Courtesy American Walnut Manufacturers Association)*

Actually, only a few veneers are produced by sawing the flitch. These are usually the very hard woods that split easily.

The rotary cut method uses the entire log rather than the smaller-sized flitch. As with sliced veneers, the log must be softened by steaming in water. The softened log is the placed in a veneer lathe and rotated against a stationary knife. A continuous long sheet is cut from the log by slanting the knife toward the center of the log. Rotary-cut veneers also have an *open* (or *loose*) side and a *closed* side. However, it is much more difficult to tell the two apart, particularly in a well-cut veneer. Most of the veneers used today are produced by the rotary cut method.

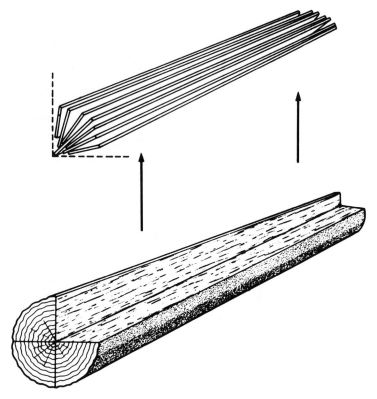

Fig. 5–27. Quartersawed.

Two important modifications of the standard rotary cut are:

1. The half-round rotary cut,
2. The back rotary cut.

The first method involves cutting the log off center, which produces a broader grain pattern. The cutting is done from the outside (or half-round side) of the log. With the back rotary cut, the cutting is done from the center of the log.

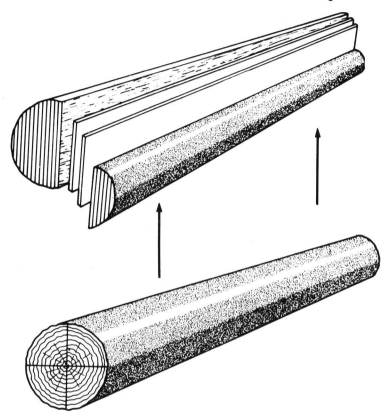

Fig. 5-28. Plain sawed.

Veneer Panels

A veneer panel is essentially a section of plywood covered on the top and bottom with thin sheets of wood selected for their high quality.

The core (everything exclusive of the face veneers) of a five-ply sheet (or all-veneer sheet) is constructed by gluing together a series of narrow (one to three inches wide) sheets of veneer. The narrowness discourages warping. In addition to being narrow, these strips of wood should also be straight grained. This is important because the grain of the next layer will be glued at right angles to the grain of the core wood. Once the glue has dried, the core must be carefully planed so that the entire surface will be even. This should be tested with a T-square. There should not be the slightest depression in the surface of the core piece. This is essential to a proper gluing of the first layer of veneers (or cross bands) across the surfaces of the core. These inner veneer pieces are relatively inexpensive, and are glued across the grain of the core to give added strength. They are eventually covered by the higher-quality face veneer (the surface exposed to view) and a lower-quality back veneer. The inner veneers are glued so that their grain runs perpendicular to the grain of the core wood. The outer veneers, however, are glued with their grains running parallel to that of the core. This change in the direction in which the grains of each layer run adds to the overall strength of the unit (Fig. 5–29).

Fig. 5–29. The various layers of a veneer sheet.

Veneer Matching

Veneer sheets cut from the same flitch are kept together so that they can be matched to form larger sheets. It is almost impossible to match veneers from other than the same sheet because of differences in coloring and figure. Not only can veneer matching produce larger sheets, but special effects can be achieved by the arrangement of the pattern. Some of the more common methods of matching the veneer patterns are:

1. The diamond match,
2. The reverse diamond,
3. The book match,
4. The end match,
5. The four-way match,
6. The slip match.

In the diamond match (Fig. 5–30) pattern, four sheets with a straight stripe in the veneer pattern are arranged so that the stripes form a diamond. The stripes in the reverse diamond (Fig. 5–31) are

Fig. 5–30. Diamond match pattern in veneer. *(Courtesy Reliance Universal, Inc.)*

Fig. 5–31. Reverse diamond pattern. *(Courtesy Reliance Universal, Inc.)*

Fig. 5-32. Book match pattern. *(Courtesy Reliance Universal, Inc.)*

arranged to run in the direction of the four outside corners. A book match (Fig. 5–32) has the two sides of veneer sheets joined so that they produce a mirror image. The end match (Fig. 5–33) uses the same principle, but joins the ends of the veneer sheets. The four way match, (Fig. 5–34) combines the book match was the end match. The veneer sheets are joined in slip matching (Fig. 5–35) side by side to produce a repetition of the figure.

These matched veneer patterns are used as table tops, the exposed fronts of dresser drawers, and the fronts of cabinets, desk tops, and wall panels.

Face veneers for matching are sold in sheets cut to a ⅟₂₈ -inch

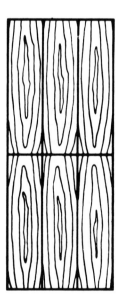

Fig. 5-33. Vertical butt match pattern. *(Courtesy Reliance Universal, Inc.)*

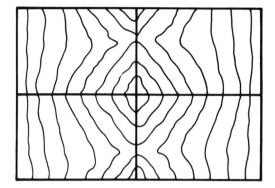

Fig. 5-34. Four-way center and butt match pattern. *(Courtesy Reliance Universal, Inc.)*

thickness. These may be purchased from mail-order houses. Most of these companies offer a wide selection of face veneers, including complete kits for the beginner.

Veneering

Veneering can be as uncomplicated as gluing a face veneer to the surface of a piece of furniture, or it can involve the complete construction of a wood veneer panel.

It was pointed out earlier in this chapter that the complete veneering process consists of the gluing of *at least* a face veneer sheet to a core unit. A back veneer sheet of slightly lower quality is also sometimes added. The core can be a lumber core center with ve-

Fig. 5-35. Slip match pattern. *(Courtesy Reliance Universal, Inc.)*

neer sheets glued to either side; an all-veneer core consisting of three-ply (three veneer sheets), five-ply, and even seven-ply constructions (note that the layers are in odd numbers, with the middle sheet acting as the core); or the surface of a piece of furniture you wish to cover.

The following is an outline of the veneering process. It can serve as a guide on your own particular projects. Remember to regard it as a guide only. Some of the steps may not apply to what you are doing. On the other hand, you may need to expand upon the steps provided.

The various stages in a typical veneering operation are as follows:

1. Decide first whether you want to use a single-face veneer or a matched veneer. Face veneer sheets in both domestic and imported woods are generally sold in 4-inch to 12-inch widths and 3-foot lengths (longer lengths can be obtained on request), with a standard thickness of $\frac{1}{28}$ inch.

2. The single-face veneer sheet will have to be cut so that no joint shows. You will also have to do the cutting if you wish to make your own matched veneers. However, matched veneers can also be ordered (the pieces taped and ready for gluing) from a number of mail-order houses in 12-inch by 24-inch sheets, 15-inch by 30-inch sheets, and 30-inch by 30-inch sheets.

3. Lightly sand the surface to which the veneer will be joined until it is free of all defects or irregularities and uniformly smooth. If several pieces of wood are to be joined together, the joints must be smooth. Any dips in the surface have to be filled and leveled. Any surface bumps must be planed and sanded so that they are even with the rest of the surface.

4. Repeat this procedure for the underside of the veneer sheet.

5. Thoroughly clean the two surfaces you just sanded.

6. Take the veneer sheet and position it on the surface to which it is to be glued. This is the time to decide the direction you want the grain to run, as well as the arrangement and positioning of the figure and grain pattern. If you estimated correctly, the total area of the veneer sheet that you purchased (either a single piece or the possible combination of several sheets) overlaps the surface to which it is to be glued at least $\frac{1}{2}$ inch on all sides.

7. Now that you have decided upon the exact positioning of the veneer sheet, and this sheet is a single one (that is, it has not been necessary to cut and join several pieces together to make a veneer sheet large enough to cover the area), take a marking pencil and mark the underside where it meets the edge of the surface to which it is to be glued.

8. You may find it necessary to join two or more veneer sheets together to make one large enough for the surface you wish to cover. Your first problem will be to find two veneer sheets that are very close in figure, grain, and color. You will want to have the grains of the various pieces running in the same direction if you wish to join them so that they appear to be one piece. Above all, the joint between the two pieces must not show.

9. Overlap the two edges that are to be joined (about 1 inch should do). Take a straightedge and draw a line across the veneer sheet at the point where you want to make the cut. X-acto has a number of blades that will cut through both veneer sheets quite well. After you have made your cut, fold the two sheets over so that the face veneer surfaces are together. Take two 1 × 4-inch boards with straight edges and a length measuring one inch beyond the edge of the two veneer sheets. Take two clamps and attach them to the 1 × 4-inch boards at a point over the outside edges of the two veneer sheets.

10. Allow only about ¼ inch of the veneer sheets to extend beyond the edge (lengthwise) of the 1 × 4-inch boards. Plane off the excess and remove the clamps and 1 × 4-inch boards (Fig 5–36). Open up the veneer sheets and place the newly planed ends together. If the match is perfect, glue the edges (Fig. 5–37). Temporarily tape the good side until you are ready to glue (Fig. 5–38).

11. The problem now is to determine how close to the core you want to cut the veneer sheet. This in turn depends upon whether the top veneer sheet is to overlap the veneer edge strip, or the reverse is to be the case. Make your decision about the type of edge you want, and then read Step 12 before continuing.

12. The excess wood must be cut away from the veneer sheet. Since it is very easy to chip or split the surface, special precautions must be taken. Place straight-edged wood blocks

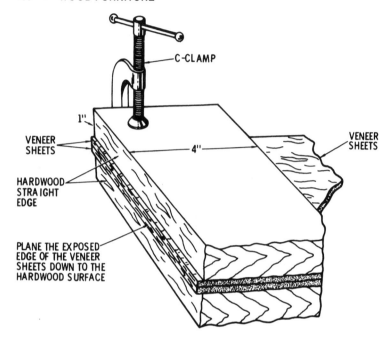

Fig. 5-36. Planning the veneer sheets.

Fig. 5-37. Gluing the edges of the veneer sheets together.

Fig. 5-38. Taping the glued veneer sheets until the edges dry.

made from 1 × 6-inch boards cut to the length of the veneer sheet on both sides of the veneer sheet so that the outer edge of each block is on the line drawn in Step 9. Use C-clamps to keep the wood blocks in place.

13. Take a veneer saw or knife and cut away the excess wood to about ¼ inch of the line drawn in Step 9. Take a jack plane and trim the rough edge down to the line. Use a sanding block and sandpaper (changing from a medium to a fine grade) to finish the edge.

14. At this point, you must decide what kind of edge you want. Any surface to which a face veneer has been glued must be finished along the edges so that the layers of veneer sheets are hidden from view.

The easiest method of finishing the edge is to take a block of wood and a rough grade of sandpaper (to be followed by medium and fine grades, in that order) and sand the edge smooth. After you have finished sanding, wipe away the excess sawdust and dirt, and paint the surface of the edge a dark color (flat black, black enamel, red brown, dark brown, ochre, etc.) (Fig. 5–39).

A more difficult method of finishing the edges is to glue a strip of veneer into place. This strip is usually selected to match the veneer sheet covering the larger surface. The cutting method is the same as the one described in Steps 12 and 13 (Fig. 5–40).

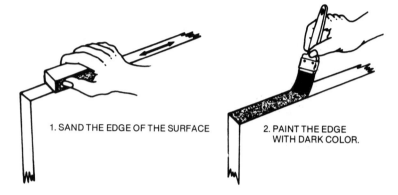

1. SAND THE EDGE OF THE SURFACE

2. PAINT THE EDGE WITH DARK COLOR.

Fig. 5-39. Finishing the edge by painting.

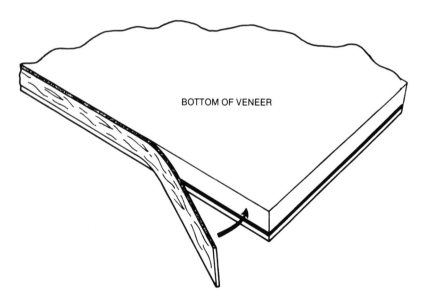

BOTTOM OF VENEER

Fig. 5-40. Gluing the veneer strip to the edge.

15. In Step 5 you were asked to dust thoroughly the bottom of the veneer sheet and the surface to which it is to be glued. Dust it again now if it needs it.

16. Coat the surfaces to be joined with a contact veneer cement. If you are applying veneer to a table top, desk top, or the top of a cabinet or dresser, coat the edge of the top with cement also.

17. Allow the contact cement sufficient time to dry thoroughly before placing the two newly coated surfaces together. The cement-coated surfaces will bond instantly on contact. Therefore, you must exercise great care.

18. Place newspaper so that it completely covers the glue-coated surface of the piece of furniture.

19. Place the veneer sheet on top of the newspaper with the glue-coated side down. The dried contact cement will not stick to the paper. It will bond only to the other surface coated with cement.

20. Press down on one end of the veneer while you pull the paper out carefully from the other end. Press against the center of the veneer and outward toward the edges. Use a small veneer roller to press the bonded surfaces into even firmer contact.

21. Press screws are used to construct veneer press frames, which are particularly well suited for the type of clamping required in veneering. In the home workshop C-clamps and ¾-inch plywood serve as an acceptable substitute. Clamping pressure is necessary when glues other than contact cement are used.

Repairing Veneers

Cut away the damaged area in such a way that as many sides of the cut as possible run parallel to the grain. Those sides that cannot do so must be cut so that they form angles that are less than a right angle to the grain. The piece that you remove from the veneer surface will be a trapezoid or some variation of a diamond.

Find a wood with a grain matching that of the damaged veneer. The likelihood of finding an exact duplicate is extremely rare unless you have saved veneer sheets from the same flitch. Therefore, it is best to use a repair piece with a lighter surface color and stain it to match the older veneer.

Measure the opening you have cut in the damaged veneer. Take a piece of stiff paper (poster paper will do) or thin cardboard and using these measurements, cut out a pattern. Place the pattern on the piece of veneer to be matched. Make certain that it is positioned in such a way that the grains of both surfaces will match. Cut out the veneer patch and insert it in the hole you cut. *Do not force it in.* If it is too tight, remove it and sand the edges. Continue to do this until it will slide smoothly and snugly into the hole. Glue it in place (Fig. 5–41).

Transveneer (Plastic Veneer Transfer)

A *transveneer* (or plastic veneer transfer) is in many respects simply a larger version of the decalcomania transfer. Transveneers are available in sheets as large as 32 inches by 48 inches, where as decalcomania transfers are sold in much smaller sheets.

The transveneer consists of at least three layers:

1. The lacquer background,
2. A paper-thin coating of lacquer over which a color print has been superimposed such as a photoengraving of wood grain or some other design,
3. A layer of paper—there are sometimes two layers of paper, making a fourth layer for the transveneer sheet.

The paper layer is removed by moistening it with a damp cloth. After the paper is removed, the glue residue is sponged off the surface of the imprinted layer of lacquer.

The glue suggested by the manufacturer of the transveneer sheet is applied to the sheet, and it is then affixed to the surface being covered. Use a roller to remove all wrinkles and air bubbles. Use a damp cloth to remove any excess glue.

Transveneer sheets are successfully applied only over small-pored (close-grained) woods. In woods with larger pores, the grain pattern has a tendency to bleed through the transveneer sheet. If you have any doubts about the surface, it would be wise to sand the surface, fill it, seal it, sand it again, and apply a thin coat of lacquer.

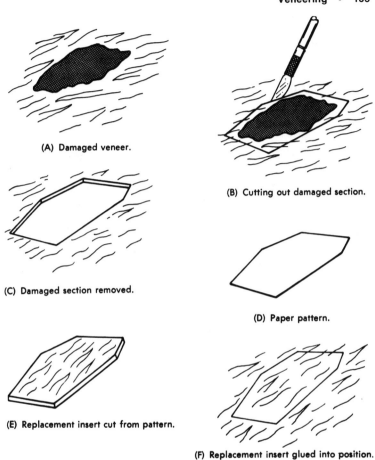

(A) Damaged veneer.

(B) Cutting out damaged section.

(C) Damaged section removed.

(D) Paper pattern.

(E) Replacement insert cut from pattern.

(F) Replacement insert glued into position.

Fig. 5-41. Repairing damaged veneer sheet.

Transveneers are used in place of veneers in the cheaper grades of furniture. The very cheaply priced "complete three-piece bedroom suite" sometimes advertised on television and in the newspaper is most likely to be of transveneer construction.

Humidity will often cause the thin transveneer sheet to peel back at the edges of the furniture. This is particularly noticeable on larger surfaces (such as dressers). A small dab of Testor's or Elmer's white glue can be used to correct this. Press the transveneer down and wipe away the excess glue with a damp cloth.

Plastic Laminates

Plastic laminates are one of several products resulting from the lamination process. The type of layering (lamina) used in lamination determines the end product. Plastic laminates use a lamina of plastic.

These plastic laminates resemble veneers in that they are built up from several layers of material. In the case of plastic laminates, there are several layers of paper impregnated with resin. The core layers are soaked in phenol-formaldehyde resin, the transparent overlay in melamine resin. The melamine overlay acts as a protective layer for the printed sheet just beneath. All the layers are bonded together under extremely high pressure and temperatures. Formica, Naugatop, and Micarta are a few of the common trademark names sold commercially.

These plastic laminates are used primarily for table tops (dining room tables, end tables, coffee tables, etc.) in furniture construction. They provide an extremely durable surface, and resist almost any kind of stain.

CHAPTER 6

Inlaying

Inlaying may be defined as the adorning of a wood surface by the insertion of different colored woods. Sometimes the inserted woods form a complex ornamental design (Fig. 6–1). Simpler forms of inlay consist of one or more woods arranged to form decorative borders (Fig. 6–2). Inlaying can be divided into two distinct types:

1. Intarsia,
2. Marquetry.

Intarsia is a true inlay process. That is, the wood inserts are glued into a groove or recess that has been cut from the background (base) wood. The wood inserts may be all one color or of several colors. The background wood may be either lighter or darker than the wood inserts, thus providing a contrasting border for the design formed by the wood inserts. The depth of the depression cut into the background wood varies according to the thickness of the inlay. Intarsia is of Italian origin and is historically a forerunner of marquetry.

Marquetry is dismissed by some as simply the French word for "inlay," and therefore different in name only. As a matter of fact, the word "marquetry" *is* derived from the French verb *marqueter*,

Fig. 6-1. Complex ornamental inlay designs.

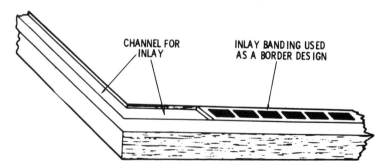

Fig. 6-2. Inlay border.

"to inlay"; however, a distinction can be made between marquetry and intarsia in the method by which the decorative pieces are attached to the background. In intarsia (which is regarded as true inlaying), the decorative wood is inserted in grooves and recesses cut from the background wood. Marquetry, on the other hand, consists of cutting a pattern out of a veneer (i.e., not a solid wood background) and inserting a decorative design made from other veneers cut from the same pattern to form a panel. The entire panel can then either be glued to a solid wood background or inlaid in that wood.

Inlaying involves not only the insertion of decorative woods in grooves and recesses cut from solid wood backgrounds, but also the insertion of such materials as stone, shell, and glass (to mention only a few) into other types of backgrounds. The inlaying of materials other than wood is known as mosaic (mosaicking), and is examined in a later section of this chapter.

Woods, Tools, and Materials

Almost any kind of wood can be used for inlays, but the best inlay woods will have one or more of the following characteristics:

1. Good workability,
2. An even grain with little or no figure,
3. A color light enough to stain,
4. The tendency to take an even, uniform stain.

Using a wood that cuts and trims easily makes inlaying (and marquetry) a lot less difficult. The inlaying procedure frequently involves the cutting and repeated trimming of a wood piece until it is just the right size to fit into the groove or recess. Some woods are subject to splintering or chipping when being cut. The cutting of such woods requires great skill and patience, and sometimes additional time to repair splintered or chipped pieces. Since this can be annoying and time consuming, I would recommend selecting the wood you use with great care.

Very dark inlay woods (e.g., ebony, oriental wood, and walnut) are used for borders or contrasting areas. The light-colored inlay woods (e.g., tulipwood, satinwood, holly, and hardwood) are often used because they can be easily stained. This is particularly useful in restoration when it is necessary to match the color of a missing piece. Stain-resistant areas, woods that crack or split easily, and woods that are difficult to cut or trim should be avoided by the beginner.

All different types of wood are commercially available to the home craftsperson. Mail-order houses that sell woodworking tools and supplies offer a wide range of inlay and veneer woods. They will be happy to send you their catalogs, and in some instances samples of their woods.

One form of inlaying consists of creating borders along square or rectangular shapes with narrow strips of wood. This is sometimes referred to as *line inlay*. The wood strips (inlay bandings) may be one solid piece of wood or built up from a number of different woods. Examples of the multicolored effect possible with the latter is shown in Fig. 6–3. Inlay bandings are of varying widths, approximately $\frac{1}{28}$ inch thick, and sold in 36-inch lengths.

Precut inlay pictures are available commercially from the mail-order houses. These are available in a number of different designs (Fig. 6–4). It is also possible to purchase inlay picture kits that

Fig. 6–3. Inlay bandings.

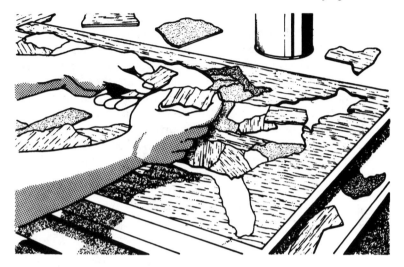

Fig. 6-4. Precut inlay pictures.

are not precut. These are complete kits containing inlay border woods, hardboard mounting panels, all the veneer wood required for the project, master patterns for cutting, and a number of other items necessary for a successful job. Cutting must be done with a suitable saw.

The tools and materials used for inlaying are similar in most respects to those used for veneering. However, some are probably more common to the former. Among the tools and materials you may find useful for inlaying are the following:

1. A jigsaw, hand coping saw, or fret saw,
2. A straight-edged razor,
3. A portable electric router or a router plane,
4. X-acto knives,
5. A veneer saw knife,
6. A veneer roller,
7. A try square,
8. Clamps,
9. A miter cutting board,
10. A suitable glue.

Three suitable saws for cutting inlay are the jigsaw, the hand coping saw, and the fret saw. When hand cutting, hold the saw so that its blade is always in a vertical position and at a right angle to the wood surface (Fig. 6–5). Use a blade with a very narrow kerf and mount it in the saw so the teeth point toward the handle.

A straight-edged razor is extremely useful for trimming the edge of inlay inserts after they have been cut out with the saw.

Use a router plane (Fig. 6–6) or a portable electric router to cut the groove or recess in the surface of the background wood. An X-acto knife is useful for cutting along the edges of the design be-

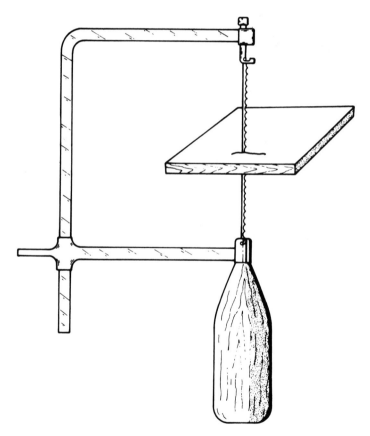

Fig. 6–5. Sawing at a right angle to the wood surface.

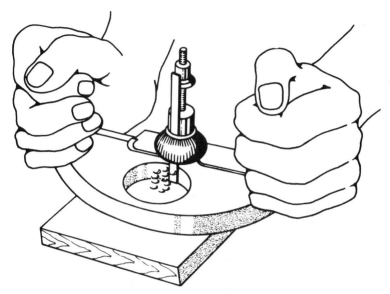

Fig. 6-6.   Using a router plane.

fore removing the wood from the recessed area. It can also be used to make miter cuts on inlay bandings. For this purpose, a miter cutting board will assist you in making the type of corners required in line inlaying.

The veneer saw knife (Fig. 6-7) is used to make cuts across pieces of veneer. Larger pieces can be reduced to the approximate size required for the job with this tool.

Pressure can be applied to inlay bandings with a veneer roller (Fig. 6-8). Clamps are also used for applying pressure to the inlay inserts.

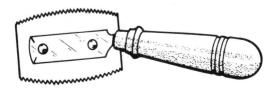

Fig. 6-7.   A veneer saw knife.

Fig. 6–8. A veneer roller.

The metal edges of a try square are useful for making both straight edge and miter cuts.

A variety of glues can be used for inlay work. Hot animal glue was once a favorite with many cabinetmakers because it did not discolor the wood. However, it required special preparation and has been replaced in many shops by glues more convenient to use. Casein glue, rubber cement, and a number of others are used today. Premixed animal glue is available that has longer work life and is reversible. Whatever your selection, the glue you use should be easy to apply, should form a strong bond, and should not discolor the wood.

Line Inlay

There are three basic types of inlaying:

1. Line inlay,
2. Corner inlay,
3. Center inlay.

Line inlay consists of creating borders along square or rectangular shapes with narrow strips of wood. These strips of decorative wood (inlay bandings) are inserted into grooves parallel to the edges of the larger wood surface.

The procedure for applying inlay bandings is as follows:

1. Use a ruler and pencil, and outline the position of the groove for the inlay banding.
2. Rout out the groove. The groove must be cut so that it is slightly shallower than the inlay piece. The width of the groove will be exactly the same as the width of the inlay banding.

3. Coat the bottom of the recess with glue (some prefer coating the bottom of the inlay banding instead).
4. Place the inlay banding in the groove. If the fit is tight (which is more desirable than too loose), force it in with a hammer. Do not strike the inlay banding without placing a piece of felt or cardboard between the hammer and the wood. If the fit is loose, it will be necessary to clamp the inlay banding until it has dried.
5. Allow enough time for the glue to dry thoroughly.
6. After the glue has dried, lightly sand the inlay banding until it is level with the surface.
7. Cover the inlay banding with a shellac washcoat before doing any filling or staining of the rest of the surface. Otherwise, you may ruin the inlay colors. It is best to line the edge of the inlay banding strip with masking tape before applying the washcoat.

Corner and Center Inlay

Corner inlays consist of decorative designs inserted at corner positions on the wood surface. Center inlays are positioned in the exact center. A decorative design for a center inlay may be relatively small, or it may cover most of the surface area. Regardless of size, the design expands outward from a center point on the surface. The size of corner inlays is somewhat limited by the angle of the corner.

The procedure for making corner and center inlays is similar to the one described for line inlay. However, the problem of obtaining a close fit between the inserted piece and the recess cut into the wood surface is usually greater with corner and center inlays than with line inlay work. A more detailed description follows.

The Inlaying Procedure

The inlaying procedure for line inlay work has been described above. This particular section is devoted to a description of the procedure for inserting inlay pictures and other decorative designs into the background wood surface. It is slightly more difficult than line inlay, but most of its procedural steps apply equally well to the latter.

Proper fit is a major problem in inlaying. The inserted pieces must fit snugly into their recesses and grooves. An insert consisting of a few straight edges (e.g., inlay bandings, squares, and rectangles) is relatively easy to use. The problems begin with curved or irregularly shaped designs.

The inlaying procedure for center inlay (or corner inlay) is as follows:

1. Take a piece of paper and draw an outline of the decorative design you want to use as an inlay. This will serve as a pattern.
2. Cut out the pattern, position it on the inlay wood, and trace the outline of the design.
3. Using a jigsaw (other suitable cutting tools are suggested in the section WOODS, TOOLS, AND MATERIALS), cut out the inlay design.
4. Lightly sand the edges of the inlay until they are smooth. Do *not* round them. All edges must be vertically straight and square to the surface of the inlay. If this is not accomplished, then the inlay will not fit properly.
5. Place the inlay on the surface of the background wood, position it carefully, and trace its outline.
6. Cut out the area you have outlined with a machine router. Hand cutting can also be done, but it is slower and much more difficult. Before you use the router, cut straight down with a sharp knife along the edge of the outline. This will form the edges of the recess.
7. Be very careful when you cut the recess for the insert. Take your time, because your cuts must be made with absolute accuracy; otherwise there will be a space between the edge of the inlay and the edge of the recess. This will fill with glue and give the appearance of a dark, uneven border when the glue dries.
8. The recess should be cut slightly shallower than the thickness of the inlay insert. This will cause the inlay to protrude slightly above the surface, but it will be sanded smooth after the glue has thoroughly dried.
9. The glue may be applied either to the bottom of the insert or to the recessed area. For many years hot animal glue was a favor-

ite for inlaying because it left no glue film or discoloration. Specially prepared rubber cements with these same characteristics, though perhaps not the same adhesive strength, are now becoming available. Casein glues are also popular.

10. Press the inlay insert into the recess and immediately wipe off any excess glue that may have squeezed through the edges with a clean, dry cloth.

11. A tight-fitting inlay, preferably one that requires the use of a hammer to force it into the recess, will generally not require clamping.

12. Allow the glue enough time to dry thoroughly before sanding. The inlay may be subject to both swelling (by absorbing the moisture from the glue) and shrinking (contracting during the drying). Consequently, the true position of the inlay with respect to the surface can only be established after the glue has thoroughly dried.

13. Sand the surface with a fine grade of sandpaper. Dust it with a clean, dry cloth, and sand it again with a very fine grade.

14. See FINISHING INLAYS AND OVERLAYS for suggested finishes.

Repairing and Restoring Inlays

Repairing an inlay may appear difficult, but it need not be so. It is essentially a problem of replacing an inlay piece with one that matches it in color and shape. Since the procedure for making inlay repairs is identical to the one used for repairing marquetry, all information given in this section will pertain to both.

There are three basic types of repairs associated with inlaying. Beginning with the easiest type of repair and progressing to the most difficult, these are:

1. Regluing a loose piece,
2. Replacing a missing piece,
3. Replacing a chipped or broken piece.

Sometimes a piece of inlay will become loose or fall off. Since you have the inlay piece in your possession, you do not have the problem of obtaining a replacement. Take the piece of inlay, remove it from its backing if it is still partially glued to it, and clean off all traces of glue on its underside. You will also have to remove any glue found in the groove or recess from which the inlay piece came; a new coat of glue will generally not adhere well if there are traces of old glue on the surface. When you have cleaned all traces of the old glue from both contact surfaces, give the inlay piece a new coating of glue and reposition it in the groove or recess.

You are faced with a slightly more difficult problem if the piece of inlay is completely missing. You will have to substitute another piece that matches the color and shape of the missing one. Since many mail-order houses that deal in woodworking supplies carry a full line of woods used in veneering and inlaying, it is not too difficult to find a wood that matches or comes very close to matching the wood type and color of the missing piece. You might also be able to find a suitable substitute around your own shop. In any event, once you have obtained a wood to be used as a replacement for the missing piece of inlay, the procedure is as follows:

1. Take a piece of tracing paper, place it over the hole in the inlay, and trace its outline. This serves as a pattern for the new piece of inlay.
2. Cut the pattern out slightly larger (about $\frac{1}{8}$ inch larger) than the traced lines indicate.
3. Place the inlay pattern on the piece of wood you obtained and cut out the inlay.
4. Since the inlay pattern was cut out slightly larger than the tracing indicated, it stands to reason that the new inlay piece will also be slightly larger. This was intentional. The new inlay piece will be trimmed down with a razor until it fits.
5. Place the new, slightly oversized piece of inlay over the groove or recess. Take a single-edged razor or an appropriate X-acto knife, and trim the edges of the inlay piece until it fits snugly into the groove or recess. A good fit will require a certain amount of pressure (hammering, etc.) to force it into the depression in the background (base) wood. Do not trim away too much excess wood, or the inlay piece will fit too loosely. Trimming should proceed carefully and slowly.
6. After you have trimmed the inlay piece to the desired shape, lightly sand the edges so that they are smooth and straight. Do *not* round the edges as you sand them.
7. Coat the underside of the inlay piece with glue and position it

in the recess or groove. Do not use an excessive amount of glue, or it will squeeze up between the edges of the inlay piece and smear the surface with a glue film, which will interfere with the finishing operation. Wipe away any excess glue with a clean, damp cloth.

8. If the piece needs to be clamped, use ¼ -inch thick clear plexiglass as a clamp pad. This allows you to see the fit.

9. If the piece of inlay you are using to replace the missing piece does not match the latter in color tone, you can correct this by staining. I would recommend experimenting on a piece of scrap wood first.

Attempting to replace a broken or chipped off piece of inlay is only slightly more difficult than the last-described operation. In addition to the eight steps recommended for replacing a missing piece of inlay, you will have to include an additional, preliminary step of cutting off any sharp corners or edges along the break. This can be done with an X-acto knife or a straight-edged razor. Make your cut as straight as possible, so that the joining edge of the new piece will meet an equally straight edge.

Overlays

Overlays are wood decorations that are glued directly to the wood surface without routing out a groove or recess (Fig. 6–9). They therefore extend or project slightly above the surface of the wood.

Overlays purchased from mail-order houses or other retail outlets have a protective paper covering the side that faces up. After the glue has dried, remove the paper by moistening and then sanding. Remove the dust left by the sanding operation with a dry, lint-free cloth. The surface of the overlay is now ready for a natural finish or a shellac washcoat.

Finishing Inlays and Overlays

If a natural finish is used, the inlay or overlay wood does not require any additional protection. However, the use of stains or

Fig. 6-9. Various overlays.

fillers requires that the inlay and overlay woods be protected. A washcoat of shellac will be quite adequate for this purpose. Without this protection, the inlay and overlay woods will tend to absorb color from the stain and filler.

Mosaic

Mosaic (or *mosaicking*) is the process of inlaying small pieces of tiles, colored glass, stone, or other materials into a background (base) to form a design for a surface decoration.

The most commonly used and readily available material for creating mosaics are the ceramic tiles that can be purchased at most hobby and homecraft centers. These come in several shapes (square, triangular, circular, and rectangular) and a variety of sizes and colors. Usually they are used to decorate table tops, but they can also form decorative inlays for chair legs or border strips for furniture frames.

These mosaic tiles may either be inserted into the wood surface or laid across the top. If the former, then it is necessary to cut away a portion of the surface for the insertion of the tiles. The procedure is similar to that described for inlaying pieces of decorative wood (see THE INLAYING PROCEDURE above). If the tiles are laid across the surface, then an edging is necessary. This can be either a wood strip or a strip made of metal. Whichever is used, it must be screwed into position or glued to the surface with epoxy glue.

The procedure for creating a mosaic is as follows:

1. Cut a piece of thin cardboard or heavyweight art paper to the exact shape of the area to be covered by the mosaic tiles.
2. Using this cardboard or paper pattern as a temporary guide, arrange the mosaic tiles in the design you wish to create on the furniture surface.
3. The next step is to prepare the surface of the wood. The entire surface must be completely finished before laying the mosaic tile. In the case of an older piece of furniture, this may require removing the old finish, sanding, and applying a new finish. The complete process is described in detail in the appropriate chapters of this book.

CHAPTER 7

Repairing and Restoring

This chapter covers repairing surface defects. Repairs that affect the structure (frame) of the piece of furniture are only described briefly, so you will recognize when they are needed. Surface defects may involve only the finish, or may be serious enough to have damaged the wood in some way. Crazing, lifting, and cracking are examples of the former; gouges, scratches, and dents, of the latter.

Restoring is essentially a touch-up operation involving minor repairs of either, or both, the finish and the wood portions of the piece of furniture. The old finish is retained, but measures are taken to restore some of its former beauty. Old wax, polish, dirt, grease, and other matter are removed with a suitable cleaning preparation (i.e., one that will not damage the original finish). Sometimes the finish is reamalgamated to eliminate cracks or crazing. Shellac stick and other touch-up materials are used to repair the surface. Minor repair work (such as regluing joints) is also commonly done. The overall purpose of restoration work, however, is to retain as much of the original finish and structure as possible.

Always attempt to clean or restore a finish before considering the more expensive and time-consuming operation of stripping it. After all, if your restoration attempts fail, you can still remove the finish as well as any evidence of your failure to restore it.

Stripping is the process of removing an old finish down to the bare wood surface. It should be considered only if the original finish is in too poor a condition to be effectively restored. Stripping is both messy and time-consuming. Restoring a finish can be reduced to a minimum by careful planning. I strongly recommend that you take your time and work carefully.

Wear old clothes, old shoes, and gloves when you are refinishing. No matter how careful you try to be, some of the finishing materials always seem to splatter onto clothing or the skin. These materials are also usually inflammable, so I must caution you once again against working near flames, electric coils, and other heat sources. Sparks are also dangerous because they could set off an explosion. Proper ventilation in the work area is a must, because prolonged inhalation of the fumes from these materials could damage your health. I would recommend using finish removers outdoors. See the chapter on safety for more on using hazardous materials.

Tools and Materials

Many of the tools and materials used in repairing furniture and in restoring or stripping old finishes have already been described in Chapter 2. Some other items that lend themselves specifically to this type of work are included here.

Those tools and materials that will make repair work easier are as follows:

1. Sandpaper,
2. Sanding block,
3. Wood fillers,
4. Glue,
5. Clamps,
6. X-acto knives,
7. Small and medium size saws,
8. A hand or power drill.

White, yellow, and epoxy resin glue are very useful in repair work. Yellow glue is commonly used for gluing furniture joints together. Although in the past epoxy resin glue has been more frequently used to join nonporous materials (glass, metal, etc.), it is finding increasing use in woodworking. For example, it is useful for regluing a loose joint that you do not want to disassemble. It will even fill in spaces between the frame joints.

A hand or power drill is essential for making new dowel or screw holes. I do not recommend nailing, because it results in the weakest type of construction. Small saws (a jigsaw, coping saw, etc.) are used for cutting wedges or inserts. Larger saws (a hand-saw, crosscut saw, etc.) are useful for larger cutting operations such as removing damaged legs or extensive remodeling. X-acto knives come in a variety of sizes and shapes, and are excellent tools for trimming.

The clamps illustrated in Figs. 7–1, 7–2, and 7–3 suggest the variety of ways in which pressure can be applied while a joint or surface is being glued.

Sandpaper, sanding blocks, and steel wool are covered in Chapter 2, *Finishing Tools and Supplies.* The various types of

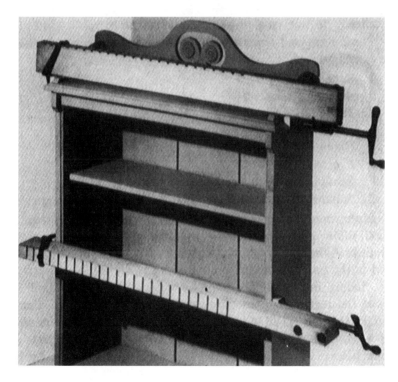

Fig. 7–1. Wood bar clamp. *(Courtesy Adjustable Clamp Company)*

Fig. 7-2. Band clamps. *(Courtesy Adjustable Clamp Company)*

wood fillers used for patching wood surfaces (e.g., stick shellac, wax stick, plastic wood, and wood putty) are described in the section WOOD PATCHING COMPOUNDS. Do not confuse these with the type of filler used to fill wood pores during the initial stages of a finishing schedule.

Identifying Finishes

Not all cleaning preparations are suitable for every type of finish. Some are simply not chemically compatible, and will cause serious damage to the topcoat. Therefore, it is absolutely necessary that you first correctly identify the type of finish with which you are working before you proceed.

Most of the furniture finishes with which you will be dealing can be classified under one of the following types:

Fig. 7-3. Steel bar clamps. *(Courtesy Adjustable Clamp Company)*

1. Shellac,
2. Shellac-lacquer,
3. Lacquer,
4. Varnish,
5. Paint,
6. Enamel.

The easiest method for identifying these finishes is to test them on some inconspicuous spot with a solvent. If you cannot determine the type of finish on the piece of furniture, you will have to identify it through the process of elimination by testing it with a number of different solvents. The identification will be made when you find a solvent that will dissolve it.

It is best to start with denatured alcohol, because this solvent will dissolve a shellac finish (and partially soften a shellac-lacquer finish), but it will not affect other types of finishes. Soak the end of a clean rag in denatured alcohol and rub it on an area of the finish that is not normally exposed. If the finish begins to dissolve, you are dealing with a shellac finish. However, if your efforts succeed in only partially softening the topcoat, it is more than likely a combination shellac-lacquer finish. Adding an equal amount of lacquer to the denatured alcohol will completely dissolve the topcoat if it is a shellac-lacquer finish. Denatured alcohol will not dissolve any of the other finishes listed above. Consequently, if there is no reaction whatsoever, try the same test with lacquer thinner.

Lacquer thinner will partially soften a shellac-lacquer finish and completely dissolve one consisting only of lacquer. However, it has no effect on varnish, paint, or enamel finishes. These can be dissolved by any of the commercial paint and varnish removers. Table 7–1 lists the various types of finishes and the solvents used to dissolve them.

Table 7–1. Finishing Materials and their Solvents

Finishing Material	Solvent
Synthetic Varnish	Turpentine or Mineral Spirits
Oil Base Varnish	Turpentine, Mineral Spirits, or Paint Thinner
Enamel (Varnish Type)	Turpentine, Mineral Spirits, or Paint Thinner
Shellac	Denatured Alcohol
Lacquer	Lacquer Thinner
Lacquer Sealer	Lacquer Thinner
Lacquer Enamel	Lacquer Thinner
Paint and Varnish Remover	Denatured Alcohol
Water Stain	Soap and Warm Water
Spirit (Alcohol) Stain	Denatured Alcohol
Oil Stain	Turpentine, Paint Thinner, Naphtha, Kerosene
Paste Wood Filler	Mineral Spirits
Paint (Latex)	Water
Linseed Oil	Turpentine or Mineral Spirits
Paint (Milk Base)	Ammonia

Cleaning

Wax, polish, grease, and dirt can be removed from the finish with a suitable cleaning preparation. Mineral oil, or a cleaning preparation containing a mineral oil base, is recommended because it will not harm a shellac finish. Preparations containing alcohol will dissolve the shellac. The mineral oil should be warmed slightly and applied to the surface with a soft, clean, lint-free cloth. Lacquer thinner or naphtha, should be wiped across the wood surface *after* the finish has been removed to eliminate any residue left by the solvent, otherwise the new finish will not dry easily. (Lacquer thinner and naphtha produce hazardous fumes. See Chapter 20, *Safety*, for more on handling hazardous materials.)

Wood Patching Compounds

Wood patching compounds are used for filling gouges, dents, scratches, and other types of imperfections found on wood surfaces (Fig. 7-4). The five wood patching compounds most commonly used for repairing damaged wood surfaces are:

1. Plastic wood,
2. Wood putty,
3. Stick shellac,
4. Wax stick,
5. Latex wood patch.

Plastic wood and stick shellac are more popular with wood finishers for reasons that will be pointed out below. It will be seen that each product has certain advantages and disadvantages.

Plastic wood (also referred to as *wood plastic* or *wood dough*) is actually a trade name for a wood dough product. Owing to popular usage, the trade name is gradually replacing the generic one.

Plastic wood is a quick-drying filling material so tough that it can be sawed, drilled, sanded, or carved without crumbling or loss of strength. In short, its workability is excellent. Furthermore, it holds nails or screws as well as wood does. Unfortunately, it produces an ungrained, opaque surface that is very noticeable unless used under an opaque finish or in areas not normally exposed. Plastic wood is used primarily to (1) repair sections of the frame that

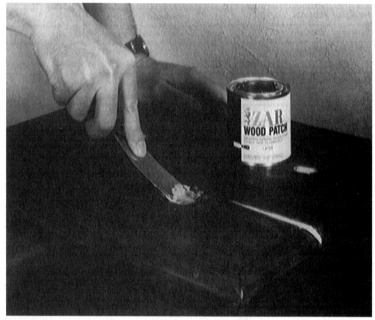

Fig. 7-4. Using latex wood patch to repair cracks and other surface blemishes. *(Courtesy Wood Finishing Products/United Gilsonite Laboratories)*

require strengthening, (2) fill large dents, gouges, and deep holes (especially knotholes), and (3) build up carvings, moldings, and edges that have been chipped or broken off.

Plastic wood is available in cans and tubes. If it seems too dry (crumbly), it can be restored to a workable consistency by adding denatured alcohol, lacquer thinner, or a solvent recommended by the manufacturer. Plastic wood that has dried too hard cannot be restored regardless of the amount of thinner you add. Therefore, when not being used it should be stored in an airtight container.

Coloring plastic wood to match the surrounding areas has always been a problem. Some finishers prefer to color it before application, others afterward. In the former method, stain somewhat darker than the finish is added to the plastic wood as it is being mixed with the thinner. Apply a portion of the mixture to a piece of wood and let it dry. Drying will lighten the stain slightly. Compare the color of the plastic wood with the color of the wood finish. If you are close to a color match, use it. It is probably as close as you will be able to get.

The method of coloring plastic wood after its application should also be tested experimentally on a piece of scrap wood first. Apply the plastic wood and give it sufficient time to dry. After it has dried, stain it and match the dried stain color with that of the finish.

The procedure for using plastic wood to repair and restore damaged areas is as follows:

1. Carefully read the manufacturer's instructions, and prepare the plastic wood accordingly. Prepare enough to do the job and have a little left over.
2. Clean the area to which the plastic wood is to be applied. All wax, polish, grease, and other possible contaminants must be removed. Remove any old finish with a suitable solvent. The area to be repaired must be completely dry before applying the plastic wood.
3. Pack the plastic wood into the depression as deeply as possible, and build it up until it protrudes slightly above the surface. Allow it sufficient time to dry thoroughly. Drying will cause it to shrink to a certain extent. The rest can be sanded level with the surface.
4. The plastic wood may be colored (stained) at this point. Coloring can also be added at Step 1 (thereby eliminating Step 4).
5. Proceed with the various steps in the finishing schedule.

Wood putty (also referred to as *water putty*) is also used to fill cracks or other imperfections on wood surfaces that are either not generally exposed to view or will be covered by an opaque finish (e.g., paint or enamel). The reason for this is that it has no grain and there is some difficulty in coloring it to match the rest of the wood. In this respect, wood putty very closely resembles plastic wood.

This is an extremely rapid-drying filler, and must be applied almost immediately. It is subject to less shrinkage than plastic wood, and will result in a smoother finish.

Wood putty is available in a powder form at most hardware

and paint stores. Water is added to form a working paste. Wood colors in powdered form can be added to tint the putty the desired color.

The procedure for using wood putty as a wood filler is as follows:

1. Select a container for mixing the wood putty.
2. Pour enough powder into the container to make all the putty you will need to do the entire job.
3. Add the coloring powder, and mix it thoroughly through the wood putty powder. The result should be slightly darker than the finish. It will lighten as it dries.
4. Add water a little at a time to the powder until you have the consistency you want.
5. Dampen with a wet cloth the area to be filled.
6. Pack the wood putty into the depression until it extends slightly above the surface at every point. Wipe excess putty from the surrounding areas with a wet cloth.
7. Let dry and sand the wood putty until it is smooth and level with the rest of the surface.
8. Continue with the rest of the finishing schedule.

A semihard putty stick under a number of different trade names (e.g., Patchal Pencil, etc.) can be used for filling scratches and other minor defects. It is rubbed into the depression until the area is built up to surface level, and the excess wiped away with a cloth or a piece of fine steel wool. No melting or sanding is necessary, which makes it a little more convenient to use than stick shellac. However, it is not as durable as the latter. Putty sticks are already colored.

Stick shellac is a wood filler consisting of hard pieces of shellac in a variety of different colors. It is also available in a very light color (neutral in tone) that can be stained to match other colors. Stick shellac is variously referred to by a number of other names, including *shellac stick* and *sealing wax*, but they are all one and the same. It is becoming more and more difficult to find stick shellac in the stores, and many manufacturers apparently are no longer making it.

Stick shellac is produced in both transparent and opaque forms. The latter shows no grain. Therefore, when it is used to fill relatively large areas, simulated grain patterns must be put on by hand. This can be done with stain and a pencil brush, but it is a rather difficult technique and requires both a good eye and a steady hand.

When using shellac stick to make surface repairs, select the color that most closely matches the rest of the surface and proceed as follows:

1. Place the shellac stick over a file or the blade of a table knife to shield it from the direct heat of the flame.
2. Hold the file or blade over a hot, carbonless flame. The flame must not emit smoke, or it will be incorporated in the melting shellac. Cheap alcohol lamps (available through mail-order houses dealing in finishing supplies or local paint and hardware stores) are recommended for the heat source.
3. Keep the file or blade over the flame until the shellac stick begins to melt.
4. Pass the file along the surface of the piece of furniture, holding it in such a way that the melted shellac can run into the depressed area. Use enough melted shellac to form a slight ridge above the surface.
5. Moisten your finger and run it along the top of the melted shellac, pressing it lightly as you go. You may then use the flat side of the file or blade to smooth out the shellac filler. If it is still not smooth and level, try rubbing it with a felt pad dipped in FFF grade pumice stone and rubbing oil (only a small amount of rubbing oil is necessary). Use rottenstone and water to complete the rubbing operation. Always rub in the direction of the grain, regardless of the position of the surface imperfection (e.g., if it lies across the grain).

Wax stick is a filler-type material made from colored wax and designed for patching. It is much easier to use than stick shellac. Wax stick is commercially available in a variety of colors, or it can be made in the home workshop by melting paraffin or beeswax and coloring it with aniline dye powder.

Not only is wax stick easy to apply, it can also easily be removed if the repair work does not look right. It is simply a matter of prying it loose and starting over again. Among its principal disadvantages are its low durability and lack of resistance to wear.

Moreover, it has a tendency to bleed into other finishes. The application of a shellac washcoat will eliminate the bleeding tendency and protect the wax stick somewhat.

The *latex wood patch* compound shown being applied to the surface in Fig. 7–4 may be used to repair cracks, gouges, scratches, nail holes, broken corners, and other types of damage or blemishes. It accepts stain uniformly and may be sanded, sawed, or drilled one hour after being applied.

Repairing Surface Defects

Surface defects range in severity from wood damage to various types of problems with the finish. They include dents of various sizes, gouges, scratches, minor splitting and cracking, pit marks, old nail, screw, and dowel holes, burns, stains, and a number of other imperfections that ruin the overall appearance of a finish unless dealt with properly. They can be divided into the following three basic categories:

1. Defects that lie on the finish,
2. Defects that have penetrated into the finish,
3. Defects that have damaged the wood.

Each type of surface defect will be carefully examined in the sections that follow. The suggested remedies will be based on the degree of damage they have caused (see the three categories listed above).

Spots and Stains

The terms "spot" and "stain" are largely synonymous as used in wood finishing. I suppose if you wanted to be technical about it, a spot could be defined as a *deposit of foreign matter on the finish*. A stain, on the other hand, could be regarded as *discoloration caused by a deposit of foreign matter*. There is only a slight difference in definition.

The types of spots and stains you will encounter on finishes include the following:

1. Water spots,
2. Alcohol spots,

3. Ink spots,
4. Grease, oil, and dirt spots,
5. Milk spots,
6. Citrus acid spots.

Spots and stains caused by water or moisture on the surface appear as white spots or rings (i.e., blushing) on lacquer and shellac finishes. They can also occur on some cheap varnish finishes. Try wiping the spot lightly with a cloth dampened in naphtha or turpentine. If this fails to remove the spot, wipe the surface with denatured alcohol. Be careful—too much alcohol will dissolve the finish.

Alcohol will cause shellac finishes, some varnish finishes, and wax finishes to spot white. Wiping the surface with turpentine or denatured alcohol will sometimes remove them.

Ink spots can be removed by rubbing lightly with soap and water or pumice stone (FFF grade) and water. The latter is recommended only if the stain resists the soap and water treatment. If the ink has penetrated the finish (particularly through cracks), you will have to strip it and bleach the stain out of the wood.

Treat milk spots and citrus acid stains in the same manner as ink stains. Spots other than those caused by water or alcohol can also be eliminated by one of the following methods:

1. Mild soap and water,
2. Mineral oil,
3. Lemon oil,
4. Vinegar and water,
5. Turpentine,
6. Very fine steel wool,
7. Pumice stone and water (or oil),
8. Rottenstone and water (or oil).

Alligatoring, Scratches, and Cracks

Minor scratches and cracks can usually be eliminated by reamalgamating the finish (i.e., redissolving it with a suitable solvent so that it will flow together and eliminate the defect). It is very important to identify correctly the type of finish you are dealing with *before* attempting to reamalgamate it. I suggest that you read the section IDENTIFYING FINISHES in this chapter before proceeding any further.

Alligatoring refers to the development of intersecting cracks or ridges on a finish. In effect, it resembles the skin of an alligator. It usually occurs as a result of overexposure to sunlight. The finish can be restored and the alligatoring effect eliminated by reamalgamation. This consists of partially dissolving the finish with its solvent (Table 7–2). Apply the solvent with a clean, soft cloth wiped gently across the surface. When the alligatoring cracks and ridges disappear, stop wiping. If the sunlight has affected the stain or wood color, I would recommend stripping the finish and applying a new one. This holds true for crazing or cracking caused by sunlight (see below).

Crazing consists of irregular patterns of minute cracks caused by shrinking, excessive moisture, or exposure to excessive amounts of sunlight. You can eliminate crazing by reamalgamating the finish (see Alligatoring).

A *hairline crack* refers to a single, minute crack extending partway or completely across the finish. One or more can occur, but they need not intersect. They are caused by the same conditions that produce crazing or alligatoring. Hairline cracks can also be removed by reamalgamation (see Alligatoring).

A *crack* is a split or break in the finish considerably larger than those caused by alligatoring, crazing, or hairline cracks. However, the conditions causing the crack (i.e., shrinkage, excessive moisture, or too much sunlight) are the same. Reamalgamating the finish should eliminate most cracks.

Table 7–2.   Recommended Solvents for Reamalgamation

Type of Finish	Reamalgamation Solvent
Shellac	Denatured Alcohol
Shellac-Lacquer	Denatured Alcohol (3 Parts), Lacquer Thinner (1 Part)
Varnish	Turpentine (1 Part), Boiled Linseed Oil (1 Part) or Strip the Finish
Lacquer-Base Enamel	Lacquer Thinner or Strip the Finish
Lacquer	Lacquer Thinner

A *scratch* is caused by a foreign (i.e., externally-directed) object being drawn across the surface with enough force or pressure to break the finish. The depth of the scratch will determine the method you use to remove it. Suggested removal methods are:

1. Reamalgamate,
2. Rub with pumice stone (FFF grade) and oil,
3. Fill with white shellac and stain.

Remove all wax, polish, and other possible contaminants before attempting to repair a finish scratch. Varnish and lacquer can be substituted for white shellac; rottenstone for pumice stone.

Lifting, Peeling, and Blistering

Lifting, peeling, and *blistering* are often used interchangeably to describe a condition in which the finish is losing its adhesion to the wood surface. That is to say, it is lifting or peeling off the wood. This condition can usually be traced to one of the following causes:

1. Incorrect application methods,
2. Using two or more chemically incompatible finishing materials,
3. Excessive moisture in the wood.

Because the causes are of internal origin and usually too extensive to repair effectively (in cases where excessive moisture is the cause), a complete stripping of the finish is recommended.

Blistering might prove to be the only exception. If the blisters are large and cover the entire finish, strip it. On the other hand, if they are isolated in one area or resemble tiny blisterlike bubbles, try reamalgamating the finish first.

Dents, Gouges, and Deep Scratches

Dents, gouges, and deep scratches are all depressions in the surface caused by pressure, or impact externally applied. The wood fibers may be torn (as with gouges and scratches), or simply depressed (dents). The force that causes the dent may or may not break the finish.

These types of surface defects can be repaired in several ways, depending upon their size. The methods commonly used to make this kind of repair include:

1. Raising the grain,
2. Filling,
3. Fitting wood inserts.

Raising the grain is probably the easiest method, but it can be used successfully only on relatively shallow dents. The grain-raising is accomplished by placing a damp cloth with water over the dent and pressing a heated iron against the cloth. The absorption of water by the wood (in combination with the heat) should cause the fibers to rise and fill the dent. With some woods, only the application of water is necessary. A few hardwoods will resist both the water and the heat, and will have to be filled and sanded.

Large dents, gouges, and deep scratches can be removed by packing them with a filler material and sanding them smooth. Plastic wood, wood putty, shellac stick, and wax stick can be used to repair these surface defects under certain conditions (see WOOD PATCHING COMPOUNDS in this chapter). For example, shellac stick and wax stick can be used to repair most scratches unless they have penetrated the wood too deeply. If such is the case, then plastic wood or wood putty are recommended. These two filler materials are also recommended for repairing large dents and gouges. Both plastic wood and wood putty shrink when drying, so be sure to pack enough of either into the depression to extend slightly above the surface. Whatever remains after shrinking can be removed by sanding. Sawdust mixed with glue (or varnish) can also be used to fill depressions. If a sawdust mixture is used, the sawdust should come from the same wood as the rest of the furniture. All splinters should be removed and sharp edges rounded before attempting to repair dents, gouges, or scratches. Except in the case of grain-raising, the area should also be thoroughly cleaned of all wax, polish, grease, dirt, old finish, and other substances that might interfere with the proper adhesion of the finishing materials used in making the repair.

If the dents or gouges are particularly large, they can be repaired by cutting a piece of wood to the size and shape of the depression and gluing it in position. Sand the area and apply a stain.

Plastic wood or shellac stick can be used to fill any cracks if the fit is not tight enough. This should also be stained, or it will leave a noticeable border around the wood insert.

Holes

Holes in the surface are usually the result of missing screws, nails, dowels, or knots, and will probably extend completely through to the other side of the wood. Tightly-fitted wood inserts used in combination with plastic wood or shellac stick are the recommended method of repair (see above).

Burns

A burn can be caused by a cigarette, cigar, or burning match dropped on the finish. It can also be caused by setting a hot pan or plate down on the surface. Usually this will make the finish blister or dissolve. If a cigarette or cigar is allowed to remain long enough, it could burn into the wood and result in a dentlike depression.

Superficial burning of the finish on a small area can be repaired by first sanding the spot smooth with a very fine sandpaper, and matching the rest of the surface with an appropriate shade of shellac stick or wax stick (see WOOD PATCHING COMPOUNDS in this chapter). After the shellac stick has cooled, rub it down with linseed oil and a lightweight emery cloth. The whole surface may then have to be rubbed in order to make the overall gloss (or lack of gloss) uniform.

If the burn is deep enough to have caused a dentlike depression, it may have to be filled in with plastic wood, stained, and sanded. This is particularly true along edges (where most such burns occur), because you will have to do a certain amount of rebuilding of the edge.

Missing Pieces of Veneer and Inlay

The problem of replacing missing pieces of veneer and inlay is described in Chapter 4, *Veneering*, and Chapter 5, *Inlaying*.

Worn Edges

Worn edges can be caused by heavy use over a period of time or careless handling when moving the piece of furniture. If the former is the case, then the wear will be evenly distributed over those portions of the frame where one would normally expect to find it. If you are dealing with a genuine (or suspected) antique, I would recommend not doing anything about it. These naturally acquired signs of wear will add a certain charm to the furniture, and do not reduce its monetary value, while refinishing it most certainly will.

Wear caused by improper or careless handling is usually unevenly distributed on the frame. This can be repaired by either replacing a section of the frame (e.g., the top of a table, a table leaf, a chair leg, etc.) or by building up the defect with wood filler.

Frame Repairs

The preceding sections of this chapter described various types of surface defects that can cause damage to the finish or the wood surface. A second major category of furniture repairs involves damage to the structure or frame.

Following is a brief description of common conditions and the basic approach for repairing. This is provided so you will at least recognize when more extensive repairs are needed. If structural repairs are needed, consider taking the piece to an experienced furniture repairer or check the information resources section for a book on structural repairs.

Split or Missing Frame Sections

If any portion of the wood frame has been split, it is best to remove that particular section and replace it with a new piece of wood. It is important that this new piece be seasoned (kiln-dried), because unseasoned wood will shrink. This could result in unsightly gaps after the glue has dried. The best solution to this problem would be to take an identical section from damaged furniture of the same age and style.

All of the old glue must be removed from the surfaces to which the split section was attached as a new coat of glue applied over an older one will result in a weak joint. A glue used in furniture construction must penetrate the wood in order to set properly.

It is not difficult to replace pieces of the seat foundation or the back because for the most part they are hidden from view. However, arms and legs present a totally different problem, since they are in full view and must therefore be identical in appearance to the remaining original sections after the repairs have been made.

Some legs and arms are quite ornate and consequently difficult to replace. If they are badly damaged, you may be able to obtain a matching leg or arm from an identical piece of furniture in a similar condition. In other words, it may be possible to make one good chair from two damaged ones.

Whether you are reassembling the entire frame or simply reattaching a certain piece (arm, leg, etc.), the following steps are recommended:

1. Remove all glue from both surfaces. Never place a new layer of glue over an older one.
2. Before regluing, test the pieces for fit.
3. Do not use nails in the reassembly. If these were used in the original construction, remove them, and fill in the holes with wood filler. Should you feel that a reinforcement is needed in addition to gluing, use such recommended forms as wood corner blocks, wood screws, wood dowels, or metal fasteners.
4. If the frame consists of mortise and tenon joints, use thin pieces of wood (shims) or cloth glued to the tenon to tighten the fit.
5. Reglue the frame. Remember: clamping pressure is necessary.

Broken or Missing Hardware

Sometimes you will find that one or more pieces of furniture hardware (knobs, handles, hinges, etc.) are broken or missing. If you have an antique, you should make every effort to repair the broken piece of hardware or replace it with an identical piece of reproduction. Remember, though, that there is an inverse ratio between the amount of replacement and the value of the antique. The more you replace, the more it drops in value. This is not, however, a problem with furniture not classified as antique. In that case, I would recommend one of two possible solutions. Order a completely new set of hardware from a mail-order house that sells wood finishing materials, or use hardware from an identical piece of furniture in too poor condition to restore.

Warping

Warping results from a piece of wood being able to absorb moisture from one side but not from the other. In wood finishing, the finish will serve as the waterproofing coat. Since the bottom of a table leaf, table top, or other section is often left unfinished (it is cheaper that way), it is this side of the wood that absorbs the moisture and causes the warp. The result is a shape having both a concave (unfinished) and convex (finished) side (Fig. 7–5). In some cases, the warp can be removed by applying both moisture and pressure (with weights or clamps). Lay the board on wet grass with the concave side down and place some heavy weights on the convex side for pressure. If the warp disappears, clamp the board in a flat position so that the warp will not return as the board dries. After the wood has thoroughly dried, apply a finish to *both* sides. Wet burlap folded flat can be substituted for the wet grass as a source of moisture.

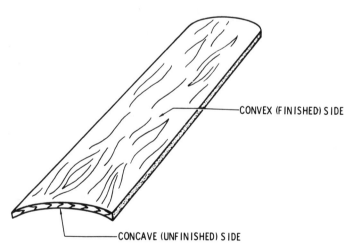

CONVEX (FINISHED) SIDE

CONCAVE (UNFINISHED) SIDE

Fig. 7–5. The convex and concave sides of a warp.

Other methods of removing warp include cutting grooves into the underside of the board or sawing the board into strips and regluing it. These are really too complicated for anyone but the professional to attempt. If you are not successful with the pressure and water method, I would recommend replacing the warped section or taking it to a cabinet shop.

Loose Frame

Examine the frame for loose joints. If you do not intend to refinish the piece of furniture, the frame can be reinforced with wood blocks. Sometimes a damaged section (table top, frame side, the back of a dresser or cabinet, etc.) will cause the looseness in the frame. If the part is salvageable, it should be refastened with wood screws and glue. Should you have to replace it, try to find a section the same age as the one being replaced. This can be taken from another piece of furniture that is in too poor condition to be repaired.

If a joint is loose without being damaged, try to pull it apart and remove all the old glue. This is important because new glue applied over old glue seldom forms a strong bond with the wood. A frequently effective method of removing glue is to pour hot white vinegar over the surface. Allow the vinegar time to work on the glue and wipe it off with a rag (some of the modern glues have to be chipped off). Sand the surfaces of the joint, and wipe them with turpentine to remove any traces of the old glue. The joint can be made especially tight by coating the glued surfaces with ground steel wool, inserting a thin shim, or wrapping the tenon (of a mortise and tenon joint) with a small piece of cloth.

Loose joints that cannot be separated can be reglued by drilling a hole into the joint, and inserting the glue with a glue injector. This is not as satisfactory as complete disassembly of the joint, because there is no way of removing the old glue.

If the entire frame is loose, it would be best to disassemble it completely, remove all glue from the exposed surfaces, and reglue it.

Wood Dry Rot

Moisture not only causes the wood to warp, it also indirectly contributes to dry rot. Dry rot is a crumbling or powdery condition of the wood resulting from a fungus that feeds on moist wood. This condition generally develops over a long period of time, but it can be corrected quite easily. Simply scrape out the dry rot area. If the area is not too extensive, fill it with plastic wood or wood putty and stain it to match the rest of the surface (see WOOD PATCHING COMPOUNDS). Smaller areas can be patched with shellac stick.

Covering an Old Finish

If the old finish is still in good condition, then you can save yourself a great deal of time and trouble simply by covering it with paint or enamel. By good condition, I mean that the finish is not cracking, is not brittle, and still adheres firmly at every point on the surface. Run your hand over the surface of the old finish. If it feels smooth to the touch, then it will probably accept a covering coat well. If even minor repairs (small areas of cracking, etc.) are required, I would recommend that you refinish it. The time spent preparing the area so that it will match the rest of the finish would be better spent removing it completely. Remember: a paint or enamel finish is opaque, and should only be applied over wood surfaces that are not particularly attractive.

A much more detailed description of painting or enameling furniture is given in Chapter 14, *Paint and Enamel Finishes.* A much briefer outline for the procedure for covering an old finish with paint or enamel is as follows:

1. Thoroughly clean the surface of the old finish. This means removing all the dirt, furniture wax and polish, and other contaminants that have accumulated over the years. It is quite possible that a good cleaning will restore the surface to a condition that will not require covering. Use warm water and a mild detergent for cleaning (or another suitable cleaning preparation if you are working with a shellac or lacquer finish). Work quickly—do not allow water to soak in or stand on the surface. If you have done your job well, the water will run off the surface without beading (the formation of moisture beads on the surface is an indication that some wax still remains). Decorative carving can be cleaned with a soft toothbrush.

Wipe the surface clean with a clean, lint-free cloth and allow plenty of time to dry.

2. If the old finish has a gloss, it will have to be removed. The new finish will not adhere to a glossy surface. Use a very fine grade of sandpaper to scuff the surface lightly. This will satisfactorily remove the gloss and provide a base for the topcoat.

3. It may be necessary to reglue joints loosened by the cleaning. When you have accomplished this, check the wood surface for glue film. This must be removed, or it will prevent the topcoat from adhering properly to the surface.

4. Brush on the first coat of paint or enamel. Allow it about 24 hours drying time, and then apply the second coat. Read Chapter 14 for further and more detailed instructions.

CHAPTER 8

Stripping Finishes

by Bob Flexner

Stripping is the process of removing an old finish to expose the bare wood surface. Stripping is usually considered the most disagreeable step in refinishing furniture. It is messy, smelly, boring, and can be unrewarding if you find problems underneath the paint. There is no way to totally eliminate the drudgery and unpredictability, but stripping can be made easier if you understand how different strippers work and a few tricks and precautions about how to use them.

There are two ways to remove old paint or finish: by mechanical means such as sanding, scraping, or heating with a heat gun; and by chemical means using a stripping solvent. Mechanical processes are often effective for removing paint from outside siding and from inside woodwork, but they are generally too harsh for furniture. Sanding and scraping usually removes some of the surface wood along with the paint or finish. This damages the aged

---

Bob Flexner is a professional refinisher with twenty years experience. During that time he has studied finish technology to understand how finishes work and to solve finishing problems he has faced. He restores antique furniture at his shop, The Workbench, in Norman, Oklahoma. The material in this chapter was previously published in American Woodworker magazine.

character that makes old furniture valuable. Sanding also rounds over the crisp lines of carvings and turnings and risks cutting through veneer. Heating the paint or finish hot enough to cause it to blister risks scorching the wood and dissolving the glue that holds the joints together and the veneer on. In contrast, stripping solvents, most of which do not damage the wood or dissolve the old glue, are almost always the better choice for removing paint or finish from furniture.

The question of whether to remove the finish or leave it intact should be considered carefully. Sometimes all that an old finish needs is a good cleaning. Once the old dirt is removed, you might be surprised and pleased with the attractiveness of the finish. Try washing the surface with soap and water, then wipe dry immediately.

Not all finishes should be removed even if they show signs of age. This is particularly true of an antique. The original finish is an intrinsic part of its monetary value, and removing the finish will considerably reduce this value. *Never* remove finish from an antique without first obtaining professional advice. Retain any old finish if it is attractive and in reasonably good condition. Signs of aging will frequently enhance the overall appearance of a piece of furniture rather than detract from it.

Paint strippers are composed of a solvent or combination of solvents that have the ability to penetrate into and eventually through a paint or clear finish film. They act on that film in one of three ways depending on how the particular solvents in the stripper react with the film being stripped. They may *dissolve* the film into a gunk that can be wiped off; they *swell* the film so it blisters and can be scraped off; or they *break the bond* of the film to the wood so the film will lift off in sheets when you get under it with a putty knife. Generally speaking, shellac and lacquer dissolve, varnish and enamel paint blister, latex paint dissolves *and* blisters, and polyurethane and catalyzed lacquer lift off in sheets.

Until recently almost all strippers available would remove almost all paints and finishes found on old furniture and woodwork. It was not necessary to understand a great deal about these strippers or about the paint or finish you were trying to remove. Chances were success would result no matter which stripper you used. But the development and use on furniture of far more solvent-resistant paints and finishes over the last thirty years, and the recent introduction of safer-to-use but less powerful solvents in paint strippers have changed all this. It is now much more common that the paint stripper you choose at the paint store will not remove the paint or finish on your furniture, so it is increasingly necessary that you understand the differences in the paint strippers in order to have success using them.

Types of Strippers

There are four solvents, or groups of solvents, that are commonly used in strippers: methylene chloride; a mixture of acetone, toluene, and methanol (ATM); n-methyl pyrrolidone (NMP); and dibasic esters (DBE). Some of these names probably sound strange to you, hence the abbreviations which are easier to remember.

One or more of these solvents will be listed somewhere on every container of paint stripper. With the information supplied here you will understand what you can expect from every paint stripper available by looking at what solvents it contains (Table 8-1).

In addition to the four solvents, lye (also called sodium hydroxide or caustic soda) can be used to remove paint and finish.

Methylene Chloride

Methylene chloride has been the primary active ingredient used in most paint and varnish removers for the past three or four decades. It is the most effective stripping solvent available to the general public. You can buy methylene chloride-based strippers in liquid or semi-paste consistency and in three different formula-strengths.

The consistency of the stripper is important to consider if you are working on vertical surfaces—liquid will run off, semi-paste will cling. The consistency has very little to do with the strength of the stripper.

The strength of the stripper is primarily dependent upon the formulation. There are three classes of formulations. All three use methanol (methyl or "wood" alcohol) as an "activator" to increase

Table 8-1. Breaking the Code: An Overview of Finish Strippers

Listed Contents	Approximate Percentages	Relative Strength	Potential Problems	Safety Concerns	Comments
Methylene Chloride, Methanol	75–85% MC, 4–10%, Methanol.	Effective on all but the toughest coatings.	Contains wax which must be removed before applying a finish.	Fumes can be a health hazard.	Work outside or in a room where you've arranged cross-ventilation.
Methylene Chloride, Methanol, Ammonium Hydroxide	75–85% MC, 4–10% Methanol, 1–5% Ammonium Hydroxide.	Strongest of all over-the-counter paint and varnish removers.	Same as above. Will stain many hardwoods.	Fumes can be a health hazard.	Same as above. Use on unusually tough coatings.
Methylene Chloride, Acetone, Toluene, Methanol	25–60% MC, 10–40% of each of the others.	Will remove most old paint and finish.	Contains wax which must be removed before applying a finish.	Fumes can be a health hazard. Fumes and liquid solvent can be a fire hazard.	Same as top. A good inexpensive choice for removing most old paint and finish.
Acetone, Toluene, Methanol (ATM)	10–40% of each.	Same as above.	Same as above.	Same as above.	Same as above.

Solvent	Concentration	Effectiveness/Speed	Cautions	Safety	Notes
Acetone, Toluene, Methanol (ATM) (liquid "refinisher")	10–40% of each.	Will dissolve shellac and lacquer. Ineffective on everything else.	Limited effectiveness on many finishes and all paints.	Same as above.	Same as top. Many people become discouraged when refinisher doesn't work.
Di-basic Ester (DBE)	25–60% DBE Water	Works very slowly. Often requires leaving overnight.	Trying to rush it. Water may blister veneer and warp thin wood.	Fairly safe to use.	It will take from three hours to overnight to work.
N-Methyl Pyrrolidone (NMP)	40–80% NMP	Works two to three times slower than methylene chloride strippers.	Trying to rush it.	Fairly safe to use.	Most expensive of all stripping solvents.

the effectiveness of the methylene chloride. One uses methanol alone; another adds an alkali or an acid to increase further the strength of the stripper; the third dilutes the methylene chloride/methanol combination with acetone and toluene in order to reduce the cost. Each formulation has advantages and disadvantages.

The most commonly available strippers are combinations of methylene chloride and methanol. Other alcohols may also be added to the formula. These strippers are strong enough to rapidly remove all but the most solvent-resistant paints and finishes, such as epoxy and polyester coatings. They are also nonflammable and non-polluting. Methylene chloride, which makes up 75% to 85% of the formula, is nonflammable, and is not considered an ozone depleter or smog producer by the EPA. The primary disadvantages are cost and potential health hazards. Methylene chloride is a relatively expensive solvent, so strippers made with high percentages of methylene chloride are also relatively expensive. Recently, methylene chloride has been listed as a possible carcinogen, a development you should consider before using this type of stripper (see the section, SAFETY WITH STRIPPERS, later in this chapter).

In order to increase the strength of methylene chloride/methanol strippers, an alkali or an acid is added. The alkali is usually ammonium hydroxide (common ammonia) and it is usually, but not always, listed on the container. The acid is usually oxalic acid. Since acid is not very stable in the mixture, this combination is only sold to commercial stripping shops.

Alkali-fortified strippers are available in most paint stores, and boat and auto-body supply stores. They are often sold as "marine" strippers. The advantage of these strippers is, of course, their increased effectiveness on exceptionally tough coatings such as epoxy, polyester, catalyzed lacquer, and baked-on boat and car finishes. Their disadvantages are their price, the health hazards associated with methylene chloride, and their tendency to stain hardwoods such as oak, mahogany, cherry, and walnut. The staining is caused by the ammonium hydroxide which reacts with the tannic acid contained naturally in these woods (see the section, SOLUTIONS TO COMMON STRIPPING PROBLEMS).

The third category of methylene chloride-based strippers is methylene chloride/methanol diluted with acetone and toluene (toluol). Sometimes methyl ethyl ketone (MEK) is substituted for the acetone, and xylene (xylol) for the toluene. The addition of these cheaper solvents lowers the cost, which is a plus. But it also reduces the strength of the stripper, and it introduces potential air pollutants and the element of flammability. Though weaker than simple methylene chloride/methanol blends, this class of paint stripper is still strong enough to remove most old paint and almost all finishes used on furniture before the 1960s.

The solvents in both liquid and semi-paste strippers of all three strengths evaporate very rapidly, so paraffin wax is almost always added to retard the evaporation. The wax operates by rising to the top of the stripper, even on vertical surfaces, and forming a skin that holds the solvents in. Everytime you disturb this wax skin you allow the release of some of the solvents. Some of these strippers are made to be water-washable by the addition of a detergent to the formula.

Acetone, Toluene, Methanol (ATM)

Acetone, toluene, and methanol are three of the basic ingredients in lacquer thinner. If you've ever put lacquer thinner on a finish, you know the damage this blend of solvents can cause. It will dissolve shellac and lacquer, and it will soften and sometimes wrinkle varnish. Manufacturers take advantage of this solvent strength to make non-methylene chloride-containing strippers. There are two types. One contains wax to retard evaporation and usually contains thickeners to make it a semi-paste. It is marketed as a stripper, and is used in the same way as the methylene chloride-based strippers. The other contains neither wax nor thickeners and is marketed as a "refinisher."

ATM-based strippers work quite well on almost all old paints and finishes. They perform as well, in fact, as many of the methylene chloride-based strippers, making them a viable alternative to methylene chloride for most situations. ATM-based strippers are effective because the wax holds the solvents in contact with the coating long enough for them to penetrate. Their advantages are that they are cheap, and they perform well without the inclusion of methylene chloride. Their disadvantages are that they are highly flammable, and some contain an alkali that will stain hardwoods.

The vapors of all three solvents—acetone, toluene, and methanol—are toxic in high concentrations. Toxic fumes in concentrated amounts can impair your central nervous system, cause illness, and in extreme cases, cause death. So you should take the same precautions when using ATM-based strippers (and refinishers) as you do with methylene chloride-based strippers (see section SAFETY AND POLITICS).

Without wax to retard evaporation, ATM-based refinishers are ineffective on paints and all finishes except shellac and lacquer. This is because the rapidly-evaporating solvents in refinishers cannot stay in contact long enough to penetrate and blister these other films. The solvents only soften them enough so they can be scratched off the wood with steel wool. This largely mechanical removal of the softened film is the procedure usually recommended.

The ineffectiveness of refinisher on old varnish and all the tough new finishes, together with the universal lack of instructions for identifying what type of finish you are trying to strip, is the most serious deficiency of this product. Many people have become discouraged because of the great amount of effort they had to expend scratching off old varnish with steel wool.

N-Methyl Pyrrolidone (NMP) and Dibasic Esters (DBE)

N-Methyl Pyrrolidone (NMP) and Dibasic Esters (DBE) are not new solvents, but they are new to furniture strippers. NMP is commonly used in industry as a cleaning and petrochemical-recovery solvent. DBE is a combination of the esters of several acids—adipic, glutaric, and succinic (which may be listed separately on the container). Both NMP and DBE are being tried as replacements for methylene chloride, acetone, toluene, and methanol in strippers, because they are less toxic. They are also low in flammability and evaporate slowly, which means there is no need for added wax and thus the extra step to remove it. A small amount of unevaporated NMP or DBE stripping solvent remaining in the wood should not interfere with any stain or finish. But there the similarity between the solvents, at least as they are currently being formulated into strippers, ends.

The only version of an NMP-based stripper currently available performs much like methylene chloride- and ATM-based strippers—it is a little slower than these strippers and a little weaker. But on all but the toughest coatings, which may not be penetrated, you will not notice much difference. Until now, higher cost has prevented NMP from being used in furniture strippers. NMP-based strippers cost about twice that of methylene chloride-based strippers. An increased awareness of the potential dangers of working with methylene chloride and the ATM solvents has made people willing to pay the extra amount to get a safer stripper.

DBE is also a safer solvent to use which is not as expensive as NMP. But it penetrates films much slower than NMP and thus takes much longer to dissolve or blister finish and paint. The extended time is especially noticeable on shellac and lacquer—the finish used on well over half of old furniture. It can take from four or five hours to overnight to penetrate and dissolve these finishes thoroughly.

The most troubling problem with DBE-based strippers, however, is not the time they take to work. The problem is the length of time the water included in these strippers to reduce the cost is in contact with the wood. In my experience working with DBE-based strippers, the water almost always roughens the surface of the wood enough to require fairly heavy sanding. Worse, the water is in contact with the wood for so long that it can warp thin parts and blister veneer that has been glued down with water-based glue. All old furniture was glued with water-based animal-hide glue.

The problem with water is made still worse if you follow manufacturers' instructions which direct you to scrub the dissolved or blistered film with more water and a coarse pad or strong detergent (steel wool will cause rust spotting in the wood). The hard scrubbing further increases the damage to the wood.

New technologies often take a while to be perfected and understood. The current generation of strippers based on DBE solvent leaves a lot to be desired. In order to make these strippers into a viable alternative, something will have to be done to reduce the time the wood is in contact with water.

Lye

Lye is probably the oldest of the paint strippers. It is also the most effective, the most dangerous to use if any should get on your skin, and the most damaging to the wood. Lye is often used by commercial strippers who dissolve about a pound into every three to five gallons of water they use to fill a vat. The vat is heated and furniture dipped into it. All the paint or finish is dissolved off the wood, but so is most of the glue that formerly held the joints together and the veneer on. And if the furniture is not removed from the lye quickly enough, the lye begins turning the surface of the wood into pulp. The surface becomes soft and punky and requires heavy sanding to get through to good wood again. A great deal of furniture has been ruined by having been dipped into a lye bath, and strip shops have gotten a bad reputation because of their often indiscriminant use of lye for stripping.

Lye is not all bad, however. It can be used sparingly to dissolve stubborn paint out of pores without doing too much damage to the wood. It can be used effectively to strip metal objects (except aluminum) without causing damage to the metal. And it is a cheap, effective stripper for large surfaces of outdoor siding, masonry, and concrete; or indoor plaster and softwood trim. See Chapter 20, *Safety*, for more on the use of hazardous materials.

Choosing Which Stripper to Use

So how do you choose between all of these possibilities? You first decide whether you are willing to use a methylene chloride-based stripper considering the health risks. If so, choose the cheapest one that will do the job. Methylene chloride reduced with acetone, toluene, and methanol will be the cheapest and will strip almost all old paint or finish. So will ATM-based strippers, which are cheap and allow you to avoid the use of methylene chloride. Tougher coatings will require strippers that are made with just methylene chloride and methanol, and the toughest coatings will require the addition of an alkali.

If you want to reduce your exposure as much as possible to toxic solvents and are willing to pay more, your best choice is an

NMP-based stripper. If you can wait longer for the stripper to work, and your stripping project would not be severely harmed by extended contact with water, you can choose a DBE-based stripper.

Safety and Politics

In the last few years methylene chloride has become a very controversial solvent. Evidence has been found that it may cause cancer. It was already known that excessive exposure to methylene chloride could cause temporary headaches, dizziness, impaired mental alertness, reduced physical coordination, and even heart attacks in people with heart problems. Methylene chloride metabolizes into carbon monoxide in the blood stream, causing the heart to have to work harder to get enough oxygen pumped around the body—do not use a methylene chloride-based stripper if you have a heart condition. When researchers in the mid-1980s succeeded in inducing cancer in mice and benign tumors in rats, methylene chloride was quickly bumped up to a class B2, "probable human carcinogen" by the Environmental Protection Agency.

If methylene chloride could be clearly shown to cause cancer in humans, no one would object to its being regulated and possibly removed from the consumer market. Unfortunately the evidence is not at all clear. While the mice in the studies definitely developed cancer, there is disagreement in the scientific community over the validity of the studies because the particular strain of mice used is highly prone to contracting cancer anyway, even without exposure to chemicals. The rats, which did not develop any malignant tumors, are less prone than the mice, and humans are even less prone than the rats to contracting cancer. So finding cancer in those mice is not at all conclusive for humans. In addition, studies done on humans, who have been exposed daily for many years to low doses of methylene chloride, have so far failed to show any increase whatsoever in the incidence of cancer. Using the same data available to the EPA, the British Health and Safety Executive does not believe methylene chloride has carcinogenic potential for humans.

With such ambiguity, it is only natural that politics should enter the debate over whether methylene chloride should be regulated or not. Recently, I attended a conference on paint strippers organized by the EPA to discuss existing alternatives to methylene chloride. Before the conference was an hour old, an employee of a major manufacturer of one of the alternative solvents asked not so subtly, "When is the CPSC (Consumer Product Safety Commission) going to require that warnings on containers of methylene chloride-based strippers be made larger and clearer?" He was followed immediately by a spokesman for users of methylene chloride-based strippers who replied, "Consumers aren't so dumb. They know that warnings just mean the stuff works!"

Thus began the debate, with the manufacturers of methylene chloride solvent and manufacturers and users of methylene chloride-based strippers on one side, and manufacturers of alternative solvents and strippers on the other. The EPA and CPSC played neutral, but it is hard to believe that in our increasingly regulated society these agencies will be neutral for long. Sooner or later they will feel the pressure to "play it safe" and begin regulating the use of methylene chloride.

So how should you, the consumer, "play it safe" in the meantime? First, you should decide if you're willing to risk using methylene chloride, keeping in mind that the history of solvents demonstrates that the more we learn about them the more we discover problems with all of them. In the 1970s, benzene was removed from strippers after it was shown to be carcinogenic and replaced by methylene chloride which was thought, at the time, to be safe. Reports are now surfacing that DBE causes blurred vision when used in poorly-ventilated areas, and that NMP may have a harmful effect on the blood of rats following subchronic exposure.

Second, you should expose yourself as little as possible to the fumes of all solvents by working outside or in a well-ventilated room. "Well-ventilated" means arranging an air flow through the room. It means *cross-ventilation*. Cross-ventilation is far more important, even, than wearing a charcoal-activated respirator mask. Respirator masks have been shown to have very limited effectiveness for impeding methylene chloride fumes. Though the use of respirator masks is usually a good idea in combination with airflow, used alone they can give you a false sense of safety. Cross-ventilation is the only means that can be relied upon to keep the concentrations of methylene chloride, and all other solvents, at a minimum. (See Chapter 20, *Safety*, for more on health-related issues.)

Using Strippers

Tools and Materials

The following tools and materials are essential for stripping finishes:

1. Removers and solvents,
2. Finish lifters,
3. Coarse steel wool,
4. Cheap brushes,
5. Rags and paper towels,
6. Cardboard boxes,
7. Newspapers,
8. Masking tape.

You will need a suitable liquid finish remover, such as a paint and varnish remover, denatured alcohol, or lacquer thinner. Putty knives, scrapers, or wedge-shaped blocks of wood will be useful for lifting the finish. A liquid finish remover can be applied with a brush (a cheap one with natural bristles) or a pad of coarse steel wool. Use a coffee can to store the pieces of furniture hardware.

Use large metal cans or cardboard boxes to catch the finish. It is quite a mess and should be carefully stored as the stripping operation progresses. By keeping it in containers, you will drastically reduce the clean-up time at the end of the stripping operation. Plastic containers may be dissolved by the finish remover. Many synthetic-bristle brushes will dissolve in methylene chloride-based strippers.

Rags or paper towels are used for wiping, and should be soft and absorbent. Using masking tape to mask off areas you do not want stained by the remover. Newspapers will protect the floor and surrounding areas from splatter.

You may not wish to use all the tools and materials suggested in this section, or you might want to add a few items to the list. After a little experience, you will be able to determine what works best for you.

Preparation

Stripping paint or finish requires no particular skill, but it can be messy, bad for your health, and some strippers are flammable. Use an organized and thoughtful approach to the work. Good housekeeping is important.

Work outside in the shade or in a room where you have arranged cross-ventilation. Do not work in the vicinity of an open flame or source of sparks if you are using a flammable stripper.

Wear a long-sleeved shirt and long pants, chemical-resistant (butyl or neoprene) gloves, a respirator, and safety goggles.

Protect the surrounding surfaces and area from splattering stripper.

Stripping Procedure

The stripping procedure described here is a general one, and cannot be expected to fit every situation. As you gain experience substitute your own variations.

1. Try cleaning the surface with soap and water.
2. Examine the cleaned finish and decide whether you want to remove it, restore it, or leave it in its present condition. If the finish is too deteriorated, consider removing it.
3. Decide which type of stripper to use.
4. Read the instructions on the container of stripper you are using. There are variations in the way different strippers work. In most cases following directions will increase your chances of success. Follow all safety and health instructions exactly.
5. Remove all hardware. If it requires stripping, soak it in a metal coffee can filled with stripper.
6. Remove any wood parts that can be disassembled easily, such as doors or drawers.
7. Open the container of stripper carefully. Cover it with a cloth and open the cap slowly to allow for a gradual release of pressure buildup. Then pour the stripper into a wide-mouthed jar or can.
8. Brush the stripper onto the surface, preferably in one direction, using an old or inexpensive new paintbrush. Brushing in one

Fig. 8-1. Applying chemical stripper solution. *(Courtesy Star Bronze Copmpany)*

direction helps lay on a thick coat and reduce solvent evaporation which occurs when you stir the stripper around by brushing back and forth. (Fig. 8–1)

9. Allow the stripper time to work on the paint or finish. Test the film now and then to see if it can be lifted from the wood. Add more stripper if the original has almost all evaporated. All strippers will lift many layers of paint at one time if kept wet and allowed time to penetrate.

10. Remove the dissolved, blistered, or softened film in one of six ways depending upon the situation:

    a. Scrape the film off flat surfaces into a bucket or cardboard box with a plastic scraper or a wide, dull, putty knife that is clean and smooth and has had its corners rounded with a file so it does not scratch the wood (Fig. 8–2);

    b. Soak up and wipe off dissolved film with paper towels;

Fig. 8-2. Scraping stripper and old paint off the surface. *(Courtesy Star Bronze Company)*

    c. Soak up dissolved or blistered film into wood shavings (from a jointer or planer), and then brush them off with a stiff bristle brush;

    d. Break blistered or softened film loose from moldings, turnings, and carvings with #1 steel wood or a fiber stripping pad;

    e. Pull a coarse string or rope around the recesses of turnings to work blistered paint or finish out;

    f. Pick the softened paint or finish out of cracks and recessed areas with sharpened sticks or dowel rods, which won't damage the wood like sharp metal picks.

11. Coat the wood with more stripper and scrub out any paint or stain that remains in the wood pores with a soft brass-wire bristle brush. Scrub with the grain of the wood.

12. Wash the wood with paint thinner, naphtha, lacquer thinner, or alcohol to remove the residue of wax that remains from all wax-containing strippers.

13. Let the solvent evaporate out of the stripping sludge, then dispose of it properly. (See Chapter 20, *Safety*, for more on proper disposal of hazardous materials.)

Solutions to Common Problems

If you have ever done any stripping, you know it is seldom as easy as the instructions just given. This is due partly to misunderstandings about what to expect and partly to an unpredictability caused by not knowing exactly what it is you're stripping. Here are some of the most common problems and their solutions.

The Stripper Does Not Work

If the stripper you are using does not dissolve, blister, or break the bond of the paint or finish film to the wood, then you are either not allowing enough time for the stripper to work, or you need to use a stronger stripper. You should first allow more time. If the temperature is below 65°, the stripper will be slow anyway, because chemical reactions in general are slower in cold weather. If the temperature is above 85°, the stripper may be evaporating before it has had time to work. You need to keep the surface wet with more coats of stripper, or cover the surface with plastic wrap to prevent the stripper from evaporating.

If you still have problems, you should try a stronger stripper. Use the information provided in the text as a guide for what to try. You should be able to remove any paint or finish with one of these solvent-based strippers, with the exception of milk paint. Milk paint is paint that uses milk (casein) as the binder. It was used fairly commonly in the 18th century and in rural areas of the United States in the 19th century. You can remove it with lye (sodium hydroxide) or with Behlen's "PDE" remover, which is safer to use than lye because it is less caustic.

You may find that layers of paint and finish respond differently. Your stripper may remove three coats of paint, for example, but not have any effect on the next coat below. If this happens, change to a stronger stripper. If all else fails, remove the film mechanically.

With clear finishes, it is sometimes difficult to tell when you have removed all of the finish. Don't be misled by the existence of stain in the wood. Stain can remain even though all the finish is off. When the finish is off and the wood is dry, there will not be any sheen or shiny places on the wood or in the pores. The wood will look and feel like raw wood, though it may not have the original color.

You Cannot Get Paint Out of Pores

Enamel paint does not dissolve; it swells and blisters. The same is often true for latex paint. But in the pores of wood, the paint has no place to swell to. It softens, but it just sits there in the pores until something jars it loose. Therefore you need to combine some mechanical force with the chemical action of the stripper to knock the softened paint out of the pores.

The best technique I've found is to scrub the stripper-wet wood in the direction of the grain with a soft brass-wire bristle brush available from most paint stores. Remove the gunk with rags or paper towels which you may want to wet with more stripper. It is usually necessary to repeat this procedure several times. The brass bristle brush will not damage hardwoods.

You may find situations where this procedure does not work,

especially on softer woods like pine and poplar. Try using a solution of lye before you resort to sanding. Use about a quarter pound of lye to a gallon of warm water, and be sure to pour the lye into the water, not the other way around, or the sudden chemical reaction may "boil over" onto you. Use as little as necessary to dissolve the paint so the wood is not damaged. Protect your skin and eyes from splashes. If you use lye, neutralize it with an acid or it will continue its chemical activity and slowly destroy the wood and the new finish you apply. Vinegar is a good choice for neutralizing lye.

You may still not be able to get all the paint out of the pores. In these cases, you can try masking the paint with a stain or paste wood filler or with a glaze applied between coats. In extreme situations you may be forced to repaint.

You Cannot Get Stain Out of Wood

The existence of stain under the finish often causes problems for beginners, because they do not realize that all the finish can be off and there still be color in the wood. There are several types of stain, and whether a stripper will remove the stain or not depends on how that particular stain is affected by the stripper. There are no strippers or refinishers that either do or don't remove all stains. Water dye stains, which were the most common stains used on old furniture, can be partially removed by water and totally removed by chlorine-type bleach. Solvent-based dye stains will be partially removed by the same solvent they were originally dissolved in and by bleach. Pigment stains are not dissolved by any solvent. They act like thin paint lodged in the pores and can be removed in the same way paint is removed.

It is not necessary to remove the stain in order to restain or refinish. You can stay with the stain color remaining in the wood or you can stain right over it with any type of stain you want in order to change its shade or darken it. But you cannot lighten the color without removing most or all of the stain first.

The Stripper Streaks and Darkens the Wood

Lye and any stripper that contains an alkali may darken the wood. This often shows up as ugly streaks in the pattern you used applying the stripper. You can bleach out the dark stains in the same way you bleach dark water rings out of the wood. Dilute some oxalic acid crystals, which you can buy in many paint stores and at pharmacies, in warm water. I usually make a saturated solution though this degree of strength is not always needed. Brush the solution over the entire surface, not just over the stains. Otherwise you may create lighter spots in these areas, and you will have to recoat the entire surface anyway to even the color. Let the oxalic acid dry back into crystal form. Then wash the crystals off the wood with a hose or well-soaked sponge or cloth. Wash the surface well with water and then add some borax, a small amount of household ammonia, or other mild alkali, to some clean water, and wash once again to neutralize the acid. Oxalic acid will seldom bleach the wood itself to any noticeable degree.

Sandpaper Gums Up After Stripping

Sanding is seldom necessary after stripping because the wood is almost always smooth. The wood was probably well-sanded when it was first finished. But sanding is often recommended because it insures the total removal of the finish. If you do choose to sand and you find that your sandpaper is gumming up, it means that all the finish has not been removed or the stripper has not totally evaporated. You are most likely to encounter unevaporated stripper when working with DBE- or NMP-based strippers. You can remove the excess with a solvent such as denatured alcohol, mineral spirits, or lacquer thinner. Denatured alcohol will be the least toxic in keeping with the spirit of the low-toxic strippers themselves.

Stain Will Not Take Evenly After Stripping

It could be that you did not remove all the old finish. If so, you will have to resume stripping until all the finish is off the wood or out of the pores. Uneven stain penetration could also be caused by uneven density or swirling grain in the wood itself.

The New Finish Will Not Dry, or Peels After Curing

Both of these problems are caused by your not having removed all the wax included in almost all methylene chloride- and ATM-based strippers. Wax requires a good deal of washing to be removed, not "neutralization" as is often suggested. Wash the wood thoroughly with any solvent for wax, refolding, and turning your wet cloth a number of times so you lift the wax from the wood and do not just slosh it around. Mineral spirits and naphtha are the best solvents to use. Lacquer thinner and alcohol will also work.

How to Choose a Commercial Stripper

Stripping shops have become much more professional in their approach over the last two decades as they have become increasingly tied in with one of several national companies that provide equipment, supplies, and instruction. The odds are better that you will get quality work if the stripping shop you are dealing with has established this tie.

The best way, however, to judge a stripping shop is to look at its work. Stripped wood should have the true color of wood, no fuzz, and feel like wood. Veneer and glued joints should be in good shape. The owner or manager of the shop should be able to intelligently explain the procedure he or she would use on your furniture.

CHAPTER 9

Wood Preparation

The first step in any finishing or refinishing procedure is the preparation of the surface for the finishing materials. If this is not done properly at this stage, the results will be very disappointing. This cannot be emphasized too strongly. Remember: the quality of the finish is directly related to the care you take in preparing the wood surface. Take your time. Many beginners are in such a hurry to see how the final finishing coat will look that they take shortcuts and try to use labor-saving techniques. The results are usually disappointing.

You are faced with one of two possible situations:

1. An old finish that needs to be removed or covered,
2. A new wood surface that requires finishing.

The procedures involved in removing or covering over old finishes were described in considerable detail in the last chapter (see also Chapter 14, *Paint and Enamel Finishes*). This chapter concentrates on the procedure to be followed when preparing a bare wood surface, and includes those surfaces from which previous finishes have been completely removed.

Wood is a highly complex material and extremely varied in its characteristics. Two pieces of the same type of wood can vary in color, moisture content, and porosity. Different types of woods will show an even greater variance. Nonuniformity is the rule rather than the exception. The worker must therefore employ a variety of techniques to create a suitable surface for whatever finish has been selected.

A number of operations have become standard procedure in wood preparation. They include:

1. Sanding,
2. Grain-raising,
3. Bleaching,
4. Wood coloring,
5. Applying a washcoat,
6. Using a filler,
7. Sealing.

Some of these operations are optional. For example, if the color of the wood is uniform and the shade you desire, there is no need to bleach it (remove the color) or stain it (add color). Sanding, on the other hand, is an operation used at various stages in the finishing schedule right up to the application of the final finishing coat (Fig. 9–1). The finishing operations that you use will depend upon the overall effect you are trying to achieve.

Sanding and Smoothing the Surface

The various coding and numbering systems used to identify the different grades of sandpaper were described in Chapter 2. The four principal categories, "coarse," "medium," "fine," and "very fine," not only identify the sandpaper grade, but also their most suitable applications (Table 9–1).

The types of sandpaper or abrasive papers commonly stocked by most paint stores, hardware stores, or building-supply outlets include flint, garnet, and aluminum oxide. An aluminum oxide sandpaper is generally recommended for finishing and refinishing applications.

Sanding is the first step in wood preparation. The wood must be sanded so that it provides a smooth and uniform surface for the finishing materials. All surface imperfections (scratches, dents, pits, etc.) must be removed, or they will ruin the overall appearance of the finish. Wood fibers raised above the level of the surface have to be cut down so that the finish appears completely uniform. You must be careful when sanding not to scratch the surface. If you are using a portable electric sander, it is all too easy to leave machine

SANDING BARE WOOD

APPLYING FIRST FINISHING COAT

SANDING FIRST FINISHING COAT

APPLYING SECOND FINISHING COAT

Fig. 9-1. Sanding should be done on the bare wood surface and on the various coats of finishing material.

Table 9-1.   Sandpaper Grades and Applications

Grade	Application
Coarse	used to remove old finish (paint, varnish, enamel, etc.), also deep gouges, scratches, stubborn stains and smudges. Use of coarse paper must always be followed by medium then fine paper, because scuff marks made by coarse paper are not only visible but sometimes magnified after a clear finish is applied.
Medium	used to remove less severe scratches, stains, smudges, etc.—also, scuff marks resulting from coarse sandpaper.
Fine	used to obtain smoothness; also to remove slight traces of scratching or scuffing remaining after previous sanding; also to remove raised grain resulting from sealing or bleaching.
Very Fine	used to obtain maximum degree of surface smoothness, the key to the finest possible natural wood finish.

(Courtesy Pierce & Stevens Chemical Corporation)

marks on the surface. Hand sanding across the grain or using a grade of sandpaper too coarse for the wood will also leave unsightly scratches. Remember: any type of imperfection left on the surface will be readily apparent once the finish is applied. At that point it will be too late to correct without going to the trouble of stripping the finish and starting all over again.

As a general rule, sanding a surface in preparation for the finish begins with the coarser grades of sandpaper and progresses to the finer ones. Normally, a satisfactory surface can be produced by starting with a 3/0 sandpaper, switching to a 4/0 sandpaper, and finishing with a 6/0. Once again, the coarsest grade you use will depend upon the softness of the wood. If the sandpaper is too coarse, it will scratch the wood and damage the fibers. It is probably better to use too fine a grade of paper, although then you encounter the possibility of clogging the wood pores and reducing stain penetration.

Use a sanding block with some sort of backing inserted between the paper and the surface of the block. Cork or hard rubber sanding blocks are better than the metal or hardwood variety because they greatly reduce the possibility of scratching the surface with the hard edge of the block.

Sand with the grain, in long, even strokes, almost as if you were ironing a piece of clothing (Figs. 9–2 and 9–3). Do not bear down

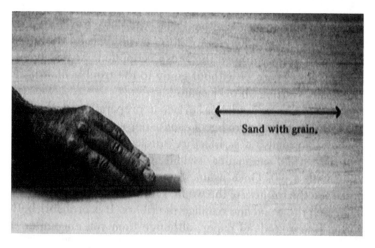

Fig. 9–2. Sanding with the grain. *(Courtesy ZAR Wood Finishing Products/United Gilsonite Laboratories)*

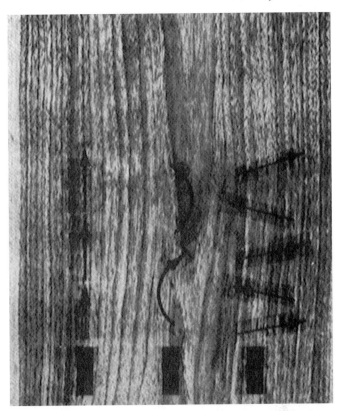

Fig. 9-3. Correct and incorrect sanding techniques: (A) Correct sanding straight and parallel with the grain; (B) Incorrect sanding with strokes that cut into the grain; (C) Incorrect sanding with strokes across the grain.

heavily, or you will lose some of the handling and directional control necessary to good sanding. You also run the risk of cutting too deeply and unevenly. Use a moderate to light pressure, and take your time. The old adage "haste makes waste" is certainly appropriate here.

Change your sandpaper frequently. If you continue to use it after it has become worn smooth, it will burnish the surface of the wood. This will prevent stains from penetrating into the wood, because the pores will have become blocked. This can also occur if you use too fine a grade of sandpaper.

Use a tack cloth, a clean, dry, lint-free cloth, or a brush to clean the dust and debris left by the sanding operation from the surface of the wood. As a final touch, pass a damp clean cloth over the surface of the wood. This will cause the grain fibers to swell and raise slightly. For a more detailed description of this aspect of wood preparation, see GRAIN RAISING in this chapter. Sand these raised fibers down level with the surface, and brush away the sawdust.

Whether you have an old furniture frame from which a finish has been removed, or a new one that has never had a finish, the wood surface probably has some dents and scratches. These must be removed before the preliminary stage of sanding is completed.

Raise the dents by applying a wet cloth to the area of the dent, or by applying an iron to a wet cloth held over the dent (Fig. 9–4). This causes the wood fibers to swell and raise above the surface. Shallow dents can be filled in by this grain-raising action. The raised fibers are removed by sanding. Make certain that the cloth you use is clean, or you may leave dirt and grease blemishes on the surface.

Scratches, pit marks, old nail and screw holes, gouges, and deep dents can be removed by filling them with wood putty, plastic wood, wood patch, or a stick shellac. The latter is recommended for use beneath natural finishes. Stick shellacs are particularly useful because they are available in a number of different colors. This enables you to match very closely the color of the wood. Additional information on removing surface defects can be found in Chapter 7 (see REPAIRING SURFACE DEFECTS).

Fig. 9–4. Removing shallow dents by using a moist cloth and a hot iron.

Grain-Raising

Most woods are subject to a certain amount of grain-raising when the surface comes into contact with moisture. When some of the wood fibers become wet, they rise above the surface, dry, and stiffen. The result is a rough, uneven surface that destroys the overall appearance of the wood. The task of the wood finisher, then, is to reduce the effects of grain-raising. This is accomplished by deliberately raising the wood fibers and sanding them down to the level of the surface. This operation *must* be done before the first of the finishing coats is applied. It is recommended that it be completed before you do any staining.

Sizing is an operation used by the furniture industry to remove wood fibers and fuzz, and is done just before the last sanding stage in wood preparation.

Size is made by dissolving a stiffening material (such as certain types of glue) in water until it reaches a very thin consistency. The sizing solution is then applied to the wood surface, causing the wood fibers to rise and stiffen. These raised and stiffened fibers are then removed by sanding. This reduces the amount of grain-raising at later stages in the finishing schedule, such as applying a water stain. Sizing also acts as a sealer coat for soft areas on the surface. As such, it allows the stain to be applied more uniformly, and reduces the chance of a splotchy appearance. In this respect, it has the same function as a prestain washcoat.

Rags, pads, or sponges are used to apply size. Be certain that the size is completely dry before attempting to sand it. Remember: sizing is a pretreatment stage in wood preparation. It is not intended as a filler or sealer.

Another method of raising and stiffening wood fibers is by applying a sanding sealer. The sanding sealer functions in the same way as sizing.

Many finishers accomplish grain-raising simply by sponging the surface of the wood with cold water (Fig. 9–5). Sponge the water onto the surface until it is thoroughly soaked, wipe off the excess, and let it dry. As soon as the fibers have dried and stiffened, lightly sand them down to surface level. Remove the dust and the residue left by the sanding operation with a tack rag or a clean, lint-free cloth.

Fig. 9–5. Sponging water on the surface in order to raise the wood grain.

Bleaching

Examine the surface of the wood. Sometimes an old finish has penetrated deeply into the wood pores. This stains the wood, making it somewhat darker than its original natural color. You will also find cases in which the coloring is uneven or too dark. This can occur with unfinished wood or wood from which a surface has been removed. Bleaching is used to remedy this situation.

Bleaches are used to lighten coloring or to remove it from a wood surface. Whatever the sought-after results, they must be *completely uniform*. You have not bleached properly if there are spots still on the surface showing different shades of coloring. The bleach may be applied to local areas or over the entire surface. In any event, the main purpose in applying the bleach is to obtain not only a lighter coloring, but also the even distribution of the same shade. A good bleaching, then, will succeed in removing all dark spots from the surface (spots that will ruin the appearance of clear and semiopaque finishes). It will not affect the grain pattern of the wood.

Synthetic (*not* natural) fiber brushes are recommended for applying bleach. Brushes made from natural fibers show a tendency to break down when they come in contact with the strong chemicals found in bleaches. Commercial one-solution bleaches can also be applied to the surface with a sponge (Fig. 9–6).

Bleaches should be mixed in glass or enamel-lined containers.

Fig. 9-6. Apply liquid bleach with a sponge.

Other types of containers may also be used, as long as they prove resistant to the bleaching solution chemicals.

Although both one- and two-solution bleaches are available commercially, the latter is by far the more effective form with woods that resist lightening. In the two-solution bleaches, the first solution produces the chemical change in the pigments and the second solution removes the residue.

Bleaching should be used only as a last resort, because (unless extreme care is taken) the strong chemicals used in the bleaching process can harm the skin or ruin the wood surface by destroying the fibers.

The procedure for mixing and using your own bleach to lighten a wood surface is as follows:

1. Use a brush with a synthetic fiber. Natural-fiber brushes disintegrate under the action of the bleach solution. Wear rubber gloves to protect the hands, goggles to protect the eyes, and make certain that you have proper and sufficient ventilation.
2. Apply an oxalic acid-water solution to the surface of the wood. A mild bleach can be produced from three ounces of oxalic acid (usually obtained in crystal form) dissolved in a quart of hot water and allowed to cool.
3. Mix sodium hypochlorite (household bleach) with hot water in the same proportions as the oxalic acid solution. Allow it to cool before application.
4. After the two solutions have been prepared and cooled, apply the oxalic acid solution. After it has dried, then apply the second solution.
5. As soon as the sodium hypochlorite solution has dried, wipe the

surface with a solution of borax and water. Again, allow the solution enough time to cool before applying it to the surface. The borax will neutralize the acid in the bleaching operation.

Step 3 will lighten the wood further, although it is not absolutely necessary to apply sodium hypochlorite after the application of the oxalic acid solution. Household bleaches work best at lightening natural wood colors, although they can also be used with success on water stains and ink. Oxalic acid-water solutions also work on water stains, and as a color lightener. If you would prefer not mixing your own bleach solution, a number of commercially prepared bleaches are available.

Commercially prepared two-solution bleaches enjoy widespread use. A popular brand name is Dexall, a commercial wood bleach manufactured by the Sherwin-Williams Company. Other reliable two-solution bleaches are Albino and Blanchit.

Clorox is a well-known one-solution bleach. It is a chlorinated liquid that will continue to lighten the wood with successive applications.

A special word of warning should be given about bleaches. Do not allow them to come into contact with your skin. The ingredients in the bleaches will frequently cause extreme skin reactions. This can be avoided by wearing rubber gloves and using some caution. Bleaches using oxalic acid solutions are particularly dangerous to the eyes and lungs. The threat is greatest when sanding a wood surface that has been treated with an oxalic acid solution. The dried oxalic acid adheres to the sawdust particles and is easily inhaled and brought into contact with the eyes. Excessive inhalation can cause the throat muscles to contract. It is recommended that you wear some sort of protective face mask (with goggles) when working with this type of bleach. I also recommend that you work outdoors. See Chapter 20, *Safety*, for more on working with hazardous materials.

Washcoating

Washcoating involves the application of a thin, fast-drying material over a stain, toner, or the bare wood surface prior to filling or using a pigment uniform stain.

The purpose of applying washcoat over a stain or toner is to seal these two materials and prevent them from bleeding through into the filler and subsequent finishing coats. It also provides a better surface for the application of the filler. Finally, it serves to raise loose wood fibers so that they may be sanded down close to the surface. When a washcoat is applied directly over a bare wood surface, it seals off the wood (particularly important if a bleach has been used) and provides a base for the stain. Stains will be much more uniform if applied over a washcoat. This is particularly true of open-grained woods.

Sometimes the terms "washcoat" and "sealer" overlap in meaning, causing a certain amount of confusion. The difference between the two is in their functions, and to a lesser extent in their composition. A sealer should be a thinned coating of whatever finish is to be placed on the wood. If the surface is to be varnished, then the sealer should be a much thinner varnish. A washcoat, on the other hand, may be a thinned shellac (50% shellac, 50% denatured alcohol), a thinned lacquer (or vinyl-type material), or a sealer. Sealers are always used after staining and after filling. Either a sealer washcoat or one of the other types of washcoats is used after a stain or on the bare wood surface. With these possibilities in mind, you could follow either of the two finishing schedules illustrated in Table 9–2. Finishing Schedule B should be used only with close-grained woods. Otherwise, the stain will penetrate too deeply and unevenly into the wood.

A good washcoat properly applied will coat the inside of the

Table 9–2. Finishing Schedules for Washcoats and Sealers

Finishing Schedule A	Finishing Schedule B
1. Sanding	1. Sanding
2. Washcoat or Sealer	2. Staining
3. Staining	3. Washcoat or Sealer
4. Sealer	4. Filler
5. Filler	5. Sealer
6. Sealer	6. Various Coats of Finish
7. Various Coats of Finish	

wood pore, not close it off. The pore must remain open so that the filler can be packed into it. Thinning, then, is a very important consideration when making a washcoat.

As was mentioned before, the three basic types of washcoats are:

1. Thinned shellac,
2. Thinned lacquer (or vinyl-type material),
3. A washcoat sealer.

Shellac washcoats are made by thinning orange or white shellac with denatured alcohol. The mixture is commonly 50% shellac thinned with 50% denatured alcohol, although thinner solutions can be used effectively. Shellac washcoats are preferred by many finishers because they are inexpensive, easy to make, and easy to apply. However, they should be used immediately and not stored, because shellac has a tendency to break down over a period of time and lose its effectiveness. Non-grain-raising and water stains will frequently bleed in a shellac washcoat and give the appearance of greater depth (particularly with cordovan and dark mahogany finishes), brilliance, and clarity.

Sealer washcoats (made from a lacquer sealer) are reduced with a lacquer thinner on a one-to-one basis. However, not all lacquer sealers can be properly reduced, and you might encounter some difficulty in making this type of washcoat. It all depends on the quality of the sealer.

Lacquer washcoats are fast drying (faster than shellac) and easy to use. They are also very easy to sand. I recommend purchasing a lacquer washcoat rather than attempting to make one. It is not as simple as reducing a lacquer with a lacquer thinner.

All bleached surfaces must be sealed with a washcoat, because the alkali contained in bleach has a tendency to cause other finishing materials to decompose. The best washcoat for this purpose is the vinyl type, since it is not as susceptible to the decomposing action of bleach as are the other washcoats. Vinyl washcoats are very similar to the lacquer type, except that they are based on vinyl or modified vinyl resins. As such, they serve as an excellent sealer for some resinous woods.

Washcoats can be lightly colored or pigmented with dye in order to create certain color effects. They are very similar to toners in both function and composition.

Always lightly sand the washcoat after it has thoroughly dried. This will cut down any wood fibers that may have been raised, and produce a smooth, even base for the stain or filler.

Staining

Stains are frequently used to add color to a wood by darkening some areas so that they match other, equally dark areas of color. Using stains to add color to the wood *before* a final finish is applied gives to staining a function exactly the opposite of bleaching, that is, the addition rather than the removal of color. It is that function of staining in the wood-preparation stage of finishing that will be discussed here. Because staining is a very complex subject and only one aspect of it pertains to the preliminary stage of wood preparation, both stains and staining techniques will be discussed in detail in the next chapter.

A typical staining procedure is illustrated in Fig. 9–7. More detailed finishing schedules for specific types of stains are found in Chapter 10.

Sealers

A sealer or sealing coat functions primarily as a barrier between two mutually incompatible substances. For example, a sealer is frequently used over fillers or stains to prevent bleeding through into the finish. An abbreviated schedule including the sealer step is as follows:

1. Staining,
2. Sealer,
3. Final finish (varnish, shellac, lacquer, etc.).

The addition of a filler would expand this schedule to the following steps:

1. Staining,
2. Sealer,
3. Filler,

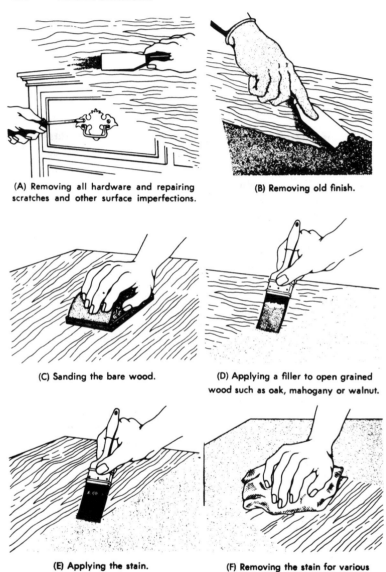

(A) Removing all hardware and repairing scratches and other surface imperfections.

(B) Removing old finish.

(C) Sanding the bare wood.

(D) Applying a filler to open grained wood such as oak, mahogany or walnut.

(E) Applying the stain.

(F) Removing the stain for various tone effects.

Fig. 9-7. Preparing the wood surface for staining. *(Courtesy Sherwin-Williams Co.)*

4. Sanding,
5. Sealer,
6. Final finish.

Note that a sealer coat is used after the application of both the stain and filler to prevent any possibility of combining with the next layer. Fillers are not required for close-grained woods (those having small pores). With these types of wood, the sealer functions as a substitute for the filler.

Sealers are available commercially, or they may be made in the home workshop. The latter is simply a washcoat of white shellac (one part shellac mixed with one part denatured alcohol).

The shellac washcoat is applied to the surface with a brush. Allow the wood to absorb the sealer. If the wood is particularly porous, it may be necessary to apply several coatings before the pores are completely filled. You will know that a sufficient amount of sealer has been added to the wood surface when it no longer soaks into the pores. Wipe off the excess sealer and allow the surface to dry for one to two hours. These shellac sealers are frequently used as base coats for a varnish finish.

Commercial sealers containing penetrating oils and resins are also available. These commercial sealers are variously referred to as *sealers, penetrating sealers, sealer stains,* or *penetrating resin finishes,* and may be purchased in a clear form or with stains added. The sealer is applied to the surface until it is sufficiently saturated. It is then allowed to sit for 10 or 20 minutes, and the excess is wiped away with a soft cloth. The sealer provides a protective coat as tough as varnish, but (unlike varnish) it penetrates deeply into the pores of the wood, where it hardens to form its special lamination-like effect. Moreover, these commercial sealers enhance and emphasize the grain of the wood. At least 24 hours of drying time should be allowed between each layer of sealer.

Shellac or varnish may be applied over the commercial sealer, or it may be waxed and serve as the finish itself. In the latter case, it is recommended that the dried sealer be rubbed with steel wool (000 grade), and then wiped clean *before* waxing.

Sanding sealers are usually vinyl-based finishing materials designed to make the sanding operation easier. They are sold in liquid form and are brushed or sprayed onto the surface. If the sanding sealer is sprayed, it should be thinned to the proper spraying consistency. A sanding sealer properly used will make sanding smoother and will reduce the amount of dust that adheres to the sandpaper.

A sanding sealer may be applied to the surface of the wood to stiffen fibers raised by wetting. In this respect, it has a function similar to that of a shellac washcoat or sizing.

When varnishing, a sanding sealer is sometimes used before the first coat of varnish is applied. It provides protection to the wood, stain, and filler. It also functions as a smooth bonding surface for the varnish topcoat.

Wherever you use the sanding sealer, it should be lightly sanded afterwards. Make certain that it is thoroughly dry before sanding. Use a tack rag or a clean, lint-free cloth to remove the dust and other residue left by the sanding operation.

Fillers

Open-grained woods (those having large pores) must have their pores filled before the finish coats are applied; otherwise the finish will seep down into these large pores, resulting in a very uneven coat. Another reason for filling is to provide a color contrast between the pore and the flake of the wood.

Fillers are produced in either paste or liquid form. Both are manufactured from a base that includes quartz silica mixed with some sort of drier, a thinner (usually turpentine or oil), and a vehicle.

Fillers may be sprayed or brushed onto the surface; the latter method is the most common in the home workshop.

The procedure for brushing a filler onto a wood surface is as follows:

1. Apply a washcoat to the untreated wood surface.
2. Thin the filler to the thickness you find suitable for working. Follow the manufacturer's recommendation for the selection of a thinner. The filler can be tinted at this point with your wood stain to make a better match with the rest of the finish. As a rule of thumb, add about 10% to 30% stain, depending on the wood.

3. Brush in the filler in the direction of the grain. Allow the filler sufficient time to dry to a dull sheen. Do not let it completely dry, or it will be difficult to rub off.
4. Rub the filler *across* the grain with a piece of burlap.
5. Take a clean burlap cloth and rub across the grain a second time.
6. Take a clean, soft cloth and wipe the surface in the direction of the grain.
7. Allow the filler enough time to dry completely, remove the excess filler with a putty knife (Fig. 9–8), burlap, or a rough cloth, and then sand lightly to restore the smooth surface.

Most filling problems can be traced to one or more of the following causes:

1. Improper application,
2. Poor drying,
3. Use of the wrong filler.

The most common problems related to the improper use of a filler are:

1. Puffing,
2. Shrinkage,
3. Ashing,
4. Pinholing.

Puffing refers to the swelling of the filler after the sealer and topcoat have been applied. It results in the filler pushing itself out

Fig. 9–8. Removing excess filler with a putty knife.

of the wood pore, and is caused by not allowing sufficient time for the filler to dry. *Shrinkage* has the opposite effect. Although a filler will be subject to some shrinkage as it dries, excessive shrinkage is caused by coating the filler before it is completely dry.

Ashing refers to the grayish color a filler will acquire after a topcoat has been applied. This too is due to improper drying. *Pinholes* are also caused by applying a sealer or topcoat to a filler before it has had time to dry. However, pinholing can also be traced to other causes unrelated to the filling procedure, such as vapor trapped in the pores or excess moisture in the wood. The pinholes resemble tiny eruptions on the surface of the finish.

The filler has been improperly applied when it is wiped too vigorously and before it has dried sufficiently. This results in removing some of the filler from the pores and giving the surface an appearance similar to one caused by excessive shrinkage.

Poor filling can also be caused by any of the following factors:

1. A washcoat that is too thick or thin,
2. A filler that is too thick or thin,
3. A surface that is poorly sanded.

A washcoat that is too thick will bridge (close) the pores and prevent packing by the filler. A washcoat that is too thin will cause the filler to wipe hard. This produces a nonuniform appearance. A filler that is too thick will not pack the pores properly, while one that is too thin will not fill them adequately. Poor sanding produces rough spots and results in a nonuniform application of the filler.

All of these filling problems can be prevented by properly preparing the wood surface and carefully following the manufacturer's instructions for using the filler.

CHAPTER 10

Staining

A *stain* is a solution of coloring matter, usually an aniline dye or a pigment, in a solvent. The coloring matter is dissolved or suspended in the solution, depending upon the type of stain. Dye-type stains are transparent unless modified with opaque pigments, while pigment-type stains are characterized by a certain degree of opacity. It all depends on the amount of pigment color suspended in the solution.

Staining is the process of applying a stain to a wood surface. Stains may be applied over a smoothed, bare wood surface (almost always close-grained woods), over a washcoat or sealer (open-grained woods), or over finishes (shading, antiquing, etc. See Chapter 17). They may be applied to portions of the surface, or to the entire surface.

The primary purpose of staining is to alter or change the color of a wood, and *not* to provide a protective coating. Generally, a stain is unsuitable as a protective coating because it lacks toughness and its color is subject to fading. A *stained finish* is usually one that has some sort of clear, transparent finish or wax applied over the stain to lock in the colors and to provide a protective coating. This protective finish is applied after the stain has dried. Examples of how a stain can be finished are:

1. A shellac washcoat and a wax,
2. A sealer and a clear varnish,
3. A lacquer sealer and a lacquer.

The washcoat or sealer prevents the stain from bleeding into the wax or clear top coat, but at the same time does not obscure or alter the color of the stain.

Reasons for staining wood vary. For example, the colors of many woods are too light or pale, and the figure and grain are indistinct. Staining these woods will enhance their beauty. Frequently too a wood surface will have a number of spots that are lighter or darker than the rest of the wood. Staining will correct this unevenness. Another way in which a finisher can use a stain is to give a wood the color of one more expensive or more difficult to obtain. Finally, staining can be used to create special coloring effects. There are red, green, and other non-wood-color stains on the market that can change a cheap, uninteresting wood surface into an attractive addition to any room.

Wood stains can be purchased in hardware stores, paint stores, art supply stores, and many other retail outlets. Stains may also be purchased from mail-order firms that specialize in wood finishing materials.

The finisher should carefully follow the instructions and recommendations of the manufacturer when using a stain. One word of caution: Always purchase enough stain of a particular brand to complete the job. The color produced by one manufacturer does not always match the same color made by another manufacturer, and many complications can be avoided by not mixing the two brands.

Before applying a stain to a wood surface, the finisher is advised to test it on a piece of wood of similar composition. If this is not available, select a section of the piece of furniture (e.g., a back rail, underside, etc.) that is usually out of view, and apply the stain. If, when testing the stain, you find that it is darker than you want, thin it with turpentine. Stains that appear to be too light can be darkened by adding a second coat. After the stain sample has dried, coat it with the various finishing materials (e.g., filler, sealer, and topcoats) you plan to use. This will give you a very good idea of how the completed job will look. Remember, even a clear finish will alter a stain color slightly.

Stains can be applied with a brush, pad, lint-free cloth, or by spraying them onto the surface (Figs. 10–1, 10–2, and 10–3). The last method finds its greatest use in shading, toning, or applying stain to areas that are difficult of access. Brushes with synthetic bristles and rubber ferrules are recommended for brushing on a stain.

In addition to the surface preparation procedures described in Chapter 9, it is recommended that the following additional precautions be taken when applying stains:

Fig. 10–1. Spraying a stain coating on a wood chair.

Fig. 10–2. Brushing on a stain.

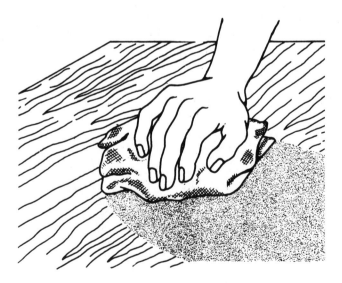

Fig. 10–3. Wiping on a stain.

1. Whenever possible, place the surface being stained in a horizontal position (i.e., the working surface face up). This will minimize the problem of the stain running.

2. Overlap only wet surfaces. If a wet brush stroke overlaps a dry one, it may result in unsightly lap marks on the surface. This is always a problem with water stains; however, it decreases in varying degrees with other types of stains.

3. Work from a light to a dark tone when staining. It is always easier to darken a color by adding more stain.

4. Apply the stain in the direction of the grain whenever possible.

5. Remove badly stained areas with a commercial bleach.

6. For large surface areas, mix two or three containers of the same stain color before starting the work. Mix only stains from the same manufacturer. Different manufacturers may have different chemical formulas for the same stain color. Mixing them may cause problems.

7. If the stain is too dark, lighten it before application by adding a lighter stain of the same type and from the same manufacturer.

8. If you have already applied the stain and feel that it is too dark, you can lighten it considerably by wiping part of it off the surface before it has had time to penetrate very far into the wood.

9. Always stain the largest exposed areas of a piece of furniture last.

The type of stain used and its application procedure will often be determined by whether you are staining a softwood or hardwood surface. To obtain the best results with a softwood, such as pine or fir, use a stain that penetrates the surface slowly, to obtain a more uniform effect. The softer spring growth of softwoods absorbs the stain more rapidly than the harder summer growth, creating the effect known as *wild grain* (Fig. 10–4). This is frequently a problem when applying a dark stain such as walnut or mahogany over a softwood surface. The wild grain effect can be avoided by applying an alkyd-base filler-sealer to the surface to equalize the absorption rate of the wood grain and provide a more uniform stain effect (Fig. 10–5). Be sure to use a liquid filler-sealer that is compatible with the stain applied over it.

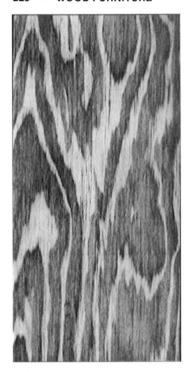

Fig. 10-4. Example of the wild grain effect on a softwood surface. *(Courtesy Benjamin Moore Paints)*

Fig. 10-5. Uniformly stained softwood surface. *(Courtesy Benjamin Moore Paints)*

Hardwoods usually absorb stains uniformly. A penetrating stain will penetrate the hard grain in depth, resulting in a finish that emphasizes the natural pattern of the wood (Fig. 10-6).

Many of the stains used in wood finishing can be grouped into three broad categories, depending upon the base used in their composition. These three categories of stains are:

1. Oil stains,
2. Water stains,
3. Spirit (alcohol) stains.

Fig. 10-6. Stained hardwood surface. *(Courtesy Benjamin Moore Paints)*

Oil Stains

Oil is used as the base in the production of oil stains. These types of stains, also called *oil-base stains*, are commercially available in a wide variety of colors, are relatively easy to apply, and will usually not raise the grain of the wood. On the other hand, oil stains do show a tendency to fade over a period of time. Although an oil stain will impart a deep, rich tone to the wood, it also has a tendency to reduce the clarity of the grain pattern. Finally, untreated end grains will become considerably darker than the rest of the wood when covered with an oil stain. This can be avoided by applying a coating of linseed oil, thinned shellac, or mineral spirits as a sealer before staining.

Oil-base stains are the easiest for the beginner to apply. If the surface is carefully prepared and the manufacturer's instructions are faithfully followed, even the most inexperienced should have no difficulty.

The procedure used for applying an oil stain to a new wood surface may be summarized as follows:.

1. Prepare the surface according to the instructions described in Chapter 9.
2. Cover all end grains with a washcoat of thinned shellac, linseed oil, mineral spirits, or a similarly suitable sealer. This will prevent excessive penetration of the porous end grains by the stain. Excessive penetration by the stain will result in a darker color at the end grains than the rest of the wood.
3. Try out the stain on an inconspicuous section of wood similar to that of the exposed surfaces (Fig. 10–7).
4. Turn the piece of furniture upside down and begin applying the stain to the legs and other exposed surfaces with a brush or a lint-free cloth (Fig. 10–8). Wipe away the excess stain to blend in the color or tone you desire (Fig. 10–9). Brush or wipe with long straight strokes in the direction of the grain or flat surfaces. After completing an area, inspect it for skips and misses, particularly along the edges. Do this by viewing the surface at an angle. Missed spots will show up dull in comparison to the newly applied coating and should be touched up immediately. If they are discovered after the coating has begun to set, allow it time to dry and then lightly touch it up.
5. Continue to apply the stain until the wood pores will absorb no more.
6. After about 15 or 20 minutes, wipe off the excess stain. Wipe the dark areas more than the light ones to obtain greater uniformity in tone and color.

Fig. 10–7. Trying out the stain. *(Courtesy Carver Tripp)*

Fig. 10-8. Staining the legs. *(Courtesy Benjamin Moore Paints)*

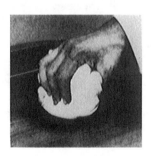

Fig. 10-9. Wiping away the excess stain to obtain desired color and tone. *(Courtesy Carver Tripp)*

7. After staining the underside, return the piece of furniture to an upright position and apply the stain to the exposed surfaces. Follow the same procedure used to stain the underside.

8. Table tops should be stained in workable segments and then wiped before continuing in order to maintain a uniform effect (Fig. 10–10). If the stain appears darker than you wish, dampen a cloth with mineral spirits and wipe away some of the stain.

9. Allow the stain to dry according to label directions, usually about 24 hours.

10. Smooth the surface with a very fine grade of steel wool *only* if you feel it is absolutely necessary. The danger of using an abra-

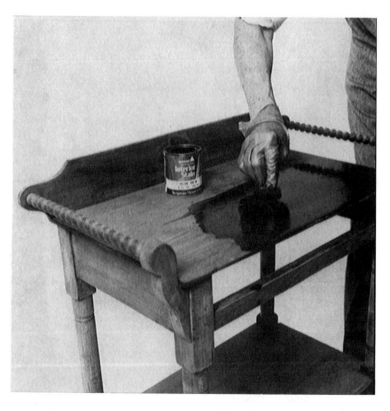

Fig. 10–10. Staining the surface in manageable segments. *(Courtesy Benjamin Moore Paints)*

sive on a newly-stained surface is that you may cut through it and make light spots. It is far better to remove all rough spots from the surface before staining.

11. Wipe the surface carefully with a tack cloth to remove all lint, dust, and other residue.

12. Turn the piece of furniture upside down again and apply a clear finish to the dry stained surface. When coating legs and braces, avoid overloading the brush with varnish, which may cause runs.

13. Return the piece of furniture to an upright position after the underside work has been completed. Working on an area of manageable size, apply the clear finish across the grain (Fig. 10-11).

Fig. 10-11. Applying the clear finish. *(Courtesy Benjamin Moore Paints)*

Final brush strokes are made with the grain to distribute the finish evenly. Continue coating the surface in the same manner, always working back into the previously coated area.

14. After allowing the coating to dry according to label directions, rub the surface lightly with a very fine steel wool and then clean it thoroughly with a tack cloth or lint-free cloth. Apply the second coat of clear finish following the same procedures.

A stain may also be applied over a previously stained, waxed, finished, or varnished surface if it is properly prepared. Cleaning is an important first step when staining this type of surface. If the surface is not clean, the stain will not take evenly. The procedure for applying a stain to a previously stained, waxed, finished, or varnished surface may be summarized as follows:

1. Clean the surface with a mild paint remover or a mild detergent, and then rinse it thoroughly with clean water. A fine-grade nylon scrubbing pad will help remove builtup grease. If there is a heavy buildup of grease on the surface, use a paint thinner with the nylon scrubbing pad.

2. Touch up bare spots, if necessary (Fig. 10–12). These are areas where old finish has worn away, usually because of repeated touching or wear, and where grease has built up. Clean the area thoroughly, sanding out the grease if necessary. Apply a clear finish tinted with a small amount of stain to the bare spots. Let it dry, and then sand the surface to smooth it out. This will allow the stain to cover the surface uniformly. If you

Fig. 10–12. Bare spot where hardware has been removed. *(Courtesy Carver Tripp)*

stain before this procedure, you will find that the bare spots will absorb more stain, resulting in a different color.

3. Sand the entire area with a fine grade of sandpaper to roughen the surface. A roughened surface will provide better adhesion for the stain.

4. Use a tack cloth or a clean, lint-free cloth to remove dust and other debris from the surface.

5. Apply the stain and then the clear finish by following the same procedures described for staining new wood. Note: For best results, always cover a lighter stain with a darker one.

Oil-base stains may be divided into several types, depending upon their composition. The two types most frequently used in furniture finishing are:

1. Pigment oil stains,
2. Penetrating oil stains.

Pigment Oil Stains

Pigment oil stains, not to be confused with pigmented wiping stains, are composed of ground color pigments suspended in a solvent (e.g., turpentine, linseed oil, or naphtha). These are nonpenetrating oil stains that at one time enjoyed widespread use in furniture finishing. They have now been largely replaced by non-grain-raising stains, water stains, spirit (alcohol) stains, and others more convenient to use.

Pigment oil stains are particularly useful for blending and retouching colors. This is primarily due to the fact that the stain is mixed by the finisher himself to match the color of the surface, and there are literally hundreds of different color tones possible.

The disadvantages of using pigment oil stains are as follows:

1. The color pigments have a tendency to settle to the bottom of the container and must be thoroughly stirred before and during use.

2. Oil pigment stains have a tendency to fade as well as cloud the finish.

3. These stains require a comparatively longer drying time.

Penetrating Oil Stains

Penetrating oil stains consist of aniline dyes dissolved in a solvent (turpentine, naphtha, toluol, or some other hydrocarbon solvent). These stains are available in a ready-mixed liquid form or powders.

Penetrating oil stains are very easy to apply, and the lightness or darkness of the overall color can be controlled by wiping. Unfortunately, they tend to penetrate unevenly on certain woods. These stains generally penetrate the wood more deeply than other types, and are therefore much more difficult (and sometimes impossible) to remove once they have dried. Penetrating oil stains are produced in clear, transparent colors and are used most effectively on open-grained woods (those having large pores). Their primary advantage is that they will not clog the pores of these woods.

The color of penetrating oil stain has a tendency to fade. Moreover, this type of stain tends to bleed badly, particularly under lacquer or varnish topcoats, where it usually bleeds through and creates a spotted or mottled appearance.

Water Stains

Water stains (sometimes called *water-soluble* or *latex stains*) are produced by dissolving powdered aniline dye in hot water. These stains are particularly effective in bringing out the natural color of the wood. The most serious drawback encountered when using water stains is their tendency to raise the grain of the wood. As a result, certain wood fibers swell and harden, extending permanently above the surface of the wood. They must be removed by sanding before the finishing schedule can proceed any further. The problem of raised grains can be handled in several ways, including:

1. Raise the grain *before* applying the stain by sponging the surface with warm water, allowing it to dry (one to three hours), and sanding down the raised grain.
2. Sand down the raised grain after having stained the surface. This is the least desirable method, because you run the risk of sanding through the stain.
3. Use a non-grain-raising (NGR) stain.

The procedure recommended for applying a water stain to a wood surface is as follows:

1. Prepare the surface according to the instructions given in Chapter 9.
2. Raise the wood grain by sponging it lightly with warm water. Allow the surface sufficient time to dry and the wood fibers time to harden.
3. Sand the raised grain down with a fine grade of sandpaper. Do *not* sand against the grain.
4. Remove all dust caused by the sanding operation. Use a soft, clean cloth for this purpose.
5. Apply the water stain with straight, even brush strokes. Do not wipe off the excess. This will be absorbed by the wood, or it will evaporate during the drying period.
6. Allow the stained surface to dry for approximately 24 hours.
7. Sand the surface lightly with a fine grade of sandpaper if further grain-raising has occurred. It may be necessary to apply a second coat of stain, especially if the sanding has caused light spots to appear. Always sand in the direction of the grain, never across the grain.
8. Remove all dust caused by the sanding operation (see Step 4).

A water stain may be sprayed, brushed, or wiped onto the surface. Brushing is often followed by wiping, because a water stain can be made uniform by the wiping action. Drying time is rather long (usually 24 hours), but this allows the stain to penetrate more deeply into the wood. A water stain is flooded onto the surface. This ensures uniformity in application, but the excess stain should not be allowed to sit too long. The longer the stain is allowed to sit after it has been applied, the darker the color will be. A very light color can be obtained by wiping off the stain almost immediately after application.

Water stains are noted for their rich, deep colors. The intensity of the color is determined by the amount of water added to the aniline dye powder. As the amount of water in proportion to the powder increases, the intensity of the color decreases.

Water stains are nonbleeding, and can therefore be used safely under a lacquer or varnish topcoat. These stains should be applied on a horizontal surface in order to reduce the chance of running.

A washcoat is mandatory after applying a water stain, because it creates a smoother surface for the next layers of finishing material. It is particularly important that end grains be sealed when working with this type of stain. A shellac washcoat will do nicely.

Water stains should not be applied over surfaces that have been stripped, because oil films from the old finish will interfere with a uniform penetration of the stain.

Spirit (Alcohol) Stains

Spirit (alcohol) stains (also called *alcohol-soluble stains*) are formed by dissolving aniline dye powders in alcohol. These stains are commercially available in a wide variety of ready-mixed colors, or you can mix your own by purchasing packets of the aniline dye powder.

Like oil stains, the color of a spirit stain tends to fade over a period of time. In addition to that, these stains tend to bleed very badly, and will bleed into most finishing topcoats unless properly sealed. Never use a shellac washcoat under a spirit stain. Alcohol will dissolve shellac.

A spirit stain will dry in about half an hour. Because of its rapid drying rate, spraying is recommended as the method of application. Brushing requires quick, long, even strokes parallel to the longer edges. Overlapping should be avoided. Do not sand a spirit stain except as a last resort. Any grain-raising and sanding should take place before the stain is applied. Avoid applying a spirit stain if the humidity is particularly high. Otherwise, the wood will absorb a certain amount of moisture from the air and grain-raising will usually occur after the spirit stain is applied.

Non-Grain-Raising (NGR) Stains

A non-grain-raising stain consists of:

1. A primary solvent (e.g., methanol),
2. A secondary solvent to hold the colors in solution,
3. A coal tar dilutant to reduce grain raising,
4. An aniline powder (the same acid dye used in water stains).

Non-grain-raising stains are the most commonly used stains in furniture finishing. Among their principal advantages are:

1. Color permanency (they show very little tendency to fade),
2. Color uniformity,
3. The absence of bleeding.

The major disadvantage of using non-grain-raising stains is their relative costliness as compared to water stains. On the other hand, they are still cheaper than the spirit stains.

Non-grain-raising stains dry more quickly than water stains, usually requiring only 15 minutes to one hour. This makes brushing them somewhat difficult. Furthermore, brushing a non-grain-raising stain tends to cause a certain amount of grain-raising. For this reason spraying is recommended, because very little or no grain-raising takes place with this method of application.

Because non-grain-raising stains dry so rapidly, a relatively wide brush (2½ to 3 inches) is recommended for applying. The rapid drying speed of non-grain-raising stains also results in lap marks when brushed onto the surface. These can be reduced to a minimum by applying several thinned coats of this stain rather than one overall coat.

The most notable feature of non-grain-raising stains is that they will not raise the wood grain appreciably if properly formulated.

Varnish Stains

A varnish stain consists of an aniline dye dissolved in a varnish solvent. It should never be used on a fine wood surface, because it tends to obscure the grain pattern and color. Moreover, it has no penetrating power, and sits on the surface in a manner similar to paint or enamel.

Varnish stains are generally sold under the names of woods that approximate their color (e.g., "walnut" for a walnutlike color), and are easily applied to the wood surface with a brush. In the furniture industry, they are used to apply a quick, inexpensive stain coating to wood surfaces not generally exposed to view (chair bottoms, insides of cabinets and drawers, the backs of chests, dressers, and dish cabinets, etc.) Pigmented wiping stains are recommended for use in place of varnish stains.

Spray Stains

Wood stains are available in aerosol spray cans (16-oz. capacity) for coating areas that are difficult to reach with a brush or cloth, and for shading and toning. These are quick-drying stains requiring only about 20 to 30 minutes to become completely dry. They are produced in a number of different colors and are sold under such names as Spanish Walnut, Modern Walnut, or Cherry.

These are lacquer-base stains that both seal and stain the wood in one application. Because lacquer is used in their composition, the same safety and health precautions recommended for a lacquer topcoat should also be used when spraying with these stains.

The nozzles of some spray cans are adjustable for either a vertical or horizontal spray pattern. When spraying, hold the can approximately 12 inches from the surface, and move it according to the instructions given in Chapter 2.

Spray stains can be applied over old finishes as well as bare wood surfaces. If you are spraying an old finish, make certain that no lifting or crazing has occurred, otherwise it will have to be stripped. Clean off all dirt, grease, polish, wax, and other substances that might contaminate the new stain with a suitable solvent (e.g., mineral spirits). Do not use a solvent strong enough to dissolve the old finish. Sand the surface with a very fine grade of sandpaper and remove the dust left by the sanding operation with a clean, lint-free cloth. Spray the stain onto the surface with quick, uniform movements. Allow the stain to dry thoroughly (about 30 to 45 minutes) and apply additional coats until you have obtained the desired uniformity and depth of color. When the last coat has completely dried, spray onto the surface several coats of a clear finish compatible with the stain.

Staining Over Surface Defects

Stains are designed to reveal and enhance the wood grain. Unfortunately, they also reveal surface defects equally well. Therefore stains should not be used as finishes (e.g., stain and wax finish) over surfaces which have been extensively repaired or built up.

In Chapter 7 the use of wood putty, plastic wood, and shellac stick for filling dents and other surface imperfections was described. All of these materials can be closely matched with the natural color of the wood or the finish; however, none of them contain wood graining. Therefore, their extensive use will be quite conspicuous under any of the clear finishes. Opaque finishes (paint, enamel, etc.) are recommended for surfaces that require more than minimal repair.

Other Types of Stains and Stain Sealers

Sap Stains, Overall Stains, and Accent Stains

Sap stains, *overall stains*, and *accent stains* are terms referring to specific staining functions. For example, sometimes wood surfaces will have color streaks or nonuniform sections of coloring. *Sap stains* (water stains, non-grain-raising stains, or modifications of these two) are used to equalize the overall color of the surface by eliminating these color irregularities. Sap stains are also used to equalize the color differences between the various parts of a piece of furniture (legs, arms, rungs, etc.) and the veneer.

Overall stains (usually water or non-grain-raising stains) refer to stains applied to the entire surface of a piece of furniture. *Accent stains*, on the other hand, are stains applied to accent wood grain before an overall stain is applied. These are usually spirit or water stains. Accent stains can also be applied over the filler, sealer, or first coat of lacquer for a highlighting effect.

Toners

A toner is used to change partially or completely the natural color of a wood to a simulated one. The toner covers the surface of the wood and does not penetrate into the pores. It generally consists of an opaque or semiopaque pigment suspended in a lacquer. A synthetic or natural resin base may also be used as a vehicle for the toner. Sometimes a toner will contain a dye instead of pigment, which results in a more transparent coating than the pigment type will give.

The disadvantages of pigment-type toners is that they obscure the grain figure and often give the wood a painted effect. However, if the toner is too transparent, the uniforming effect decreases. A good toner will have the following characteristics:

1. Maximum uniformity,
2. Little buildup,
3. No obscuring of the grain,
4. A smooth base for the other finishing materials.

Equalizers

Equalizers are similar in composition to toners, but differ in their function. Toners are used to change partially or completely the color of a wood, while equalizers are designed to make uniform a wood of variegated colors.

Padding Stains

A padding stain is essentially a glaze and takes its name from the method by which it is applied. A pad moistened with shellac or lacquer (in this case, a special padding lacquer) is dipped into a colored powder and then rubbed onto an older surface for a special color effect. Note that it is not rubbed onto a bare wood surface.

Tobacco and Other Organic-Base Stains

Cornell University has developed a tobacco stain for use on pine that leaves a very interesting warm brown color.

The stain is made by mixing a cutup plug of tobacco with a pint of clear household ammonia in a quart jar. The mixture is sealed and allowed to soak for seven to ten days, and then applied to the wood surface. A soft, lint-free cloth is recommended for application. Because this is in a sense a wiping stain, the excess not absorbed by the wood should be wiped off as soon as possible. Allow the stain to dry for approximately 24 hours, remove any dust particles or other matter with a tack rag, and apply a sealer coat.

Other organic-base stains have been made from berries, roots, bark, and other types of vegetation. The coloring matter is ground and dissolved in a solvent in much the same manner as aniline dye powders used in water stains. The method of application is also similar. The colors of these stains fade more rapidly than do the water stains, and for this reason, they have been largely replaced by the latter.

Sealer Stains

Sealer stains *(or stain sealers)* are designed to add color and seal the wood in the same operation (Fig. 10-13). These stains are basically sealers produced by thinning such finishes as varnish, shellac, or lacquer and mixing in color dyes. They are available in cans for brush application or as sprays.

Sealer stains usually dry a uniform tone without the occasional dark spots found with other types of stains. They are also characterized by the absence of lap marks during their application. Sealer stains generally exhibit less surface penetration than do other types

Fig. 10-13. Example of a stain that seals and stains in the same operation. *(Courtesy of ZAR Wood Finishing Products/United Gilsonite Laboratories)*

of stains. Pigmented wiping stains and Minwax are examples of sealer stains.

Pigmented Wiping Stains

Pigmented wiping stains (known also as *wiping stains, oil stains, uniforming stains,* or *unifying stains*) consist of finely ground color pigments suspended in a solvent (naphtha, mineral spirits, turpentine, or linseed oil) that is usually combined with oil or a synthetic resin binder.

These stains are more closely related to an enamel or paint (they are actually a thin paint by composition), and are frequently used to cover or mask an undesirable grain pattern or wood color. When they do emphasize a grain, it is accomplished by filling in the open pores with color pigments. Essentially, then, the grain is outlined by the wiping stain. These stains are frequently used to imitate the color of a more expensive wood.

Pigmented wiping stains are second only to non-grain-raising stains in popularity. This is due not only to their low cost, but also to their ease and flexibility of application. They may be brushed, wiped, or sprayed onto a surface, and various color effects can be obtained by the manner in which they are wiped off. These are rather long-drying stains, and wiping generally takes place five to ten minutes after application.

Either size or a washcoat should be applied to a bare wood surface before using a pigmented wiping stain. This reduces penetration, increases color uniformity, and develops better wiping properties for the stain.

Two stain systems are possible by applying a pigmented wiping stain over a water or non-grain-raising stain. This will result in combining the best properties of the dye-base stains (depth and brilliance of color) with those of the pigmented wiping stain. An abbreviated finishing schedule for such a two-stain system is as follows:

1. Follow wood preparation steps before staining (see Chapter 9).
2. Apply a water or non-grain-raising stain to the wood surface and allow it sufficient time to dry thoroughly.

3. Lightly sand the surface with a very fine grade of sandpaper. Be careful not to scratch through the stain spots.
4. Wipe away the dust left by the sanding operation with a clean, lint-free cloth.
5. Apply the pigmented wiping stain.
6. Follow the concluding steps of a finishing schedule following the application of a stain (see Chapter 9).

A pigmented wiping stain can also be applied over a toner when the latter substitutes for the primary stain (i.e., in Step 2 of the above finishing schedule).

All pigmented wiping stains should be mixed carefully before using. The ground color pigments have a tendency to settle to the bottom of most containers when not being used. Pigmented wiping stains are available in cans, bottles (with dauber tops), aerosol spray cans, and tubes (cream or paste form).

Most pigmented wiping stains (with the exception of those in aerosol spray cans) should be thinned before use. Follow the manufacturer's recommendations for thinning.

Minwax

Minwax is a trade name for a finishing material that functions as both a stain sealer and a finish. It penetrates, stains, and seals the wood in a single action, and dries to a relatively tough scratch resistant finish.

The recommended finishing schedule for applying Minwax is as follows:

1. Prepare the surface (sanding only) according to the recommendations suggested in Chapter 9.
2. Thoroughly mix the Minwax before applying it to the surface.
3. Apply the first coat of Minwax with a brush or a clean, lint-free cloth and wait 10 to 15 minutes for it to penetrate the wood.
4. Wipe away the excess with a clean cloth and allow it to dry for about 24 hours.
5. Apply a second coat of Minwax (follow Steps 2, 3, and 4).
6. Apply a paste finishing wax and polish with a clean, soft cloth.

A tougher finish with a deeper, richer color can be obtained by modifying the finishing schedule as follows:

6. Apply a shellac washcoat and allow it sufficient time to dry thoroughly.
7. Apply one or two coats of clear varnish.

Blonding

Blonding is a staining procedure used to lighten the color of a wood without resorting to bleaching. This is accomplished by applying a very light tinted or white pigmented wiping stain to the wood and wiping it off. This procedure does not work on dark-colored woods, and produces only a slight lightening effect on the light-colored ones.

Shading Wood Stains

Wood stains can be given a shaded effect by wiping or brushing harder at the center of a wood surface than at the edges or in the corners. The stain will then be darker at these points and will appear to frame or outline the panels and other sections with a gradual change of color from very dark to very light.

The procedure for shading wood stains is as follows:

1. Follow the instructions for preparing the wood surface given in Chapter 9.
2. Apply a thinned oil stain to the surface, and wipe it off almost immediately afterwards. This will prevent the stain from penetrating the wood pores to any great extent, and provides the lighter shades.
3. Apply a second unthinned coat of oil stain to the edges and corners. Wipe off the stain with a cloth, using circular hand movements. Wipe harder on those areas that will be a lighter shade or color.

Refer to Chapter 17 for a more detailed description of shading procedures. See the same chapter for information on SHADING STAINS and GLAZING STAINS.

Gelled Wood Stains

Wood stains are also available in gelled form in ½-pint, pint, and quart cans. The advantage of gelled wood stains is that the color pigments are distributed evenly throughout the container. Consequently, there is no settling out of the color pigments (as is the case with liquid oil stains), and the same color is maintained from top to bottom.

These stains can be applied over latex or flat oil-type bases with a brush or a cloth wiping pad. They are excellent for antiquing (see Chapter 17). Gelled wood stains are available in a variety of different colors, including red mahogany, brown mahogany, butternut, fruitwood, and walnut.

CHAPTER 11

Shellac Finishes

The word "shellac" is formed by combining the words "shell" and "lac." The latter word is of ancient origin, found in Persian (as *lak*), in Hindu (as *lahk*), and in Sanskrit (as *laksha*). All three refer to the tiny lac insect and its resinous excretion used in the production of shellac. The word translates in each of the three original languages as "hundred thousand," and is descriptive of the manner in which the insect rapidly multiplies until it completely covers the host plant. The lac insect, then, is literally the "hundred-thousand bug."

The lac insect seeks out certain types of host plants to which the larvae attach themselves and feed upon the sap. However, before feeding, the lac insect covers itself with a protective cover or shell by excreting a sticky, resinous substance. It is this substance (also referred to as *lac*) that forms the basis for the manufacture of shellac.

Among the principal advantages of using shellac in wood finishing is that it is easy to apply and permits the natural grain of the wood to show through. It is a quick-drying finish, and mistakes made during application can be corrected quite easily. A shellac finish polishes well and imparts a mellow tone to the color of the wood.

Unfortunately, shellac finishes are not the most durable. They are easily scratched, they form white spots when they come in contact with water, and both water and alcohol will cause them to dissolve.

Using Shellac on Furniture

Much of the furniture of the eighteenth century was finished by applying many thin layers of shellac. This technique, known as *French polishing*, was developed in France and eventually found its way to England and America. This produces a tough, transparent finish that greatly enhances the beauty and grain pattern of such woods as mahogany, walnut, and bird's-eye maple. Although it takes many hours of painstaking care in application, this technique is still used by many finishers today in order to obtain its characteristic velvet sheen.

The introduction of production-line, mass-produced furniture in the second quarter of the nineteenth century resulted in the eventual disappearance of multilayered shellac finishes from all but the most expensive pieces. The determining factor, of course, was economic. These shellac finishes required a number of different coats, and it was quicker and cheaper to use a finish that needed only one or two applications.

Shellac has a variety of other uses in furniture finishing besides that of a top coat. For example, it enjoys widespread use as a washcoat and as undercoating for other types of finishes, such as lacquer or varnish. It functions very efficiently as a sealer to prevent other substances (e.g., stains, fillers, etc.) from bleeding through into the top coat. In Europe and elsewhere it was popular for a long time as a combination filler and sealer. In this case, the shellac was thickly applied, allowed to dry, and sanded smooth. This technique was not uncommon even as late as the 1940s.

Types of Shellac

Shellacs are available in several types and are distinguished by colors ranging from very dark (almost black) and very light (orange). Shellac can also be bleached (the so-called white shellac) and completely purified of all wax content. The latter is a clear shellac having no color at all.

White and orange shellacs (frequently referred to as *shellac varnishes*) are available in a ready mixed liquid form or in dry flakes that must be combined with a vehicle. The liquid form is the most common. Note: Because the liquid form of shellac is ready mixed, many beginners make the mistake of using the shellac directly from the can without thinning. Do *not* try to do this. The shellac is too thick and must be thinned before use (50–50 is a good rule-of-thumb formula for thinning). Otherwise the shellac will tend to thicken and pile up on the surface, causing all sorts of finishing problems.

White shellac is a purified and bleached form of shellac from which virtually all traces of color have been removed. It is used primarily to apply a clear finish to light-colored woods. Orange shellac, on the other hand, is recommended for surfaces having darker colors (e.g., redwood or gumwood). Orange shellac can be stored longer than white shellac. It will also prove a more durable finish in the long run. The major objection to using orange shellac is that it is too dark for the lighter woods. Using an orange shellac on a light-colored wood will all too frequently leave a yellowish cast.

Shellac substitutes should be avoided because they usually require refinishing long before surfaces on which a genuine shellac has been used. These shellac substitutes, as well as cheap shellacs, will gum during sanding and clog the abrasive. There is thus really no advantage to using them.

Pigmented Shellac

Anilines used to produce alcohol stains can also be dissolved in shellac. The result is a pigmented, opaque shellac that produces a finish similar to paint. The color and shade of the shellac will naturally depend upon the type of aniline dye selected and the amount used. Pigmented shellac can be used to touch up worn areas on a piece of furniture, or to refinish it completely. Because pigmented shellac is an opaque finish, it can be applied directly over an older finish.

Applying Shellac with a Brush

Soft bristle brushes, two to four inches wide, are recommended for applying shellac to wood surfaces. These are the same kind of brushes used for applying varnish or enamel. The wider brushes should be used where it is necessary to cover large areas (e.g., table tops, desk tops, etc.). The brush should be kept wet with shellac at all times. If the brush is allowed to become dry, the shellac coat will more than likely be uneven. Skipping spots, streaking, and lapping are all characteristic results of improperly using a dry brush.

If the shellac is allowed to dry on the brush, the brush can be cleaned and softened again by soaking it in denatured alcohol. Always clean shellac brushes in denatured alcohol. After the brush is completely cleaned, dry it, wrap it in paper, and store it in a flat position.

Never dip a brush wet from water into the shellac. Water is the natural enemy of shellac finishes. Not only will a wet glass bottom cause a white ring to form on a shellac finish, it is possible to remove the entire finish simply by rubbing it with soap and water.

Never allow a shellac brush to be used for any other purpose. You do not want to run the risk of contaminating the shellac when you use it for shellacking again.

Spraying Shellac

The equipment used for spraying shellac should be absolutely clean. Any dirt or residue from other finishes found in the equipment will probably be combined with the shellac and sprayed onto the surface.

Thin the shellac to approximately a 1½ - to 2-pound cut (Table 11–1) for use in the spraying equipment. Maintain a distance of 7 to 8 inches between the surface and the nozzle of the spray gun. Move the gun in a straight line parallel to the surface. Resist the temptation to swing the gun nozzle in an arc.

The major problems encountered when spraying are runs and uneven deposits of shellac. The latter results in surface sags, and is generally caused by failure to maintain an even distance between

Table 11-1. Formulas for Thinning Shellac

Desired Cut For Finish	Consistency of Purchased Cut	Alcohol	Shellac	Consistency
1-Pound Cut	3-Pound Cut	4 Parts	3 Parts	Thin
1-Pound Cut	4-Pound Cut	2 Parts	1 Part	
1-Pound Cut	5-Pound Cut	2 Parts	1 Part	
2-Pound Cut	3-Pound Cut	2 Parts	5 Parts	Average
2-Pound Cut	4-Pound Cut	3 Parts	4 Parts	
2-Pound Cut	5-Pound Cut	1 Part	1 Part	
3-Pound Cut	· 3-Pound Cut	———*	———*	Thick
3-Pound Cut	4-Pound Cut	2 Parts	1 Part	
3-Pound Cut	5-Pound Cut	1 Part	2 Parts	

*No dilution. The shellac is used at full strength.

the spray gun and the surface. Runs are caused by spraying too much shellac onto the surface.

Always spray where there is proper ventilation. If you are indoors, the work area should be equipped with an acceptable exhaust fan. Do *not* use portable electric house fans for this purpose. The smallest spark could set off a dangerous, perhaps fatal, explosion. (See Chapter 20, *Safety*, for more on ventilation.)

The shellac will have to be thinned before it can be used in a spray gun. This will generally be thinner than the consistency for brushing.

Thinning Shellac

The consistency of the shellac is determined by the size of the cut purchased and the amount of denatured alcohol used to thin it. For example, a 4-pound cut indicates that four pounds of shellac have been dissolved in one gallon of denatured alcohol. A 5-pound cut, on the other hand, means that an additional pound of shellac has been dissolved in the same amount of alcohol (one gallon), whereas a 3-pound cut contains one pound less. With each of the three different cuts (3-pound, 4-pound, and 5-pound), the same amount of denatured alcohol has been used. Regardless of the size of the cut, the consistency of the shellac can be further thinned by adding more denatured alcohol. Table 11–1 indicates the recommended amounts for the various consistencies.

Once again, no shellac should be used straight from the can without thinning. Not only is thinning a relatively simple procedure, it makes the shellac much easier to work with.

Denatured alcohol is used as thinner for shellac, and is available in most paint stores, hardware stores, and other outlets where paint supplies are sold. Do *not* use methyl alcohol or wood alcohol for thinning. Do not assume alcohol is a "safe" solvent. Wear splash goggles and a respirator. Ventilate the area. (See Chapter 20, *Safety*.)

Old drinking glasses or jars are excellent containers for mixing shellac with the thinner. Make certain that the container you use is perfectly clean and dry. Any dirt left will combine with the shellac and eventually find its way into the finish. Rubber gloves and old clothes are recommended for wear when working with shellac.

A Standard Shellac Finish

The standard shellac finish is relatively easy to apply. It does not require the addition of special oils or other ingredients as is the case with the French polish technique, nor are long drying periods between coats necessary. The steps in the finishing schedule are fairly simple and should, if followed faithfully, provide the finisher with satisfactory results.

The procedure for applying a standard shellac finish is as follows (Fig. 11–1):

1. Sand the wood surface until it is completely smooth. Wipe a damp cloth across the surface to remove the dust and raise the grain. Sand the surface a second time to remove the raised grain. Clean off all dust resulting from the sanding operation. More detailed instructions for preparing the surface are given in Chapter 9.
2. Prepare the shellac. The shellac should be thinned before use.

STEP 1	PREPARE THE WOOD SURFACE.
STEP 2	PREPARE THE SHELLAC ACCORDING TO DESIRED CONSISTENCY (BOTH WASHCOATS AND TOPCOAT).
STEP 3	APPLY A THIN SHELLAC WASHCOAT.
STEP 4	APPLY A STAIN (OPTIONAL).
STEP 5	APPLY A THIN SHELLAC WASHCOAT (IF A FILLER IS TO BE USED IT SHOULD BE APPLIED AFTER THIS STEP AND BEFORE STEP 6).
STEPS 6-10	APPLY THE SHELLAC COATS.

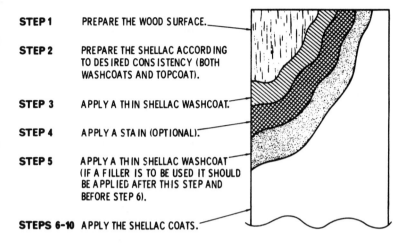

Fig. 11-1. Procedure for applying shellac.

This can be best done in a large drinking glass or glass jar. Add enough denatured alcohol to obtain the desired consistency. The initial coats of shellac will be very thin; subsequent coats are generally thicker.

3. If the wood is an open-grained one (e.g., pine, mahogany, chestnut, etc.), the pores should be sealed with a thin shellac washcoat. This will insure uniformity in the subsequent coats and prevent the stain, should one be used, from sinking too deeply into the pores of the wood. Lightly abrade the shellac sealer coat with a very fine grade of sandpaper or steel wool.

4. If staining is necessary, the stain should be applied immediately after the initial washcoat.

5. Using a stain will require a second sealer coat of very thin shellac. This is applied directly over the stain so that it will not bleed into any of the finishing materials that follow.

6. Apply the thinned coat of shellac and allow it sufficient time to dry—about two or three hours.

7. After the coat of shellac has dried, *lightly* sand it with a fine grade of sandpaper or steel wool. It is very important not to cut through the shellac coat. Otherwise, it will be necessary to start all over again, because it is very difficult to repair this

kind of mistake. Remove the dust left by the sanding operation with a dry, lint-free cloth or by other suitable means.

8. Repeat Steps 6 and 7 until at least four or five layers of shellac have been applied to the wood. These coats should be somewhat thicker in consistency than the washcoats used for sealing. Note: After the last coating of shellac has been applied, substitute a fine grade of steel wool for the sandpaper that was used in the previous steps.

9. Apply one or more coats of wax and polish with a soft, clean, lint-free cloth. If you use a self-polishing wax, the polishing operation is eliminated. However, you may buff the surface lightly with a soft cloth after the wax has thoroughly dried. See Chapter 16, *Rubbing, Waxing and Polishing Finishes*, for further information.

10. A tougher, more durable surface can be obtained by covering the final coat of shellac with a thinned coat of clear varnish. If this is desired, then eliminate Step 9 in the finishing schedule.

Semidull Finish

A semidull finish can be obtained by lightly dry-rubbing the final coat of shellac with a No. 000 or No. 0000 grade of steel wool. Do not rub too hard, or you may cut through the finish. Remember, you are only trying to reduce the sheen. Be sure to remove all dust particles left by the sanding operation before applying the wax.

Dull Finish

Some finishers recommend a rubbing paste made from pumice stone, vaseline, and paraffin oil as a means of obtaining an interesting dull finish. The vaseline and pumice stone (FF grade) are mixed on a one-to-one basis. The paraffin oil is added until the mixture reaches the consistency of thick paint. The rubbing paste is then applied to the shellac surface with a pad of No. 0000 steel wool. Rub the shellac in the direction of the grain. Once again, you are cautioned to rub lightly to avoid scratching through the surface. The paraffin oil will leave an oily residue. This can be easily removed by sprinkling a layer of clean sawdust across the surface and then brushing it off. The sawdust will absorb the paraffin oil.

Satin Finish

Allow at least 24 to 48 hours for the last coat of shellac to dry. When you are certain that it is thoroughly dry, remove the sheen by rubbing it lightly with No. 000 or No. 0000 steel wool. Remove the dust left by the steel wool rubbing operation with a dry, lint-free cloth. Lightly brush a FFF grade of pumice stone across the surface. Make certain that every portion of the surface is brushed with the pumice stone. Wipe off the pumice stone powder and lightly sand it again with a No. 000 or No. 0000 steel wool. Wipe off the dust with a dry, lint-free cloth.

French Polish

French polish is a shellac top-coat finishing technique originally developed in France some three centuries ago. It is a durable finish produced by building up layer after layer of thinned shellac after an initial application of linseed oil to the surface. The French polishing technique imparts a velvet sheen to the surface and enhances both the grain pattern of the wood and its natural color. This finishing technique gives better results when applied to close-grained woods. Open-grained woods will require a certain amount of staining and filling before the layers of shellac are applied.

The procedure for French polishing is essentially as follows:

1. Sand the wood surface until it is completely smooth. Raise the grain of the wood by wiping a damp cloth across the surface, and sand it again. See Chapter 9 for more complete instructions describing the preparation of the surface.
2. Remove any dust or other particles left on the wood surface by the sanding operation with a lint-free cloth or soft brush, or by vacuuming.
3. Stain the surface for the desired coloring. Allow the stain suffi-

cient time to be absorbed by the wood pores. Do not proceed to the next step until you are certain that the stain has completely dried. As a result of the staining operation, the surface should now have an even, uniform color.

4. Apply the linseed oil to the surface, and allow it sufficient time to soak in and dry. Wipe away any excess.

5. Sand the surface with a very fine grade of sandpaper. Remove the dust and allow about 24 hours to make sure that the wood has completely dried.

6. Apply a thin solution of shellac to a rubbing pad made from a section of soft linen wrapped around tightly wound strips of muslin (Fig. 11–2). The shellac must be distributed evenly over the entire rubbing surface of the pad.

7. Using a circular movement, rub the surface of the wood with the pad (Fig. 11–2). Add an occasional drop of raw linseed oil while rubbing. Continue rubbing the surface for 45 to 50 minutes, and then allow it to dry for approximately 24 hours.

8. Repeat Step 7 and allow 48 to 72 hours drying time.

9. Repeat Step 7 and allow one week to ten days' drying time.

10. A soft cloth (preferably one that has been used to apply shellac) slightly dampened with denatured alcohol is quickly and

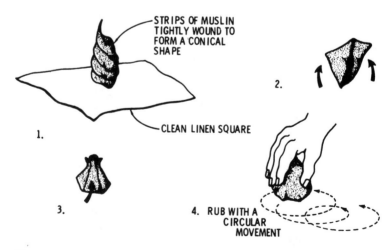

Fig. 11-2. Making and using a French-polishing pad.

lightly passed over the surface to remove any oil residue left from the raw linseed oil.

Some finishers prefer to add the raw linseed oil directly to the shellac before it is applied to the surface. This is usually in the ratio of ¼ ounce of raw linseed oil for *each* pint of denatured alcohol. If this is desired, then eliminate Step 4 in the French polish schedule.

The shellac itself will generally serve as an adequate filler for close-grained woods. On large- (open) grained woods, an additional agent is required. One method used by many finishers is to sprinkle a fine grade of pumice across the surface when applying the second coating of shellac. The pumice is rubbed into the pores of the wood with a circular movement of the rubbing pad, and the excess is removed after the operation is completed.˙The filling operation should take place after Step 7 of the finishing schedule described for the French polishing technique.

Piano Finish

A *piano finish* is obtained by rubbing a clear or pigmented shellac until the surface has a near-perfect gloss or "eggshell" finish.

The procedure for applying a piano finish is as follows:

1. Sand the wood surface until it is completely smooth. Raise the grain of the wood by wiping a damp cloth across the surface, and sand it again. See Chapter 9 for more complete instructions describing the preparation of the surface.
2. Remove any dust or other particles left on the wood surface by the sanding operation with a lint-free cloth or soft brush, or by vacuuming. Wiping the surface with a cloth dampened in denatured alcohol will remove any last traces of dirt.
3. Apply a water stain to the surface for the desired coloring. Allow the stain 24 hours to penetrate and dry completely.
4. Apply a thinned washcoat of shellac (generally about four parts denatured alcohol to one part shellac in a 3-pound cut).
5. Brush on a filler and allow approximately 24 hours to dry.
6. Sand the surface with a fine grade of sandpaper *in the direc-*

tion of the grain. Sanding across the grain may leave scratches on the surface.

7. Remove any dust or other particles left on the wood surface by the sanding operation with a lint-free cloth or soft brush, or by vacuuming.
8. Apply the first coat of shellac that will form the top coat. This will be thinned to a medium consistency (about two parts denatured alcohol to five parts shellac in a 3-pound cut).
9. Allow the shellac two to three hours to dry.
10. Lightly sand the surface with a fine grade of sandpaper. Patch the surface dents and scratches with shellac stick matching the color of the stained wood as closely as possible. Sand again with the fine grade sandpaper until the surface is smooth and even to the touch.
11. Remove all dust or other particles left by the sanding operation with a lint-free cloth or soft brush, or by vacuuming.
12. Apply the second coat of shellac, and follow Steps 8 through 11.
13. Continue to apply as many coats of shellac as necessary to obtain the desired gloss (three or four should do it), but rub each coat with pumice and raw linseed oil.
14. Before applying the final coat of shellac, allow the surface to dry for three or four days.
15. Apply the final coat of shellac, allow it sufficient time to dry, and rub it with rottenstone, a felt pad, and raw linseed oil.
16. Clean the surface by wiping it gently with a soft, lint-free cloth.
17. Wax the surface to protect it from water damage. Polish the waxed surface with a dry, soft cloth.

Shellac as a Sealer and Base Coat

Shellac can be used as a sealer coat over wax finishes, dents, and other minor defects. A shellac sealer coat will be adequate for filling in these minor surface imperfections and for providing a flat, smooth surface for subsequent finishing coats. The sealing of a wax finish will prevent the wax from bleeding through into the new top coat. This is particularly important for such finishes as varnish or lacquer.

Shellac should be applied as a sealer over all types of stains, and especially as a base coat for a varnish finish. A base coat of shellac and a single coat of varnish is far quicker and simpler to apply than the often recommended multiple layers of varnish.

A shellac sealer coat is an absolute necessity over any wax stick patching, to prevent the wax from bleeding through into the top coat. The sealer should be applied over the entire surface, not just the patched portion.

Shellac also serves well as a sealer over an old coat of paint, because the paint will not bleed through it.

Shellac is often used as a sealer over unfinished wood, particularly a wood with large, open grain. The shellac sealer results in an even, uniform surface over which fillers, stains, and finishes can be applied. Regardless of the type of finish to be used, the shellac sealer coat should be lightly abraded with a fine grade of sandpaper or steel wool. This will enable the other finishing coats to adhere better.

Reamalgamation of Shellac Finishes

Shellac finishes showing minor defects (e.g., scuffing, wear, etc.) can be restored through the process of reamalgamation. Essentially, this consists of dissolving the shellac with denatured alcohol and allowing it to re-form and thereby erase the defect. Older shellac finishes often contained special substances that increased their durability or decreased the drying time. Unfortunately, these special substances also tend to resist the dissolving effect of denatured alcohol. The addition of a little lacquer thinner to the alcohol should overcome this resistance. (Alcohol and lacquer thinner are health and fire hazards. See Chapter 20, *Safety*, for more details.)

Stick Shellac Patching

Stick shellac is sold in a great variety of colors that approximate or match the numerous different finishes and woods. It is difficult to use, and requires a period of practice before the beginner can expect to obtain satisfactory results. A detailed description of stick shellac patching is found in Chapter 9.

Points to Remember

Anyone using shellac in wood finishing should be aware of a number of precautions that must be taken to insure an acceptable standard of work. The four principal precautions are as follows:

1. Never store shellac for more than 90 days.
2. Never store shellac near a source of heat.
3. Never apply shellac to a wet surface.
4. Never use a damp brush to apply shellac.
5. Never apply shellac in a room with any appreciable degree of humidity.
6. Never use shellac near a heat source.

You will note that the avoidance of water, dampness, and heat is emphasized. Water should never be used to polish shellac. Because finishes are highly flammable, they should be kept well away from any heat source. Because shellac also tends to evaporate rapidly, it is recommended that glass containers with screw-top covers be used for storage. The container *must* be tightly sealed when the shellac is not being used.

Air bubbles in the shellac will detract from the appearance of the finish. This can be greatly minimized by *not* shaking the shellac container excessively before application.

Shellac should be applied as rapidly as possible. When using a brush, *flow* it onto the surface, always in the same direction. Never go over the shellac a second time, or you will cause it to pile up; the first application must therefore be correct. The thinner the shellac, the less likelihood there will be for mistakes of this nature to occur. You can always add two or more coats until you have obtained the desired thickness.

CHAPTER 12

Varnish Finishes

Varnish is one of the toughest finishes used on wood surfaces. It is a clear finish that enhances and emphasizes the grain, while at the same time imparting a special warmth to the wood color. Varnish finishes show an especially strong resistance to the effects of water and alcohol. Furthermore, they will resist impact, abrasion, and heat to a much greater degree than other finishes.

Although many different types of varnish are available for use on wood surfaces, this chapter will be limited to a description of the two types most commonly used as furniture finishes. These are:

1. The oleoresinous (or oil-base) varnishes,
2. The synthetic resin varnishes.

The *oleoresinous* or *oil-base varnishes* have been used in various forms for centuries. They are made by combining a drying oil (commonly linseed oil), natural resins, and other additives, such as a solvent or thinner. Turpentine was used for years as the solvent for oleoresinous varnishes, but due to its expense and increasing scarcity was later replaced by mineral spirits (petroleum spirits). A recent improvement of oleoresinous varnishes was brought about by the substitution of China wood (tung) oil for the linseed oil.

The solid film of the oleoresinous varnish is produced by the evaporation of the solvent and the curing of the oil by oxidation. The drying rate of these varnishes is rather slow when compared with the newer synthetic resin types, and for this and other reasons they have been largely replaced by the latter. Other factors contributing to the decline of their popularity include their lack of color retention, durability, and, in some cases, resistance to wear.

The *synthetic resin varnishes* are an improvement over the oleoresinous (natural resin) type. They exhibit better durability, better color retention, and greater hardness. They also show the same resistance to water, alcohol, fruit juices, mild acids, and other substances that the oleoresinous substances do. They are faster drying, but still not fast enough to compete with the lacquer finishes that have replaced them in the furniture industry. However, unlike lacquers, they exhibit good resistance to acetone-type solvents.

The synthetic resins used in the production of varnishes are basically of four types:

1. Urethane,
2. Alkyd,
3. Phenolic,
4. Vinyl.

Others are continually being developed in the laboratories and added to the list.

Not all synthetic resin varnishes will produce a completely satisfactory finish, at least, not if durability is one of your requirements. Some, such as the urethane type, will lift off the surface when the finish is cut or struck by a sharp object. The chances are that the finish will then peel off in thin, plasticlike sheets. It may be that after experimenting with different varnishes you will find that you prefer the older oleoresinous varnishes to the newer synthetic resin type. It becomes a matter of personal choice.

Color is also a problem when selecting a varnish. Some varnishes are extremely clear (e.g., the vinyl types), whereas others have traces of color (e.g., the alkyd and phenolic resin varnishes). However, their color after application will depend on so many variables, it is almost impossible to predict the results. Never hesitate to ask knowledgeable paint or hardware store sales personnel for advice. They have had a great deal of experience with these products, and will usually try to give you the one that will best suit your specific needs.

One of the major disadvantages of varnish is that it is a relatively slow-drying finish, and dust and other particles often become trapped in it before it is completely dry. This problem can be greatly minimized by observing the following procedures:

1. Apply varnishes in rooms that are as dust-free as possible.
2. Work in a room in which the temperature is maintained at 65° to 70°F.
3. Remove dust from the wood surface with a tack rag before applying the varnish.
4. Lightly sand each coat of varnish with a very fine grade of sandpaper.
5. Give the final coat a careful rubbing.

Dust particles and other objects (e.g., hair, lint, sand, etc.) can be removed by lifting them with a sharply pointed brush (an artist's brush will do) that is slightly wet with varnish. A specially constructed picking stick will also serve the same purpose (Fig. 12–1).

1. COTTON WAD GLUED TO THE END OF A STICK

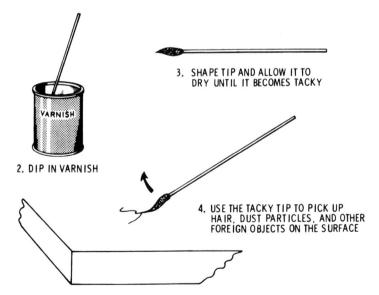

3. SHAPE TIP AND ALLOW IT TO DRY UNTIL IT BECOMES TACKY

VARNISH

2. DIP IN VARNISH

4. USE THE TACKY TIP TO PICK UP HAIR, DUST PARTICLES, AND OTHER FOREIGN OBJECTS ON THE SURFACE

Fig. 12–1. Constructing and using a picking stick.

These are sticks with small, tightly rolled balls of cotton attached at one end. The cotton ball is rolled in varnish, and then squeezed until all excess varnish has been removed. Shape the cotton so that you have a pointed end for picking up the various foreign objects from the surface. The cotton should be tacky, not wet.

Thinning Varnish

Both mineral spirits (paint thinner) and turpentine can be used to thin varnish. Usually this is in a five-to-one formula (five parts varnish to one part thinner), but it can range as high as eight-to-one, depending upon the consistency desired. Your safest bet is to use the thinner recommended by the manufacturer of the varnish. Some varnishes are formulated to be applied by brush without thinner. I would recommend testing these on a piece of scrap wood and being your own judge of the manufacturer's claim. For spraying, use one pint of VM&P Naphtha for each gallon of varnish. When using naphtha, ventilate the area to prevent breathing vapors. To prevent explosion, do not smoke or use near flame or sparks. Wear gloves and splash goggles. (See Chapter 20, *Safety*.)

Applying Varnish with a Brush

Before applying any varnish to the surface, make certain that the brush you intend to use is suitable for varnishing. It must also be perfectly clean and in fairly good condition. Examine it carefully for any loose bristles that may detach themselves during the varnishing operation. Many finishing problems can be avoided by using a new brush of good quality (a cheap price does not always indicate a bargain, particularly not when you are trying to brush varnish onto a surface).

Thinning the varnish will usually reduce brushing problems, but you should not be too concerned about minor brush marks on the surface. Varnish, like enamel, tends to flow together or level itself as it dries.

Try to work so that the surface you are varnishing is in a horizontal position. Turn the piece of furniture so that you are always working on a flat, horizontal surface.

Lighting is also very important. Place the piece of furniture in such a way that the light will reflect on the surface and indicate any spots that you may have missed. This holds true when spraying a varnish, too.

Always keep your brush wet, but be careful about overlapping it with too much varnish—otherwise the excess varnish may drop onto the surface. If this should happen, try to pick up the drops of varnish with the tip of your brush. Never allow drops or pools of varnish to stand on the surface; always remove them immediately. The problem of excess varnish on the surface is especially bad along edges. If it is not noticed and allowed to dry, it forms a hard ridge of varnish along the edge.

Try not to overlap your strokes. Begin each new stroke on a dry spot where the last one ended. One method of applying varnish is to cross and tip off the brush strokes so that a series of intersecting and interlocking bands is formed. This pattern is followed until the entire surface is covered. It is started by laying a series of parallel (but separated) strokes in the direction of the grain. Cross these with a series of strokes in the same manner *across* the grain. Tip off the brush by filling in the uncoated areas. If you intend to apply more than one coat of varnish, make certain that the previous one has thoroughly dried before applying the next.

Varnish Finishing Schedule (Brushing)

The finishing schedule for applying varnish to a wood surface bears many similarities to other types of finishing schedules, particularly during the initial steps. However, varnish does have certain unique features, especially when it is applied with a brush.

Prepare the wood surface according to the instructions given in Chapter 9. It is essential that the surface be smooth and clean. Roughness, grease or oil stains, and other surface imperfections will be emphasized by the varnish top coat. These will ruin the overall appearance of the finish.

The procedure for applying varnish to a wood surface with a brush is as follows (Fig. 12-2):

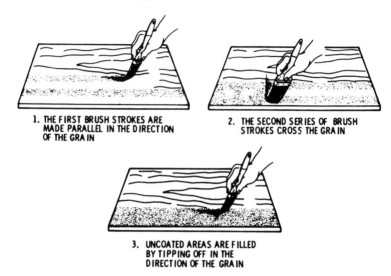

1. THE FIRST BRUSH STROKES ARE
   MADE PARALLEL IN THE DIRECTION
   OF THE GRAIN

2. THE SECOND SERIES OF BRUSH
   STROKES CROSS THE GRAIN

3. UNCOATED AREAS ARE FILLED
   BY TIPPING OFF IN THE
   DIRECTION OF THE GRAIN

Fig. 12-2.   Brushing technique used when varnishing.

1. Raise the grain of the wood by dampening the surface with water or some other suitable means. Flooding the surface with water and wiping off the excess will usually be adequate.
2. Allow the surface sufficient time to dry, and for the raised fibers to stiffen and harden.
3. Remove the raised wood fibers by sanding lightly with a fine grade of sandpaper. Sand with the grain. Sanding across the grain will produce surface scratches.
4. Remove any dust or other particles left by the sanding operation with a tack rag or clean, lint-free cloth.
5. Apply a thin washcoat of shellac to the wood surface. This is particularly necessary for open-grained woods in order to prevent uneven penetration. Washcoating will give the stain a uniform appearance.
6. Allow the washcoat sufficient time to dry thoroughly, and remove any raised fibers by sanding lightly with a fine grade of sandpaper.
7. Remove the dust left by the sanding operation with a tack rag or a clean, lint-free cloth.
8. Stain the surface. A water or non-grain-raising stain is sug-

gested for use with varnish because of its high nonbleeding characteristics. Allow the stain sufficient time to dry. Sanding a stained surface is *not* recommended, because you may scratch through it and produce light spots in the surface coloring. That is why it is advisable to complete all grain raising in Steps 1 through 7.

9. Seal the stain by applying a shellac washcoat. Allow it sufficient time to dry, and then sand it lightly with very fine sandpaper.

10. Remove the dust left by the sanding operation.

11. A liquid or paste filler can now be applied if you want a particularly smooth surface. Reread the section on wood fillers in Chapter 9, and the manufacturer's suggestions for application.

12. After you have applied a filler (and properly sanded and cleaned the surface), you will have to seal it so that it does not bleed into the varnish top coat. Apply a suitable sealer (a shellac washcoat will be adequate), and allow it sufficient time to dry.

13. Rub the entire surface (in the direction of the grain) with very fine steel wool.

14. Remove the dust left by the rubbing operation. Be particularly careful to get the surface clean, because steel wool will leave behind minute metal particles.

15. Thin the varnish with a suitable thinner and apply it to the surface. Follow the manufacturer's recommendations for thinning.

16. Brush the varnish on with light, even strokes. Do not press down with the brush. Work on one section of the furniture at a time.

17. When the surface has been completely covered, tip it off (first across the grain and then with the grain). Do not worry about a few brush marks. These will generally flow together as the varnish dries.

18. Remove dust particles, hairs, and other debris trapped in the finish with a sharp-pointed artist's brush. This should be done *immediately* after applying the varnish.

19. If additional coats of varnish are to be applied, the first one must be lightly abraded (scuffed) with a very fine grade of sandpaper. This will give the surface stronger holding power for each top coat that follows. Remove all dust left by the sanding operation with a tack rag or a clean, lint-free cloth, *before* the next top coat is applied (Fig. 12–3).

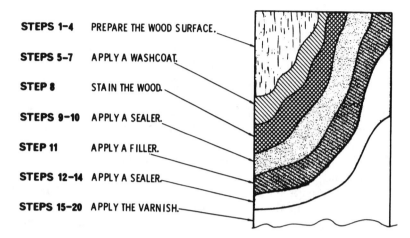

STEPS 1-4 PREPARE THE WOOD SURFACE.

STEPS 5-7 APPLY A WASHCOAT.

STEP 8 STAIN THE WOOD.

STEPS 9-10 APPLY A SEALER.

STEP 11 APPLY A FILLER.

STEPS 12-14 APPLY A SEALER.

STEPS 15-20 APPLY THE VARNISH.

Fig. 12-3. Varnish finishing schedule.

20. Do not sand the final top coat. This one will be rubbed to the desired sheen. See Chapter 16 for a number of techniques that can be used.

A sanding sealer compatible with varnish can be substituted for Step 16 (i.e., the *first* varnish top coat). This will dry more quickly than the varnish and provide a smoother finish for the next coat of varnish after it has been sanded. Make certain that the sanding sealer has thoroughly dried before you sand it. Lightly sand it with a fine grade of sandpaper in the direction of the grain. Remember to remove all dust left by the sanding operation before applying the varnish.

Shellac can be substituted for the intermediate coats of varnish (see Steps 16 and 19). These will not be as thin as a shellac washcoat, and their consistency should approach or equal that of a shellac top coat.

Cleaning the Brush

Pure turpentine is used to clean varnish from the brush. A paint and varnish remover can also be used, but with caution. Some removers will destroy the bristles of the brush.

Read the appropriate section in Chapter 2, *Finishing Tools and Supplies,* for a more detailed discussion of brush care.

Varnish Reamalgamation

Reamalgamation refers to the partial dissolving of a finish to eliminate cracking, crazing, alligatoring, and other minor imperfections on the surface of the finish. As the finish dries, it flows together (reamalgamates) and eliminates these imperfections.

The reamalgamation process is quite successful with lacquer and shellac finishes, but is generally unsatisfactory when applied to varnish. Solvents for reamalgamating varnish finishes are sold under a variety of different trade names in local paint and hardware stores.

Another method of reviving a varnish finish is to rub the entire surface lightly (always in the direction of the grain) with a very fine steel wool. Remove the dust from the surface and apply a coat of boiled linseed oil, or linseed oil mixed with varnish (on a one-to-one basis) and thinned with pure turpentine. Several coats may be necessary.

If these suggestions for restoring the finish are not successful, your only recourse is to strip it. This is usually the advice given when anyone mentions reamalgamating a varnish finish.

Revarnishing

An old varnished surface may be revarnished if it is still in good condition and adheres well to the surface of the wood. If you are planning to revarnish, you should prepare the surface in the following manner:

1. Wash it with warm water and a mild soap to remove all traces of old polish, wax, dirt, and other contaminants.
2. Sand the surface smooth with a fine grade of sandpaper.
3. Remove all dust left by the sanding operation with a tack rag or a clean, lint-free cloth.

Step 1 is important because any contaminants left on the surface will prevent the varnish from properly adhering. Remember this when you are stripping a varnish finish, because some varnish and paint removers contain wax. The wax traces can be eliminated by wiping the surface with turpentine.

The sanding operation (Step 2) roughens the surface, thereby providing a better holding action. Any gloss must be removed by sanding, or the new finish will not adhere properly.

Varnish Stains

A varnish stain is essentially a pigmented varnish. Coloring has been added to the varnish in sufficient amounts to obtain a particular shade, but not enough to obscure the wood grain entirely. It has no penetration power and remains on the surface in the same manner as a varnish. Varnish stains are not generally used on furniture surfaces exposed to view (see Chapter 10, *Staining*).

Varnish and Linseed Oil Finish

A very fine varnish and linseed oil finish has been used over the years on mahogany, walnut, and other open-grained woods. It is made by mixing one part varnish (a spar varnish is often used), one part boiled linseed oil, and five parts turpentine.

Prepare the wood surface as you would for a varnish finish (see VARNISH FINISHING SCHEDULE in this chapter), and proceed as follows:

1. Apply a sealer coat of thinned varnish (thinned one-to-one with turpentine).
2. After the sealer has thoroughly dried, sand it lightly in the direction of the grain with a very fine sandpaper.
3. Remove all dust left by the sanding operation with a clean, lint-free cloth or a tack rag.
4. Wipe on a coat of the varnish and linseed oil. Allow it sufficient time to dry completely.
5. After waiting four days, rub the surface with FFF grade pumice stone and rubbing oil.

6. After waiting another four days, rub the surface with rotten-stone and rubbing oil.

If more than one coat of varnish and linseed oil is desired, sand each coat (except the last one) with a very fine sandpaper. Be sure to remove all the dust left by the sanding operation before applying the next coat.

Varnishing Hints

Varnish is certainly not the easiest finish to apply, but a careful reading of the recommendations given in this chapter should lessen much of the difficulty. Here are some suggestions.

1. Varnish (for brushing) cannot be properly mixed by vigorously shaking the can up and down. This will cause bubbles to form in the varnish, which will result in an unsatisfactory finish. Mix the varnish by gently tipping the can back and forth, or by careful stirring.
2. Work in a room with a temperature between 65° to 70°F. Avoid working in room temperatures below 60°F, since it will interfere with drying. Varnishes should be allowed to dry in a warm room for about three or four days. If the weather is especially damp (rain or high humidity), give it twice as long. It is best to avoid altogether varnishing in wet weather.
3. *Always* wait for the varnish to become completely dry before sanding or using some other kind of abrasive. If you do not wait long enough, you will destroy the finish.
4. Observe all the precautions for safety and health described in previous chapters.
5. Use turpentine or mineral spirits for thinning and cleaning brushes, unless otherwise specified by the varnish manufacturer.
6. Always work in a well-ventilated room that is as dust-free as possible.
7. Apply in thin coats brushed out well to avoid runs and "sags." If bubbles remain, lightly brush out the coat.

8. Make sure the first coat is thoroughly dry before applying the second coat, or the top coat may mar, dent, or "print" easily.

9. To decrease drying time, tip a horizontal surface at an angle during drying to allow heavier-than-air vapors to run off the surface.

CHAPTER 13

Lacquer Finishes

Lacquer as a furniture finish originated in the Far East and was first introduced to the countries of Western Europe in the late sixteenth and early seventeenth centuries. Not long after, the cabinetmakers in France, Holland, and England were producing imitations of the Oriental pieces. In England, lacquer finishing (then referred to as "japanning") became quite popular. Although at first inferior to the Oriental product, English lacquer work was soon characterized by its high quality. Many of these early examples of English lacquer furniture indicated that the cabinetmakers preferred to cover the base wood with a veneer over which a lacquer finish was applied. Colored backgrounds of black, red, blue, green, and pale yellow were used with these lacquer finishes. After enjoying a period of relatively widespread popularity (from the late sixteenth to the middle of the eighteenth century), the interest in lacquered furniture began to decline. It was revived in the form of cellulose nitrate lacquers after World War I. The spraying technique of application contributed greatly to its revival. Lacquer now represents the most widely-used finish in mass-produced furniture.

Lacquer is a tougher, more durable finish than shellac, and it will dry much more quickly than varnish. Unfortunately, its extremely rapid drying rate (as short as five minutes) makes it very difficult to apply with a brush—particularly for a beginner. As a result, most lacquer finishes are applied with spraying equipment.

When properly rubbed, lacquer will produce a gloss or satin finish. Others, the flat lacquers, dry to a dull or flat finish. Mixing a clear gloss lacquer with a flat lacquer will result in variations of a semigloss finish.

Lacquers are available in spray cans and are particularly effective in this form for covering small areas. These spray cans may be purchased in both refillable and disposable containers. Lacquer can also be used in the various types of spraying equipment. Small spray guns and compressors are available for the home workshop and are adequate for most finishing work. However, using such equipment does require proper ventilation (see Chapter 2, *Finishing Tools and Supplies*).

It is also important to note some of the properties of lacquer that require special care and attention. Lacquer fumes are highly toxic and can damage your health if inhaled. Lacquer fumes are explosive. Do *not* use lacquer around flames or heat sources, or where sparks may occur. Even a metal spark could cause an explosion. Never apply lacquer inside a building unless you have present all the safety conditions required by the professional (suitable exhaust system, spraying booth, etc.). A common electric house fan is not considered a suitable ventilation or exhaust system for lacquer spraying. Faulty wiring in the fan could cause a fatal explosion. (See Chapter 20, *Safety*.)

The lacquer solvent is so strong that only finishing products (e.g., sealers, stains, fillers, etc.) that are compatible with lacquer should be used. Otherwise, surface defects will develop, ranging in seriousness from small pinholes to a soft surface that will not dry properly. Lacquer solvent is not alcohol, but rather a special thinner that contains acetone, the ingredient that causes the rapid rate of drying.

Types of Lacquer

Modern lacquers can be divided into two basic categories:

1. Nitrocellulose base lacquers,
2. Cellulose acetate butyrate base lacquers.

Nitrocellulose base lacquers are the most widely used as a top coat in furniture finishing.

Nitrocellulose base lacquers are composed of nitrocellulose, various resins, plasticizers, and a solvent. These are low-cost, fast-drying lacquers that produce a durable, attractive top coat. They are available in any sheen from dead flat to high gloss. It should be pointed out that a sheen can be altered by rubbing. For example, a high-gloss sheen can be rubbed to a dull flat, or a dead-flat sheen can be rubbed to a high sheen, depending upon the rubbing method used. Usually a lacquer will be chosen on the basis of the type of sheen desired on legs or other sections that cannot be easily rubbed, but where one would like to have the effect of a rubbed surface. Lacquer top coats are frequently given numerical designators that indicate the type of sheen they will impart.

Most lacquers are supplied ready for spraying. A reducer or retarder may be added to increase the flow characteristics of the lacquer or to reduce blushing under conditions of high temperature and humidity. The manufacturer of the lacquer will generally recommend the amount to be added.

Lacquer dries by the evaporation of its solvent. This usually occurs 25 to 30 minutes after it has been applied, although this should not be regarded as a complete drying. At this point, the surface is still not ready for rubbing. Complete drying takes 2 to 24 hours after the application, depending upon (1) the solid content of the lacquer, and (2) the number of coats applied. Premature rubbing will cause shrinkage.

Nitrocellulose lacquers will range in color from a very pale (the so-called "water white lacquers") to an amber. All nitrocellulose base lacquers will yellow to some extent over a period of time. Excessive exposure to sunlight will increase the rate of yellowing.

Nitrocellulose base lacquers are noted for their excellent resistance to water (hot or cold), mild soap, citric acid (in fruit juices), and other substances commonly spilled on surfaces. Fingernail polish will damage a lacquer top coat, because it contains the same type of solvents found in lacquer.

Lacquers in the second category are based on *cellulose acetate butyrate* (rather than nitrocellulose) in combination with suitable resins, plasticizers, and a solvent. Neither sunlight nor aging will cause these lacquers to yellow. For that reason they are commonly used as top coats over white finishes. All other properties (drying time, durability, etc.) are the same as those described for the nitro-cellulose base lacquers.

Lacquer Thinner

Lacquer thinner is sold in pint, quart, and gallon containers, and is used to thin both brushing and spraying lacquer. It is also recommended for cleaning spray guns and brushes. When it is used for the former purpose, the lacquer should be sprayed through the gun immediately before and after use.

Lacquer thinner contains acetone (the ingredient that causes the rapid rate of drying), and is so strong that it should be used only with finishing materials compatible with lacquer. (Lacquer thinner vapors are toxic to your health. Use appropriate eye and breathing protection. The vapors are explosive; do not work near flame or sparks. See Chapter 20, *Safety*.)

Spraying a Lacquer

Although lacquer is available in aerosol spray cans, this method of application offers certain difficulties that can prove quite frustrating for the beginner. For example, the spray can nozzles are not always reliable, and the containers cannot always be depended on to give a steady, uninterrupted pressure. Better and more efficient results can be obtained when using aerosol spray cans to apply lacquer if the following recommendations are observed:

1. Shake the container well before using.
2. Test the nozzle by directing the spray against a piece of scrap wood.
3. Spray lacquer at a greater distance than other finishes.
4. Spray lacquer horizontally (not downward) at a surface (Fig. 13–1).
5. Hold your finger back from the opening of the nozzle when spraying.

Do not try to apply all the lacquer at one time. This has a tendency to cause runs and buildup. Splattering will be the major

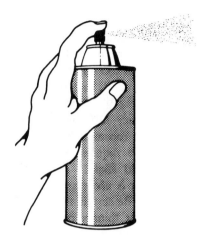

Fig. 13-1. Spraying lacquer horizontally.

problem you encounter when spraying, and is generally caused by (1) overlapping the nozzle with the finger (thereby touching and deflecting the spray (Fig. 13–2), and (2) spraying vertically (downward) against the surface.

Applying Lacquer with a Brush

The inexperienced finisher should avoid using a brush to apply lacquer. It dries much too quickly for anyone but the most experi-

Fig. 13-2. Overlapping the nozzle with the finger tip.

enced to use this method successfully. If a brush is used, one made from camel's hair is recommended. Nylon brushes will disintegrate when exposed to a lacquer thinner. The lacquer must be flowed on as rapidly as possible. A wide brush is recommended because it reduces the number of strokes that are required to complete the job. Each stroke of the brush should slightly overlap the preceding one (Fig. 13–3). A lacquer thinner is necessary to insure that the lacquer will flow freely and evenly. Be certain that you have approximately the same amount of lacquer thinner on hand as you do lacquer. If several layers are applied, lightly sand each layer before flowing on the next coat. This will remove air bubbles and irregularities caused by dust or other particles trapped by the lacquer.

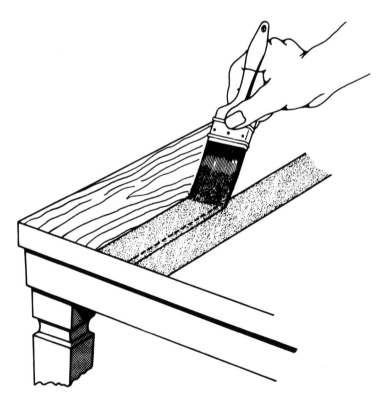

Fig. 13-3. Brushing lacquer with slight overlap of brush strokes.

Basic Lacquer Finishing Schedule

Before following any schedule for applying a lacquer finish, the surface should first be carefully prepared. This procedure has already been thoroughly described in Chapter 9, and it is recommended that these instructions be reviewed before proceeding any further.

As soon as the surface has been prepared and you are satisfied with the results, you should give some consideration to the type of stain you will be using. Water and non-grain-raising (NGR) stains work well under lacquer, but oil stains should be avoided, as they have a tendency to bleed through into the lacquer coat. However, experienced finishers have successfully used oil stains under lacquers by making certain that an adequate sealer has been laid over the stain. Shellac (1-pound or $1\frac{1}{2}$-pound cut) is recommended for the sealer. Allow the sealer to dry 24 hours before applying the lacquer.

The schedule for applying a lacquer finish is essentially as follows (Fig. 13–4).

1. Prepare the surface according to the instructions given in Chapter 9.

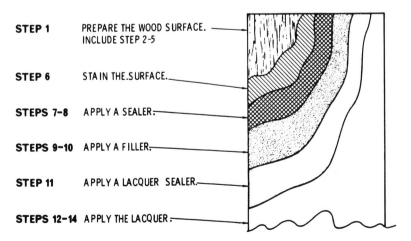

STEP 1	PREPARE THE WOOD SURFACE. INCLUDE STEP 2-5
STEP 6	STAIN THE SURFACE.
STEPS 7-8	APPLY A SEALER.
STEPS 9-10	APPLY A FILLER.
STEP 11	APPLY A LACQUER SEALER.
STEPS 12-14	APPLY THE LACQUER.

Fig. 13-4. Basic lacquer finishing schedule.

2. Raise the grain of the wood by dampening the surface with water, using a soft cloth or a sponge soaked in clean water.
3. Allow the surface to dry.
4. Remove the raised wood fibers with sandpaper (use a 5/0 or 6/0 grade).
5. Remove the dust left by the sanding operation. Some finishers prefer to remove the dust by vacuuming; others find a soft, clean cloth or a round horsehair brush effective.
6. Stain the surface with water or non-grain-raising stain. Allow at least 16 hours for the stain to dry.
7. Apply a sealer (a shellac washcoat works well).
8. Allow the washcoat about two hours to dry, then sand it very lightly with a 5/0 or 6/0 grade sandpaper. Remove the dust by the methods suggested in Step 5 above.
9. Apply a wood filler. The type of wood filler used (paste or liquid) depends upon the size of the wood pores. Paste fillers are recommended for open-grained (large pore) woods; liquid fillers for close-grain woods. A piece of burlap is suggested for applying a paste filler. Use a circular movement to ensure penetration.
10. Take a piece of burlap and wipe *across* the grain to remove the excess filler. Allow the filler sufficient drying time; follow the manufacturer's recommendations found on the container or with accompanying literature.
11. Apply a lacquer sealer (spraying is the most effective method of applying the sealer). Lacquer sealers are designed and produced specifically for the purpose of sealing the wood and providing a base for the finishing coats of lacquer. They are *always* used *after* a stain and filler have been applied.
12. Spray a coat of lacquer on to the surface. The lacquer may also be applied by brushing, but this is recommended only for the most experienced finisher (see the instructions for brushing lacquer found elsewhere in this chapter). The manufacturer's recommendations for spraying should be carefully followed.
13. Allow the first coat of lacquer sufficient time to dry and then rub it lightly with steel wool (a 000 grade of steel wool is recommended). Remove all dust left by the rubbing operation (see Step 5 above).
14. Apply one or two more coats, as described in Steps 12 and 13.

Allow at least 24 to 30 hours drying time between coats. A wax may be applied after the final coat of lacquer for added protection.

15. Varnish can also be applied over lacquer, but a lacquer sealer is recommended as a base coat.

If you are applying the lacquer with a brush, I strongly recommend that you try to make do with just one coat. Lacquer has an unfortunate tendency to dissolve previous coats of lacquer. Because of its rapid rate of drying, you cannot avoid leaving brush marks in the dissolved lacquer.

The longer you allow a coat of lacquer to dry, the smoother the surface will be. If a lacquer top coat is applied to a lacquered undercoat before the latter has had sufficient time to dry, it will damage it.

Modern Provincial Furniture

Modern provincial furniture can be finished in a soft, warm brown on walnut, and then coated with lacquer. To obtain this coloring, the following finishing schedule is recommended:

1. Prepare the wood surface according to the instructions given in Chapter 9. The essential point to remember is that the surface must be smooth and clean.
2. Trace the cathedrals* with a very dark non-grain-raising (NGR) stain. This stain can also be used to add cathedrals to an area where they do not naturally exist (e.g., in radically-cut veneer).
3. Allow sufficient time for the stain to dry.
4. Apply an overall non-grain-raising stain of warm light brown, and allow sufficient time to dry.
5. Apply a sealer over the stain. As soon as the sealer has dried,

---

*NOTE: The arch design usually found at the top (front) of furniture or wall bookcases is called the cathedral. It can be a molding design on the front or sides of furniture, or panels actually cut to produce the cathedral effect.

lightly sand the surface. Do *not* sand through the sealer into the stain.

6. Remove any dust or other particles left by the sanding with a lint-free cloth or tack rag.

7. Apply a dark wood filler (one with little staining power) to accent the grain pattern of the wood. Remove excess filler by rubbing across the grain with a piece of burlap. Allow the filler sufficient time to dry.

8. Apply an overtone that is lighter than the filler and darker than the overall stain used in Step 3. This will add depth to the finish.

9. Shade the light areas to obtain a uniform color over the entire surface.

10. Opaque spatter and distress color may be applied at this point, although it is optional.

11. Apply a lacquer sealer.

12. Apply the lacquer top coat.

Sometimes cheaper, more readily available woods are used for posts or legs. Generally woods for this purpose are also lighter in color. To minimize the amount of shading necessary, it is recommended that they be given an initial dark purplish stain before Step 2 above.

Lacquer Reamalgamation

As is the case with shellac, lacquer is also subject to the white spotting caused by water or moisture resting on the surface. The white spot (blush) can be removed through careful application of lacquer thinner. The lacquer thinner causes the lacquer finish to redissolve and flow together. This process is referred to by finishers as *reamalgamation*. Lacquer finishes are subject to cracking, too, which also can be remedied by reamalgamation.

The important thing to remember about the reamalgamation process is that too much lacquer thinner will result in the removal of more of the lacquer finish than is desired. Consequently, it is advisable to begin with as little thinner as possible and carefully watch the results before proceeding with more. It is recommended that the finisher begin with a clean, soft cloth dampened with thinner and wipe it lightly across the area containing the white spot or crack until the defect has disappeared. If the defect is not removed, add more thinner to the surface. After the successful reamalgamation of the surface, the entire finish should be lightly rubbed with steel wool (000 grade) and waxed.

Shading Lacquers

After the completion of the lacquer finishing schedule described in this chapter, a shading lacquer may be sprayed onto the surface to highlight the wood and add a special shaded effect. These shading lacquers are transparent colored lacquers formed by adding dry aniline dyes to a gloss lacquer. Although designed primarily for shading, these shading lacquers can also be used to apply a stain and a lacquer in one operation.

A shading lacquer can also be used to change slightly the color tone of the stain. This will alter the lacquer finishing schedule after Step 6 (see BASIC LACQUER FINISHING SCHEDULE). According to the schedule, the stain was applied in Step 6 and the sealer in Step 7. Change the finishing schedule as follows:

1–5. (Proceed as previously described).
   6. Stain the surface. Allow sufficient time to dry.
   7. Spray on a shading lacquer. Allow sufficient time to dry. *Do not sand.*
   8. Apply a lacquer sealer over the shading lacquer. The remainder of the finishing schedule follows Steps 8–14 described in the BASIC LACQUER FINISHING SCHEDULE.

Lacquer Toners

Lacquer toners differ from shading lacquers by being *semi*-transparent colored lacquers (shading lacquers are transparent colored lacquers). In other words, there is a certain degree of opacity to lacquer toners. This may be attributed to their composition. Lacquer toners are made by mixing color pigments with a clear gloss lacquer. The recommended mixture is approximately ½ pint of tinting color to each gallon of lacquer. If the amount of tinting in the lacquer is increased, a pigmented lacquer results.

Lacquer toners are used to color the wood but still reveal the grain. They produce a more uniform coloring than do shading lacquers. In addition to shading and applying a stain and a lacquer in one operation, lacquer toners are also used for uniforming and toning.

Lacquer Sanding Sealer

A clear lacquer sanding sealer is designed not only to seal the wood, but also to serve as a base for the finishing coats of lacquer. As such, it is chemically compatible with lacquer. If a stain or filler is used in the finishing schedule, the lacquer sealer is applied after these steps.

Points to Remember

1. Using lacquer is really not recommended for the beginner. It is difficult and tricky to apply, and requires a certain amount of practice and skill before good results can be obtained.
2. Lacquer fumes are hazardous and require special safety equipment.
3. Lacquer can be applied only over a lacquer sealer, another top coat of lacquer, or a suitable washcoat. Lacquer will dissolve most other finishes in much the same manner as a paint remover. This is particularly true of varnish.

CHAPTER 14

Paint and Enamel Finishes

Paint consists essentially of pigments suspended in a vehicle. Many other substances, such as drying oils (castor oil, linseed oil, etc.), thinners or solvents, and natural or synthetic gums, are added in various combinations to provide the special characteristics of a particular paint. The pigments (white or colored solids) give paint both its opacity (nontransparency) and its color. The vehicle or liquid must be of a type in which the pigments are soluble.

Although many different types of vehicles are used in the manufacture of paints, this chapter will be limited to a description of the following four types of paints:

1. Oil-base paints,
2. Alkyd resin-base paints,
3. Latex paints,
4. Milk-base paints.

Enamels are sometimes classified or grouped with paints, sometimes not. Enamels and paints do have many common characteristics, however, and it is perhaps for this reason that these terms are used somewhat interchangeably. For example, it appears to be an advertising prerogative to call certain types of interior wall paints "enamels," even though they are only paints. Essentially, enamel is an approved form of varnish (the vehicle used for many enamels). However, because it has many characteristics in common with paint, it will be covered in this chapter. Other paintlike, opaque finishes, such as pigmented shellacs and pigmented lacquers, will be covered in the chapters dealing with their vehicles. (See Chapter 11, *Shellac Finishes*, and Chapter 13, *Lacquer Finishes*.)

Paints are available in many different types of retail outlets, but more commonly, and in greater variety, in paint and hardware stores, arts and crafts stores, and hobby shops. Almost every imaginable color is available or can be obtained by mixing.

Paint is an opaque finish, and will completely obscure the underlying wood surface. This is especially advantageous when a finisher must cover a cheaper wood of particularly poor appearance. Another important function of paint is the decorative one. Brightly colored painted furniture can be as attractive in the proper setting as furniture done with various clear finishes. Finally, as is the case with all finishes, paint is designed to preserve the wood.

Paint finishes are easy to maintain, because they can be washed with soap and water without causing any ill effect to the finish itself.

Equipment and Supplies

The selection of a suitable brush is very important. A flat brush with a width of one to four inches is recommended for most work. This is the same type of brush commonly used to apply enamel or flat varnish. The wider brushes should be used to apply paint to large surface areas (e.g., table tops, cabinet doors, panels, etc.), the narrower ones for trim, scrollwork, and other small detail. An oval brush is frequently useful for painting round surfaces.

Brushes should always be cleaned immediately after you are through painting. The cleaning solvent is generally the solvent used for the particular paint (see the section on thinners in this chapter). Soak the brush for several minutes in the cleaning solvent and work the paint from the heel of the brush to its tip. Shake out the excess solvent and wash the brush in soap and water (lukewarm). This will remove the last traces of paint and cleaning solvent. Comb the bristles out straight, wrap them in paper, and store the brush in a flat or hanging position.

Old drinking glasses, large glass jars, or certain types of cans are useful for mixing, cleaning, and storing paints. Regardless of the type of use to which the container is put, it must be thoroughly cleaned. Dirt and other contaminants will combine with the paint and eventually find their way into the finish.

Other equipment and supplies recommended for painting include:

1. The necessary equipment and supplies for preparing the surface.
2. Several clean, lint-free cloths or tack rags.
3. A suitable thinner (follow the manufacturer's recommendations).

Brushing Techniques

Select one surface at a time for painting. Moving from one section to another before completing the previous one will cause lapping and other problems that detract from the overall appearance.

If at all possible, follow the direction of the wood grain. This will reduce the tendency of the paint to ripple. Paint with the flat side of the brush, not the edge (unless a narrow section is being painted). It is best to cover as large an area as possible with each brush stroke. Paint the edges, scrollwork, and trim first. The larger surface areas will be painted last.

Painting Procedure

Paint can be both brushed and sprayed onto a surface. Brushing and spraying instructions are basically the same as those given for other types of finishes. When spraying, the spray gun should move in a straight line at an equal distance from the surface of the piece of furniture. The finisher should not swing the spray gun so that it forms an arc, or heavy buildups and weak spots will develop. Brush marks will be left on the surface if brushing is continued too long after the application of the paint. This is particularly true of wood surfaces that are absorbent, and therefore cause the paint to dry more quickly. In this case, a sealer coat is recommended to prevent uneven penetration of the wood by the paint.

The procedure for applying paint to a wood surface is as follows (Fig. 14–1):

1. Prepare the surface according to the suggestions offered in Chapter 9. The surface must be smooth (no raised grains, dents, or scratches), clean, and dry.
2. Seal the surface with a washcoat of thinned shellac. No stain is used under a paint top coat, because the latter is an opaque (nontransparent) finish.
3. Allow the sealer sufficient time to dry thoroughly.
4. The wood grain of previously unfinished surfaces will rise and harden as a result of the shellac sealer coat. Remove the raised wood grains by sanding with a fine grade of sandpaper.
5. Remove all dust left by the sanding operation with a soft, lint-free cloth or tack rag.
6. Thin the paint with a suitable thinner until it flows fairly easily.

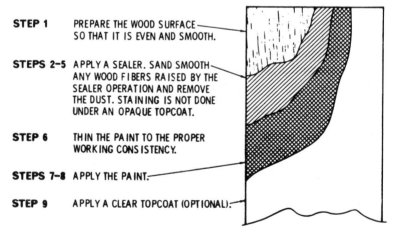

STEP 1   PREPARE THE WOOD SURFACE SO THAT IT IS EVEN AND SMOOTH.

STEPS 2–5 APPLY A SEALER. SAND SMOOTH ANY WOOD FIBERS RAISED BY THE SEALER OPERATION AND REMOVE THE DUST. STAINING IS NOT DONE UNDER AN OPAQUE TOPCOAT.

STEP 6   THIN THE PAINT TO THE PROPER WORKING CONSISTENCY.

STEPS 7–8 APPLY THE PAINT.

STEP 9   APPLY A CLEAR TOPCOAT (OPTIONAL).

Fig. 14-1. Painting procedure.

7. Do not attempt to paint the entire piece of furniture all at one time. Proceed section by section, allowing sufficient drying time to prevent the paint from running or streaking. Cover the entire section with the paint and then tip it off.

8. If several coats of paint are applied, sand each coat lightly with a fine grade of sandpaper. Be certain that the paint is completely dry before sanding. Remove the dust left by the sanding operation with a lint-free cloth or a tack rag.

9. A clear finish (lacquer, varnish, etc.) can be applied over the paint for greater durability. Make certain that both are compatible, or you will ruin the entire finish.

Oil-Base Paints

In oil-base paints, the color pigments are suspended in an oil vehicle. One of the most frequently used vehicles is linseed oil, an inexpensive, dependable drying oil derived from the crushing of flax seeds. Other oil vehicles include castor oil (a plasticizer for lacquers), China wood oil or tung oil (used in varnishes or alkyd wood finishes), Oiticica oil (pigmented enamels), and soya bean oil (a plasticizer for lacquers).

Alkyd Resin-Base Paints

The synthetic alkyd resin is used as both a plasticizer and as the liquid base (vehicle) for paints and other finishing products. Its use is quite widespread, dating back to the 1920s. Among other synthetic resins used in the production of paints and finishing products are acrylic resin, urea resin, vinyl resin, silicone resin, and styrenated alkyd resin.

Latex Paints

The water-soluble latex paints developed and used primarily for painting interior and exterior walls can also be used on furniture, particularly unfinished furniture. Some finishers resist using them because of their grain-raising effect on the wood (water is the vehicle used in these paints) and the difficulty in removing them. However, these objections are not serious ones. The raised grains can be removed by sanding and a second coat of paint can then be applied to the surface. Latex paints can be easily covered with another latex paint or some other opaque finish (if a suitable sealer has first been placed over the original finish). It is doubtful that it would ever be profitable to strip off a latex paint. Wood surfaces over which a paint has been applied are generally unattractive.

Latex paints are commercially available in a great variety of colors and shades. Special colors and shades can be mixed to meet individual needs.

A latex paint can be made more durable by covering it with a thin coat of clear lacquer or some other type of clear finish.

Milk-Base Paints

An early method used for making paints consisted of mixing berry juices, colored clays, or blood with milk. Later, dry colorants were substituted as coloring agents. Packages of these dry colorants are available at most paint and wallpaper stores, and find extensive use as tints for exterior house paints. However, by mixing them with dry powdered milk and water, a suitable milk-base paint can be produced. The dry colorants are extremely bright, and should be dulled by mixing in black or brown.

Paint Thinners

The manufacturer will generally recommend a suitable thinner for use with his paint. If not, it will be necessary to experiment on a section of furniture that is not exposed to view. Table 14–1 gives a listing of suggested thinners for various finishes. Note that latex paints use water as a thinner. Other types of paint use such thinners as turpentine or naphtha.

Table 14-1. Paints and Their Thinners

Type of Paint	Thinner
Oil-Binder Paints	Turpentine
Alkyd Resin-Binder Paints	Naphtha or Mineral Spirits
Latex Paints	Water
Milk-Base Paints	Water

Painting Fir Plywood

Fir plywood is frequently used by home craftsmen in the construction of furniture. Because good grain patterns are generally found in only the highest-quality plywood, an opaque finish (paint, enamel, etc.) is often selected as a finishing top coat.

The grain in fir plywood is subject to unequal absorption. Consequently, using a finish on fir plywood without the prior application of a sealer will result in dark spots on the surface. The use of a sealer will equalize the absorption rate. A pigmented penetrating resin sealer is recommended for use with latex paints.

The procedure for applying a latex paint to a fir plywood surface is as follows (Fig. 14-2):

1. Prepare the surface according to the suggestions offered in Chapter 9. It is essential that the surface be smooth and clean. Dirt, traces of glue, and other contaminants will combine with the finish and mar its appearance. Fill in all nail holes, dents, and scratches and sand smooth.
2. Remove any dust left by the sanding operation with a clean, lint-free cloth or a tack rag.
3. Apply a penetrating resin sealer to the surface, and allow it sufficient time to sink into the wood and dry.
4. Sand the surface lightly with a fine grade of sandpaper, and remove all dust from the sanding operation with a clean, lint-free cloth or a tack rag.
5. Apply a second coat of the penetrating resin sealer and allow sufficient time for it to thoroughly dry.
6. Sand the second sealer coat according to the instructions given in Step 4.
7. Brush on the latex paint.

STEPS 1-2 PREPARE THE WOOD SURFACE.

STEPS 3-4 APPLY A PENETRATING RESIN SEALER. SAND THE SURFACE LIGHTLY AND REMOVE THE DUST.

STEPS 5-6 APPLY A SECOND COAT OF A PENETRATING RESIN SEALER. SAND THE SURFACE LIGHTLY AND REMOVE THE DUST.

STEP 7 BRUSH ON A LATEX PAINT.

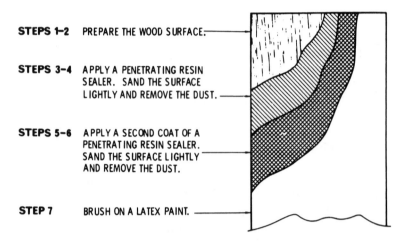

Fig. 14-2. Procedure for painting fir plywood.

Repairing Paint Finishes

The best method for repairing a paint finish is to sand it down, remove the dust, and recover it with a fresh coat of paint. If there are scratches or dents on the surface, fill them in and sand them smooth (once again removing the dust left by the sanding operation). Cover the entire surface with a washcoat of shellac. This will act as a sealer over the original paint and whatever repairs may have been made, and provide a smooth, even base for the new coat of paint.

Painting over Older Finishes

A sealer coat is absolutely necessary when painting over non-paint types of finishes to prevent reactions due to a chemical incompatibility between the paint and the original finish. A washcoat of shellac will generally serve well as an all-purpose sealer.

Painted Decoration

Painted decoration ranges from simple geometric forms and freehand designs to truly artistic motifs. To find sources of designs, look for books on painted furniture and see both early American and modern painted furniture at museums. Enamel paints are usually applied over an enamel base coat. Enamel paint holds up to the wear and tear a piece of furniture is likely to get.

Banding and Striping

Striping and banding can be learned by practically anyone. Both banding and striping (Fig. 14–3) use two-tone color effects to decorate furniture surfaces. Banding is simply a wider application of striping. Apply bands or stripes along the edge of surfaces to provide contrast and emphasis. The color of the bands or stripes usually compliments or contrasts with the color of the background surface. Most banding and striping is done over an enamel surface.

A special brush with extremely long bristles is used. Two or three widths of brush may be needed for the design you have in mind.

Begin by practicing on a waste board. Hold the brush lightly in your fingers. Trail the bristles along the surface using loose, free strokes (Fig. 14–4). Don't worry about uneven starts and stops at first. Concentrate on laying down a full coat of paint. The width of the strip is controlled by the width of the brush. After you can make nice stripes, practice starting and stopping.

Fig. 14–3. Edge striping designs.

Fig. 14–4. The proper use of a striping brush.

Once you have a good technique developed, lay out your design on the dried base coat lightly with a soft pencil. Do the stripes on the inside first, progressing outward toward the edges.

Freehand Designs

Once you have some skill at striping, progress to fancier borders with a combination striping techniques and ordinary painting (Fig. 14–5). A wide variety of decorations are possible (Figs. 14–6 and 14–7).

Artistic Motifs

If you have training and talent, the value of even very plain furniture can be enhanced greatly (Figs. 14–8 and 14–9). Begin with sketches on paper to develop ideas that reflect and interest the people who will use the furniture. Draw on your creative talent by considering the setting of the house, or the interior decoration of the room in which the furniture will be used.

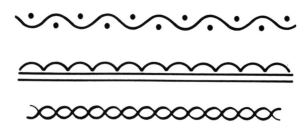

Fig. 14–5. Borders

Fig. 14-6. Freehand decoration. The design is from a nineteenth century early American chair. *(Courtesy Fancy Painters, Inc.)*

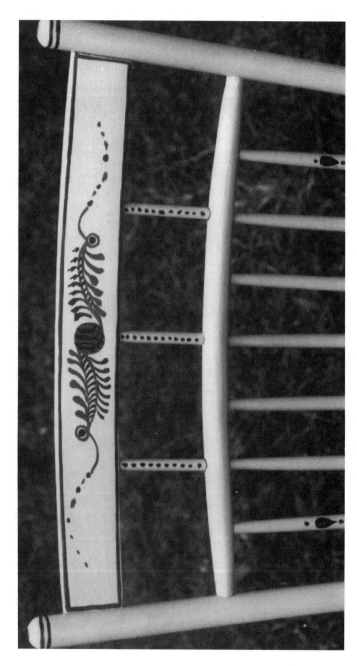

Fig. 14-7. Striping and freehand painting are combined. Note that this lively execution is less than perfect with slight variations in line width and placement. (Courtesy Fancy Painters, Inc.)

Fig. 14-8. This plain wooden blanket chest is decorated with artistic painted panels. *(Courtesy Fancy Painters, Inc.)*

Fig. 14-9. **A closeup view of the front panel of chest shown in Fig. 14-8.** *(Courtesy Fancy Painters, Inc.)*

Enamel Finishes

Enamels are often classified as paints. This may be due to the fact that enamel, like paint, is an opaque finish, and is used to cover wood surfaces that are too unattractive for a clear top coat. However, there are certain basic distinctions between enamels and paints that are important to know, because they may influence your selection of the finish.

Essentially, enamels may be regarded as finishes that belong to a broad classification of free-flowing finishing materials that dry to a smooth, hard finish in a number of different sheens. They consist of color pigments ground in a suitable vehicle, to which thinners and driers have been added. A number of different vehicles are used in the production of enamels, including alkyd base and urethane catalytic base varnishes, lacquer, and oil.

When compared with paint, enamels will generally have the following characteristics:

1. Somewhat slower drying time,
2. More finely ground color pigments,
3. Higher gloss,
4. Tougher, more durable surface,
5. Higher cost.

Types of Enamels

There are so many different types of enamel available to the finisher that selecting the right one may be confusing. For example, not all enamels are suitable for furniture finishes. Some are exclusively exterior finishes or are designed for specific conditions (e.g., water-resisting marine or waterproof enamels). On the other hand, some gloss enamels can be used for both interior or exterior surfaces, and will provide an acceptable finish for furniture. The semigloss enamels (also known as eggshell enamels or satin-finish enamels) are exclusively interior enamels, and are particularly suited for furniture surfaces. You must therefore be certain you are selecting the right enamel for the job. If you are not certain, ask a knowledgeable dealer for advice.

A final word of caution: do *not* mix enamels from different manufacturers, even if they appear to be identical in color and type (e.g., both "gloss enamels" or "eggshell enamels"). It is highly probable that differences in their chemical compositions will make them mutually incompatible. In other words, mixing them will produce a useless mess.

Enamel Thinner

The manufacturer of an enamel will generally recommend a thinner and solvent. Turpentine, benzine, turpentine mixed with benzine, and acetone have all been used as thinners and solvents for different types of enamels. Remember: not every thinner is suitable for each enamel. The selection of a thinner and solvent is determined by the chemical composition of the enamel.

Enamel Undercoating

An undercoat is usually recommended when enameling large surface areas, because it will reduce the number of top coats required to finish the piece. The undercoat also serves as a sealer, protecting the enamel top coat from substances that might bleed into it. Finally, the undercoat provides a primer-type base to which the enamel top coat can adhere.

A number of different types of undercoats can be used with enamels including latex paint, thinned shellac, or prepared undercoats. Undercoats are available in white or in colors tinted to match the enamel top coat. If the undercoat and top coat do not match, the undercoat should be lighter in shade.

Anywhere from one to three undercoats will be used on a wood surface. When they are completely dry, they should be *lightly* sanded with a fine grade of sandpaper. This will provide a better surface for the enamel top coats. Always remove all dust and other particles left by the sanding operation.

Enamel Finishing Schedule (Brushing)

Brushing an enamel can be difficult. For that reason, additional attention has been given in this finishing schedule to using a brush. If at all possible, the beginner should use a spray enamel rather than attempting to enamel with a brush the first time.

The procedure for applying an enamel with a brush to a wood surface is as follows (Fig. 14–10):

1. Prepare the wood surface according to the instructions suggested in Chapter 9. As with other finishes, it is very important that the surface be smooth and clean.
2. Apply a washcoat of shellac to seal the surface and raise the grain fibers.
3. Allow the washcoat sufficient time to dry thoroughly. After it has dried, lightly sand the surface with a very fine grade of sandpaper.
4. Remove all dust and other particles left by the sanding operation with a clean, lint-free cloth or a tack rag.
5. Mix the undercoat until it is uniform and smooth. The undercoat will either be white or tinted a color to match the enamel top coat. It is recommended that a colored undercoat be the same color or lighter than the top coat (never darker).
6. Pour part of the undercoat into a large jar or glass.
7. Dip the brush into the jar or glass, and work the enamel thoroughly into the bristles by wiping or pressing the brush against a piece of clean scrap wood.

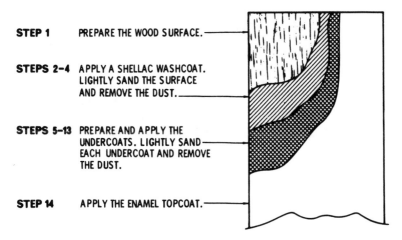

STEP 1 PREPARE THE WOOD SURFACE.

STEPS 2–4 APPLY A SHELLAC WASHCOAT. LIGHTLY SAND THE SURFACE AND REMOVE THE DUST.

STEPS 5–13 PREPARE AND APPLY THE UNDERCOATS. LIGHTLY SAND EACH UNDERCOAT AND REMOVE THE DUST.

STEP 14 APPLY THE ENAMEL TOPCOAT.

Fig. 14-10. Procedure for applying enamel.

8. When you are certain that the bristles in the lower one-third to one-half of the brush are thoroughly wet with enamel, dip the brush into the jar or glass and begin enameling the surface.

9. Brush the enamel onto the surface in the direction of the grain. Remove any excess with the tip of the brush. Do not attempt to brush the enamel smooth. Enamel will flow together of its own accord in a smooth, even coating before it dries.

10. When you have completed the undercoat, allow approximately 24 to 30 hours for it to dry.

11. As soon as the first undercoat has completely dried, *lightly* sand the surface with a very fine grade of sandpaper.

12. Remove any dust or other particles left by the sanding operation with a clean, lint-free cloth, or a tack rag.

13. A second or third coat of undercoating may be applied, but Steps 10 through 12 should be followed after each one.

14. The last coat (the top coat) is applied in the same manner as the undercoats (see particularly Steps 6 through 10). When mixing enamel, do not stir it too vigorously or you will cause bubbles to form.

15. Allow 24 hours for the top coat to dry. When you are certain that it is dry, *rub* the surface with pumice stone and oil, or pumice stone and water. Always rub in the same direction as the grain with long, even strokes. Rub along the length of a section, rather than its width. Wipe off the excess pumice stone (and oil if it is used) with a clean, lint-free cloth.

Close-grained woods are preferred for enameling. Open-grained woods require extensive filling with a paste filler. If a filler is used, allow it time to set and then wipe away the excess with a piece of burlap. Lightly sand the surface with a fine grade of sandpaper and remove the dust. Clean the surface with a clean cloth dampened with denatured alcohol, benzine, or some other suitable solvent. These steps will precede Step 2 in the enamel finishing schedules described in this chapter.

Enamel Finishing Schedule (Spraying)

Most enamel colors can be purchased in 16-oz. aerosol spray cans. These are lacquer-base enamels and are available in flat, semigloss, and gloss sheens. (See Chapter 20, *Safety*, for precautions on spraying finish materials.)

The procedure for spraying enamel onto a wood surface is as follows:

1. Prepare the wood surface according to the instructions recommended in Chapter 9. As always, the surface must be smooth and clean before applying any of the finishing coats.
2. Brush on a washcoat of shellac, and allow it sufficient time to dry thoroughly. This will serve as a sealer over the bare wood, preventing the sap from bleeding through and ruining the top coat.
3. After the washcoat has completely dried, *lightly* sand it with a very fine grade of sandpaper. Take care not to sand through the washcoat.
4. Remove all dust and other particles left by the sanding operation with a clean, lint-free cloth or a tack rag.
5. Spray the first coat onto the surface. Move the nozzle parallel to the surface and high enough so that no mist forms during spraying (an indication that it is being held too high) or runs and sags develop on the finish (too low). Do not make swinging movements of the hand, because the arc formed by the movement will cause an uneven buildup of the enamel.
6. Spray until the surface is completely covered with a smooth, even coat of enamel. There should be no uneven buildup, runs, or sags (all indications of improper spraying procedure or an excessive application of enamel).
7. Allow the first coat sufficient time to dry. Lacquer-base spraying enamels will dry much more quickly than the brush type.
8. The remaining coats of enamel will be applied in the same manner as described for brushing an enamel onto a surface. See Steps 11 through 15 of the finishing schedule for brushing. The drying time will be shorter for the lacquer base enamel. In addition, more coats of spray enamel will be required, because they are generally thinner than the brush type.

Enameling a Finished Surface

The two previously described finishing schedules dealt with spraying or brushing an enamel onto a bare wood surface. The finishing schedule for applying an enamel over an older finish is only slightly different during the initial steps. The procedure is as follows:

1. Lightly sand the old finish until it is smooth. It is not necessary to sand down to the bare wood.
2. Remove the dust or other particles left by the sanding operation with a clean, lint-free cloth or a tack rag.
3. Apply a washcoat of shellac as a sealer. This will prevent the old finish from bleeding through into the enamel top coat.
4. Allow 2 to 3 hours for the washcoat to dry.
5. After the washcoat has completely dried, sand it lightly with a very fine grade of sandpaper.
6. Remove the dust or other particles left by the sanding operation with a clean, lint-free cloth or a tack rag.
7. Apply the enamel undercoats and top coat in the same manner as described in the other enamel finishing schedules.

CHAPTER 15

Oil and Wax Finishes

Oil and wax finishes have been used for years to provide wood surfaces with durable protective coatings without obscuring the natural beauty of the wood. They are not characterized by a buildup of coats as are other finishes, but many of them do require constant, periodic renewal. The types of oil and wax finishes that will be described in this chapter are:

1. Penetrating (oil) finishes,
2. Linseed oil finishes,
3. Wax finishes.

Penetrating Finishes

Penetrating finishes (also variously referred to as *penetrating oil finishes, penetrating resin finishes, penetrating resin-oil finishes, sealer finishes,* and *penetrating sealer finishes*) consist primarily of either a resin-oil or wax-resin base to which a sealer stain has been added. Originally developed for use on floors, they are now finding widespread use in furniture finishing. Their new popularity as a furniture finish is due to a number of factors, including:

1. Ease of application,
2. Durability,
3. Beauty,
4. Ease of repair.

The major disadvantages of these finishes is that they lack depth and body, and are extremely difficult to remove.

Whether to use the resin-oil or wax base finish is a matter of personal choice. You will always find finishers who swear to the advantages of one over the other. The major difference between the two is that a penetrating finish with a wax base cannot be covered with another finish (e.g., a varnish or lacquer), because it will cause the top coat to lift. However, it can be coated with one or more layers of a paste wax, and rubbed to a very pleasing sheen. The resin-oil finish, on the other hand, is essentially a very thin varnish. As such, it can be covered with a clear varnish top coat and rubbed for a dull, satin, or high gloss.

No particular skill is required for applying a penetrating finish. It is generally brushed or wiped onto the surface, allowed to penetrate for a period of time, and then the excess is wiped off. There are no brush marks to worry about, no runs, and no surface stickiness to trap dust, hair, and other contaminants.

This type of finish penetrates into the pores of the wood and dries to form a solid, subsurface layer *inside* the wood that resists fungus (the cause of dry rot) and insect damage. Because the penetrating finish waterproofs as it seals, it enables the wood to resist shrinkage and warping due to excess moisture absorption or loss.

A penetrating finish withstands most types of wear much better than other finishes. Minor scratches and dents cannot break through the surface color to expose the unfinished wood, because penetration has usually extended below this level. However, repairing is not very difficult. You need only to clean the surface, abrade it lightly with a fine grade of steel wool, and apply another coating of the penetrating finish.

Penetrating finishes are often recommended for hardwoods such as rosewood or teak, which contain excessive amounts of natural oil. Even when the wood is kiln dried, these oils are still present and present a problem to the finisher if a lacquer, varnish, or shellac topcoat is applied. One method of eliminating the oil is to flood the surface with denatured alcohol. Let the wood dry naturally. Do not try to speed up the drying by placing the wood in the sun or using artificial means. Apply two or three more coats of denatured alcohol, letting each coat dry before applying the next one. When you feel certain that the oil content of the wood has been reduced to an acceptable level, apply the penetrating finish according to the basic finishing schedule given in this chapter (see APPLYING A PENETRATING FINISH).

A penetrating finish should be applied only over a bare wood or a stain, never over another finish. Even a surface that has been stripped will cause difficulties for a penetrating finish, because the wood pores will be clogged by the older finishing materials. Consequently, it will not be able to penetrate properly, if it penetrates at all. As you can see, a filler is not necessary, because this type of finish penetrates the wood pores and acts as its own filler.

Penetrating finishes cure initially by evaporation. As a result, the finish on the surface dries before the portion that has penetrated into the wood pores. Because there is no way of knowing exactly when the subsurface layer has dried completely, you must give it at least three days before applying certain types of waxes, just to be on the safe side. Otherwise, the undried portions of the finish may combine with the wax, and your work will be ruined. The more coatings of penetrating finish you use, the greater will be the possibility of this happening.

Applying a Penetrating Finish

As was already mentioned, applying a penetrating finish is very easy, even for the beginner. Basically, it is a matter of applying the finish to the surface, allowing it sufficient time to penetrate, and then wiping off the excess. However, you will do a much better job if you are aware of certain aspects of the application procedure before you attempt to apply a penetrating finish. For example, this type of finish requires no sanding between coats. Although this decreases the amount of work you must do during the application of the finish, it means that you must make absolutely certain that you have properly prepared the surface during the wood preparation stages in the finishing schedule. The wood must be clean, smooth, and completely free of any defects before you apply the finish, or the results will be unsatisfactory.

The procedure for applying a penetrating finish is basically as follows (Fig. 15–1):

1. Prepare the wood surface according to the instructions given in Chapter 9. Make absolutely certain that the wood surface is clean and smooth.

2. Stain the surface and allow 24 to 48 hours drying time. The stain must be compatible with the type of penetrating finish you are using. Read the manufacturer's instructions. They will generally recommend a compatible stain for use with the finish.

3. Apply a coat of penetrating finish with a brush or a clean, lint-free cloth. Keep the surface wet for 25 to 30 minutes. This "wetting" period will vary in length, depending upon which manufacturer's product you are using. The manufacturer will indicate the recommended length of time in the instructions. It is during the wetting period that the finish penetrates down into the pores of the wood.

4. At the end of the wetting period, wipe off the excess finish with a clean, lint-free cloth. Let the surface dry for about 24 hours.

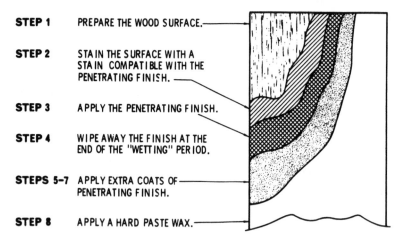

STEP 1	PREPARE THE WOOD SURFACE.
STEP 2	STAIN THE SURFACE WITH A STAIN COMPATIBLE WITH THE PENETRATING FINISH.
STEP 3	APPLY THE PENETRATING FINISH.
STEP 4	WIPE AWAY THE FINISH AT THE END OF THE "WETTING" PERIOD.
STEPS 5–7	APPLY EXTRA COATS OF PENETRATING FINISH.
STEP 8	APPLY A HARD PASTE WAX.

Fig. 15–1. Applying a penetrating finish.

5. Apply a second coat of penetrating finish (see the instructions given in Steps 3 and 4 above).
6. Wipe off the excess finish with a clean, lint-free cloth after it has been allowed to soak into the wood.
7. Continue to apply as many coats of the penetrating finish as the wood pores will absorb. Follow the instructions given in Steps 3 and 4.
8. Apply a hard paste wax to the surface with a pad of very fine steel wool, and rub with the grain. Complete the rubbing operation by polishing the surface with a soft, clean, lint-free cloth.

Applying a stain (Step 2) is optional. The color and grain pattern of some hardwoods is such that staining is not necessary.

Some finishers lightly abrade the final coat of the penetrating finish with a fine grade of steel wool. The purpose of this operation is to remove any rough spots and to create a uniformly smooth surface. Be sure to remove any steel wool residue with a clean, lint-free cloth. The last coat of finish must be *completely* dry before you use the steel wool.

Do not try to cover the entire surface of a piece of furniture at one time. Apply the penetrating finish to a small section of the surface and move immediately to an adjacent one when the previous section is finished. A penetrating finish may be applied both against and with the grain. In this respect, it is similar to a filler.

Linseed Oil Finishes

Linseed oil has been used for years as a penetrating finish and possesses many of the characteristics of the newer resin-oil- and wax-resin-base penetrating finishes. For example, it makes the wood resistant to moisture, resists minor scratching, denting, and other types of wear, and creates a hard, subsurface layer in the wood. On the other hand, it is much more difficult to apply than the newer penetrating finishes. Moreover, the finish may become sticky if the weather turns hot and humid. Another objectionable feature of linseed oil finishes is the fact that, like wax finishes, they must be constantly renewed. Reapplication of the linseed oil must take place periodically.

Linseed oil is processed from crushed flaxseed and is available as *raw* linseed oil or *boiled* linseed oil. The former is produced by taking the oil by-product obtained from the crushed flaxseed and allowing it to season in the sun for a few years. The result is an oil finish that never completely dries, except for its outer film. The nondrying characteristics of the sublayers of raw linseed oil make this a very flexible finish that is ideal for exterior surfaces. These exterior surfaces are subject to changing weather conditions that cause the wood to expand and contract. Unless the finish has a certain flexibility, it will crack under these conditions. Because of the nondrying characteristics of raw linseed oil, it is *not* recommended as a finish for furniture. However, many finishers have used it for this purpose, particularly after combining it with driers, or thinning it with turpentine or mineral spirits (which has a much faster drying rate than turpentine), or using boiled linseed oil coats after the use of raw linseed oil as the primary coat.

Boiled linseed oil has much better drying characteristics than raw linseed oil. This is brought about by the addition of driers (e.g., siccative drier, japan drier) or by boiling. Do not try to boil linseed oil yourself.

Despite the fact that boiled linseed oil has far better drying characteristics than raw linseed oil, it is still somewhat tacky as a finish and will constantly trap dust particles on the surface.

Applying a Linseed Oil Finish

The most common formula for a linseed oil finish is two parts boiled linseed oil mixed with one part turpentine. Mineral spirits can be substituted for the turpentine as a thinner. The procedure for applying a linseed oil finish is basically as follows (Fig. 15–2):

1. Prepare the wood surface according to the instructions given in Chapter 9. The surface must be sanded smooth, properly cleaned, and free of all dust. Although linseed oil does not normally raise the grain, it is best to guard against this possibility

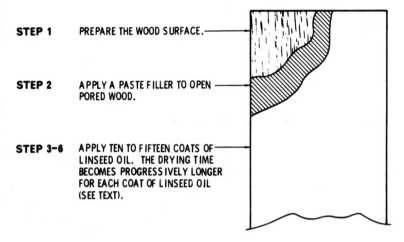

STEP 1   PREPARE THE WOOD SURFACE.

STEP 2   APPLY A PASTE FILLER TO OPEN
              PORED WOOD.

STEP 3-6 APPLY TEN TO FIFTEEN COATS OF
              LINSEED OIL. THE DRYING TIME
              BECOMES PROGRESSIVELY LONGER
              FOR EACH COAT OF LINSEED OIL
              (SEE TEXT).

Fig. 15-2. Applying a linseed oil finish.

by raising the grain during the wood preparation stage (Step 1) of the finishing schedule.

2. Apply a paste filler to open-pored woods to prevent excessive absorption of the linseed oil. See Chapter 9 for instructions concerning the correct application of a filler.
3. Take a clean cloth or brush and apply the linseed oil to a portion of the surface. Always work on limited areas and do not try to cover the entire surface immediately. Rub the oil into the surface for about 15 minutes.
4. Let the linseed oil soak into the wood pores, and then wipe away the excess oil with a clean lint-free cloth.
5. Give the first coat of linseed oil at least two days to dry.
6. Apply 5 to 15 more coats of linseed oil in the same manner described in Steps 3 and 4 above. Allow two days drying time between the first and second coats; five days between the second and third; and one month between subsequent coats.

The number of coats of linseed oil and the length of drying time between coats varies, depending upon the finishing schedule and the preference of the finisher. However, regardless of the length of drying time between the coats of linseed oil required by your particular finishing schedule, *each coat must be absolutely dry* before applying the next. If you are in doubt, lengthen the drying period between coats. Remember also that drying periods should become longer as you progress through the finishing schedule.

Other Formulas for Linseed Oil Finishes

Linseed oil finishes have been used for so many years that it is quite natural to find a great variety of formulas for their preparation. The two part boiled linseed oil and one part turpentine formula described in the preceding section is very common. Others vary in the type of thinner used, the mixing proportions between the linseed oil and the thinner, or by the use of raw linseed oil instead of boiled linseed oil. Some of the different types of formulas you may encounter are as follows:

1. One part boiled linseed oil and one part turpentine.
2. One part boiled linseed oil, one part turpentine, and one part spar varnish.
3. Three parts *raw* linseed oil and one part turpentine (first coat), followed by several coats of boiled linseed oil, followed by a coat of one part boiled linseed oil and one part japan drier.
4. Numerous unthinned coats of boiled linseed oil.

Wax Finishes

A wax finish should not be confused with wax finishing. The latter refers to the application of a polishing wax over a final finish to provide additional protection and to create a special pleasing luster. Some finishers prefer to use furniture polish instead of wax for the same purpose, although it is generally considered inferior. The merits of furniture polish and polishing wax are described in Chapter 17.

A wax finish is one in which a paste wax is applied over a sealer (thinned lacquer, varnish, or shellac), a stain, or a bare wood surface. The bare wood surface can be one from which an old finish has been removed or one that has never been finished.

Only a *paste* wax is recommended for a straight wax finish. The liquid and cream waxes should only be used for waxing a final finish. Staining waxes can also be used as straight wax finishes, but can only be applied over bare wood. They consist of wax to which a color stain has been added. Because the stain is already in the wax, there is no need to stain or seal the wood. An automotive paste wax will generally produce a very acceptable straight wax finish. Hard paste floor waxes are also good.

A wax finish does not penetrate the wood pores. Therefore, it can be applied over a wood surface from which an old finish has been removed. This is one advantage it has over linseed oil and other penetrating finishes. A wax finish possesses greater resistance to heat than linseed oil and never becomes sticky when it is humid or hot. On the other hand, it does not resist water moisture as well as linseed oil.

Applying a Wax Finish

A straight wax finish is a paste wax (e.g., a paste floor wax) applied to the surface with a soft, clean, lint-free cloth. The procedure for applying a wax finish is as follows (Fig. 15–3):

1. Prepare the wood surface according to the instructions recommended in Chapter 9. The surface must be clean and uniformly smooth. When you have finished preparing the surface, make certain that is thoroughly clean and free of all dust.
2. Apply a sealer of thinned shellac, varnish, or lacquer to the surface, and give it enough time to dry completely.
3. After the sealer coat has thoroughly dried, lightly abrade it with a very fine grade of steel wool.
4. Remove all dust left by the steel wool with a tack rag or other suitable means.
5. Apply the paste wax with a clean, lint-free cloth folded to fit your hand. Rub the wax onto the surface with a circular movement. Do not apply too much wax at one time. This first coat should be thin and evenly distributed over the surface.
6. Allow the first wax coat sufficient time to dry. The manufacturer of the wax usually recommends how long this should be.

STEP 1   PREPARE THE WOOD SURFACE.

STEPS 2-4   APPLY A SEALER, LIGHTLY SAND
                IT AFTER IT HAS DRIED AND
                REMOVE ALL DUST.

STEPS 5-9   APPLY SEVERAL COATS
                OF PASTE WAX.

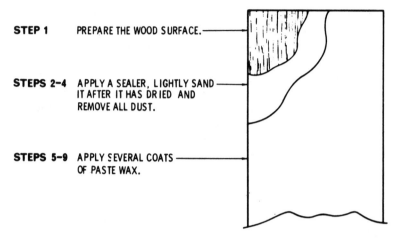

Fig. 15-3.   Applying a wax finish.

7. Rub the entire surface with a soft cloth. This will remove any excess wax.
8. When you are certain that all excess wax has been removed and that the remaining wax has been evenly distributed over the surface, polish it with a clean, hard cloth.
9. Apply one or two more coats of wax according to the instructions given in Steps 5 through 8.

The general rule for a good finish is to avoid using too much wax, because it only results in a buildup of excess wax in certain areas. Far better results can be achieved by applying two or three thin coats.

Most finishers prefer adding a wax finish over a sealer coat. This enables them to remove the finish much more easily (denatured alcohol or turpentine work well) and without the possibility of traces of the wax remaining in the pores of the wood. This condition, of course, results in the improper drying or lack of adhesion of any other finishes that might be applied. Despite these difficulties, straight wax finishes are still sometimes applied directly to a bare wood surface, particularly in the case of very fine-grained hardwoods.

CHAPTER 16

Rubbing, Waxing, and Polishing Finishes

Most furniture finishes are either waxed or polished as the final step in the finishing schedule. The purpose of these two procedures is to protect the surface while at the same time enhancing the beauty of the finish. Each has its advantages and disadvantages, and it will be these factors in relation to your needs that will influence your selection. Therefore, it is not a question of whether a polish is better per se than a wax (or vice versa), but rather which one is best suited for your needs.

Rubbing a finish is a different procedure altogether from polishing or waxing it, and should not be confused with the latter two. Rubbing a finish (Fig. 16-1) is essentially an abrading action designed to reduce the natural gloss of a shellac, varnish, or lacquer finish, while at the same time removing brush marks, runs, dust and other particles from the finish. The result should be a uniformly smooth surface with a somewhat dull appearance. A high polish can be restored to the finish by a variety of rubbing techniques. The application of a suitable paste wax or polish is usually the final step.

Rubbing is also a finishing procedure that can be used after each of the intermediate coats of finish before the top coat is applied. This is often the case with the better quality varnish finishes.

Fig. 16-1. Polish sanding to remove bubbles, brush marks, and trapped particles in the finish.

Rubbing after each of the intermediate finishing coats is another way in which the rubbing procedure is distinguished from waxing and polishing. As was pointed out before, polishing and waxing are final steps *only* in the finishing schedule. Rubbing is very seldom a final step.

Materials Used for Rubbing

Most of the materials used for rubbing a finish have already been described in Chapter 2, *Finishing Tools and Supplies*. You will probably find some new ones included in this section. In any event, the various rubbing techniques will include the following tools and materials:

1. Pumice stone (FFF grade),
2. Rottenstone,
3. Steel wool (000),

4. Sandpaper (6/0–9/0),
5. Rubbing oil,
6. Denatured alcohol,
7. Rubbing felt,
8. Naphtha,
9. Clean cloths.

Although sandpaper is listed here, and can be used for rubbing the finish, it is not as satisfactory as other types of abrasives. There is always the tendency to scratch through the finish. Steel wool is much preferred to sandpaper, but never in a grade coarser than 000. The finer the grade of steel wool used, the higher the sheen imparted to the finish.

Rottenstone will always follow the pumice stone in a rubbing schedule. The former is a finer abrasive and will produce a higher sheen.

A rubbing oil is the lubricant used with pumice stone or rotten-stone. Raw linseed oil, paraffin oil, and mineral oil can all be used as rubbing oils. Water is frequently substituted for rubbing oils as a lubricant.

Rubbing is done with rubbing felt cut and folded to form a pad. Fold the felt so that it is at least ½ inch thick. Some finishers feel they get better results by gluing the felt pad to a wood block. Another method is to rub the surface with the palm of the hand.

Naphtha is excellent for cleaning away the excess rubbing oil (or water) and abrasive residue. You should have clean cloths on hand to wipe this off the surface. If you are rubbing in between coats, you must make absolutely certain that you have cleaned all particles (abrasive powder, etc.) left by the rubbing operation. If you do not do this thoroughly, these particles will become trapped by subsequent coats of finishing materials. Naphtha is highly flammable. Use only in ventilated areas away from flames or sparks. Wear splash goggles and protective clothing. See Chapter 20, *Safety*.

Rubbing Fundamentals

Rub in the direction of the grain as much as possible. This is especially true when using a block of wood to back up the rubbing pad. Remember that abrasives are being used and will tend to scratch the grain if rubbed across it. A toothbrush is recommended for rubbing carvings, moldings, and other portions of the surface too difficult to reach with a pad. A clean cloth dampened with a lubricant and sprinkled with a powdered abrasive is very useful for polishing turnings.

Rub the surface with straight, smooth movements. Apply a uniform pressure against the rubbing pad. In other words, do not bear down at the beginning or middle of your stroke and then let up at the end. Be careful not to skip spots or create highlights by improper rubbing.

Rubbing Techniques

This chapter contains descriptions of eight different rubbing techniques used in the finishing schedule. These eight techniques are:

1. Rubbing with pumice stone and water,
2. Rubbing with pumice stone and oil,
3. Rubbing with rottenstone and water,
4. Rubbing with rottenstone and oil,
5. Rubbing with sandpaper and water,
6. Rubbing with sandpaper and oil,
7. Rubbing with steel wool,
8. Spiriting off with alcohol.

Rubbing with Pumice Stone and Water

Rubbing a finish with pumice stone and water will generally result in a smooth, dull appearance. Some finishers prefer to use an FF grade of pumice stone first, and then proceed to the finer FFF grade during the final stages. Others use the FFF grade throughout the rubbing procedure. It is a matter of personal choice.

Carvings, moldings, borders, and other areas of difficult access should be rubbed first. A toothbrush is generally very helpful for these sections. The larger flat surfaces should be rubbed with a rubbing pad, and in such a way that all movements are in the direction of the grain.

It is sometimes a good idea to sift the pumice stone through a piece of cheesecloth before using it. This will eliminate any unusually large pieces of the powdered abrasive that might scratch the finish during the rubbing procedure.

The pumice stone is applied to the surface either by dipping a water- (or oil-) dampened rubbing pad into the powdered abrasive, or by sprinkling the pumice stone across the finish as you rub.

All of the powdered abrasive must be removed from the surface once the rubbing procedure has been completed. Otherwise, the particles will mix with the next layer of finishing materials (e.g., another coat of varnish) or the wax.

Rubbing with Pumice Stone and Oil

Rubbing a varnished surface with pumice stone and oil will produce a satin finish. The luster will be noticeably higher than that resulting from a pumice-stone-and-water rubbing. Either an FF or FFF grade of pumice stone is used. A light mineral oil is recommended for the rubbing lubricant.

Rubbing with Rottenstone and Water

If the finish has already been rubbed with pumice stone and water, it can be followed with a rubbing of rottenstone and water. You should always use the same type of lubricant throughout the rubbing schedule. Rubbing the surface with rottenstone will eliminate any scratches left by the pumice stone rubbing, and will give a somewhat higher polish.

Rub the finish with the rottenstone and water not less than 24 hours after the previous rubbing (pumice stone and water) was completed. The rottenstone can be applied in the same manner as described for pumice stone. As with pumice stone, the rubbing must be done in the direction of the grain with smooth, straight, even strokes. All abrasive particles must be cleaned from the surface at the end of the rubbing operation. Any that remain will interfere with subsequent finishing materials.

Rubbing with Rottenstone and Oil

Rubbing with rottenstone and oil should follow a rubbing with pumice stone and oil. Because oil rather than water is used as the lubricant, a much longer drying period is required between the completion of the pumice stone and oil procedure and the beginning of the one using rottenstone and oil—a drying period of five to seven days is suggested.

Rubbing with Sandpaper and Water

Rubbing the finish with sandpaper and water will produce a dull surface that is somewhat smoother than the one produced by rubbing with pumice stone. However, pumice stone is usually preferred to sandpaper during the preliminary stages in the rubbing schedule, because the latter shows a greater tendency to scratch the surface. Only a very fine (7/0 or finer) waterproof sandpaper should be used. Always rub with light, even, straight strokes in the direction of the grain.

Rubbing with Sandpaper and Oil

Rubbing the finish with sandpaper and oil is not much different from the sandpaper and water technique except that there is less dust when oil is used as the lubricant. The color of the wood also tends to darken.

Rubbing with Steel Wool

Steel wool can be used to rub the finish after it has been rubbed with sandpaper and water (or oil). The effect is much the same as switching to rottenstone after having rubbed the surface with pumice stone and a lubricant. Rubbing with steel wool results in a soft, satin sheen. *Always* rub with the grain, never across it. After the surface has been thoroughly cleaned of all steel wool residue and other possible contaminants, it may be waxed.

The Spiriting-off Technique

Spiriting-off is a finishing technique used to create a brilliant, high luster on a varnish finish *after* it has been rubbed. The materials required for this technique include:

1. Denatured alcohol,
2. A mineral oil-base polish (no silicones),
3. Several clean, lint-free cloths.

The spiriting-off technique begins after the varnish finish has been polished with one of the several rubbing techniques described in this chapter. The steps involved are as follows:

1. Clean the surface thoroughly so that any traces of the powdered abrasive are removed.
2. Wipe the surface with a cleanser-polish. Remove any excess polish.
3. *Dampen* (do not soak) a cloth in denatured alcohol and wipe it lightly with circular movements across the surface. Do *not* allow it to come to rest on the finish, or the alcohol may damage the finish. The alcohol will remove polishing oil and cause the surface to gleam with a brilliant, high luster. Alcohol is highly flammable. Use only in ventilated areas away from flame or sparks. Wear splash goggles and protective clothing. Do not breath vapors. See Chapter 20, *Safety*.

Waxes versus Polishes

This section is not intended to convert you to using either a wax or a polish. Each has certain advantages and disadvantages about which you should be aware. These will be described here very generally; there are so many waxing and polishing products on the market, it is hardly possible to be more specific.

A wax will produce a thicker, more permanent coat than a polish. As a result, it provides better protection for furniture subject to heavy use. It exhibits a particularly strong resistance to alcohol and water. Finally, it has a tendency not to hold dust particles, which reduces the amount of dusting that has to be done.

Furniture polishes are very easy to apply, particularly those sold in aerosol spray cans. This is generally what is portrayed in those television commercials when furniture is polished effortlessly and is made to look as good as any wax can. And it *will* look as good—for a while. Unfortunately, dust, fingerprints, and smudges become very noticeable on any polished surface. Moreover, these surfaces require frequent dusting. This should not necessarily be regarded as a disadvantage, because no wood surface should be dry dusted. Many of the better furniture polishes are formulated to be cleaner-polishes.

A principal advantage of using a furniture polish is that it reduces the chances of certain finishing problems occurring. By sealing in the finish oils, a polish will often prevent cracking, crumbling, crazing, and related problems.

A final note: The addition of lemon to a furniture polish (or, for that matter, any other pleasing fragrance) will do absolutely *nothing* to improve its polishing characteristics. This is primarily an advertising gimmick.

Materials Used for Waxing and Polishing

Waxes and polishes are available as pastes, liquids, or sprays, and are sold under a wide variety of trade names. All manufacturers make highly confident claims about the effectiveness of their products. I would accept their claims with certain reservations. No waxing or polishing product is perfect. Be sure to read carefully the manufacturer's listing of ingredients contained in his product. A wax containing relatively high percentages of carnauba wax, for example, would indicate a fairly high-quality paste wax. High concentrations of paraffin, on the other hand, would indicate the opposite. Many finishers also avoid using waxes or polishes containing silicones, because they are sometimes difficult to remove when the finish is being stripped.

Waxes and polishes are generally regarded as two distinct categories of finishing materials, each having slightly different functions. Both waxes and polishes are designed to give the wood a special luster or glow, and are used to enhance the finish. However, another function of a furniture polish is to *clean* the surface. As you rub the polish onto the surface, it picks up dust and other contaminants without permitting them to grind into the finish as dry dusting will do. When the excess polish is wiped from the surface, the dust and other contaminants are removed with it, leaving behind a thin film or polish. This film will temporarily give the finish a very pleasing appearance, but it must be renewed frequently. It cannot give the finish the durable protective coat that a wax can provide. This is the distinction between waxes and polishes.

Each wax that you purchase contains one or more waxes mixed together to form the base, a thinner, and such other minor ingredients (e.g., coloring matter) as the manufacturer sees fit to add. The waxes used to form the base are usually one or more of the following:

1. Carnauba wax,
2. Candelilla wax,
3. Beeswax,
4. Paraffin wax.

These are listed in descending order of hardness. Silicones, though often considered polishes, are waxes by type and will be discussed at the end of this section.

Carnauba wax is the hardest paste wax used for polishing furniture finishes. It is also regarded by the experts as the best polishing wax.

An excellent polishing wax can be produced by shredding and mixing one part carnauba wax with one part beeswax or caresin wax (a beeswax substitute) and thinning the mixture to a good working consistency with pure turpentine.

Another formula for a carnauba base polishing wax is one part carnauba wax, one part paraffin, and five parts pure turpentine. The two waxes are shredded and mixed together, and then thinned to the proper working consistency by adding the turpentine. In this formula (as well as the previously described one), mineral spirits can be substituted for the turpentine as a thinner.

Candelilla wax is a hard paste wax derived from a plant grown in Mexico. It is not as hard as carnauba wax, having a melting point about 30°F lower than the latter. Its color ranges from yellow to brown. Candelilla wax is used in the same way as a carnauba wax.

Beeswax is not as hard as carnauba or candelilla wax, but it still possesses excellent polishing characteristics. It is available in either a yellow or a white type, and is always thinned 50% or more with paraffin, pure turpentine, or other suitable means. Beeswax added to a paste rubbing wax or other type will tend to reduce the gloss and give a dull finish.

Paraffin wax is a white, translucent substance generally obtained from distillates of petroleum (coal and shale oil have been used). Paraffin wax is the basis for most commercial waxes used today. It is far softer than the other waxes mentioned so far. The more paraffin added to a paste wax, the greater will be the ease with which it can be worked. On the other hand, the wax will not be as hard or hold up as well as it would have had it not been diluted by the addition of paraffin.

Although manufacturers often refer to *silicones* as "polishes" in their advertising, these types of finishing materials are actually more closely related to waxes. These silicone waxes are available in 16-ounce spray cans, and are most effectively used as dusting sprays. Some finishers do not like to use them, because they can cause refinishing defects.

Trying to list all the different formulas for furniture polishes would require a separate book. A majority of them appear to be oil-base polishes. That is to say, some sort of oil acts as their principal or base ingredient. The two oils used in furniture polishes are linseed oil and mineral oil. The former is restricted to its use in linseed oil polish. The latter, mineral oil, provides the major ingredient for almost every other kind of oil-base furniture polish. For example, lemon oil polish, cream or white polish, colored polish, and all so-called oil-base polishes use mineral oil as their basic ingredient. The cream or white polishes basically consist of mineral oil emulsified in water. It is a good polish, generally producing a very acceptable sheen without that "wet" appearance. You can obtain similar results with the colored polishes that are produced by mixing dark brown aniline dye powder with mineral oil. The lemon oil polishes are simply mineral oils to which a lemon fragrance has been added.

Waxing a Finish

A new finish should be thoroughly dusted before applying a wax. Old finishes should be cleaned and any traces of old furniture wax or polish removed.

Use a section of heavy linen to make a wax rubbing pad. The linen can be folded to a suitable size and used both to apply the wax and polish the finish. Apply the wax with circular movements, so that the rubbing movement goes both with and across the grain.

CHAPTER 17

Antiquing (Glazing) and Related Techniques

Antiquing and *glazing* are terms used interchangeably to describe a furniture-finishing process that generally involves the application and removal of a glaze (a pigmented stain or thin wash). The purpose of this process is to create highlighting, shading, or other effects on the finish in order to suggest an aged appearance. This is a total process. That is, the entire surface of the piece of furniture is covered with the glaze.

Glazing is used to produce such well-known finishes as Pickled Finish, Bone White Finish, and the various Old World Finishes (e.g., French Provincial). This chapter covers the various steps in the basic finishing schedule for antiquing (glazing).

Tools and Materials

The contents of a typical antiquing kit, along with various tools needed, are shown in Fig. 17–1. You will notice that the tools needed include a screwdriver and a pair of pliers for removing the hardware from the piece of furniture. The tack rag serves the same purpose as the lint-free cloth mentioned in the finishing schedule for antiquing. All of these tools and finishing materials can be purchased separately, and most of them are available at local paint and hardware stores.

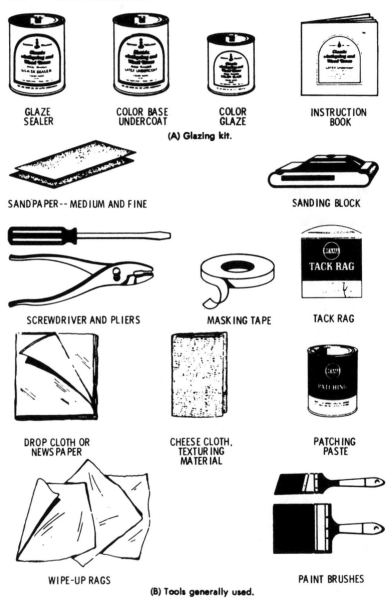

GLAZE
SEALER

COLOR BASE
UNDERCOAT

COLOR
GLAZE

INSTRUCTION
BOOK

(A) Glazing kit.

SANDPAPER-- MEDIUM AND FINE

SANDING BLOCK

SCREWDRIVER AND PLIERS

MASKING TAPE

TACK RAG

DROP CLOTH OR
NEWSPAPER

CHEESE CLOTH,
TEXTURING
MATERIAL

PATCHING
PASTE

WIPE-UP RAGS

(B) Tools generally used.

PAINT BRUSHES

Fig. 17-1. Typical antiquing kit. *(Courtesy Sherwin-Williams Co.)*

The Antiquing (Glazing) Procedure

Antiquing (glazing) is probably one of the easiest finishing techniques for the beginner to use, because it does not require the extensive wood preparation steps found in the other finishes. Most antiquing kits contain a base coat finishing material that can be applied over varnish, paint, and other surfaces. The base coat functions as a sealer, preventing the older finish from bleeding through into the glaze coat.

Most antiquing procedures will consist of the following basic steps:

1. Prepare the surface by sanding it lightly with a very fine grade of sandpaper. The purpose is to create a smooth, uniform base for the finishing materials used in the antiquing process. All surface imperfections such as dents, gouges, and scratches should be patched with a suitable wood filler, and sanded smooth. (Fig. 17–2).
2. Remove all dust left by the sanding operation with a clean, lint-free cloth.

Fig. 17-2. Removing hardware and repairing dents and scratches with wood filler. *(Courtesy Sherwin-Williams Co.)*

3. Brush on a base coat (undercoat) and allow it sufficient time to dry thoroughly (Fig. 17–3).
4. When the base coat has dried, brush a coat of glaze onto the surface (Fig. 17–4).
5. While the glaze is still wet, wipe it off with a folded piece of cheesecloth before it has time to dry. The effect you create will depend on a number of factors, including the colors you use and your wiping procedure (Fig. 17–5).
6. A clear varnish top coat or a wax can be applied over the antiquing glaze for additional protection; however, this is optional (Fig. 17–6).

Step 1 in the above described finishing schedule for antiquing should also include the removal and storage of all furniture hardware. Trying to mask these off so that the finishing materials can be applied around them is never completely successful. Some of the liquid always seems to get onto the metal.

Not only must the surface be sanded smooth, but all old wax, polish, dirt, grease, and other contaminants must be cleaned from

Fig. 17–3. Applying the colored undercoat for the antique glaze.
(Courtesy Sherwin-Williams Co.)

Fig. 17-4. Applying the glaze. *(Courtesy Sherwin-Williams Co.)*

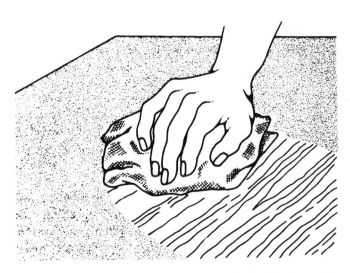

Fig. 17-5. Wiping the glaze until the desired effect is achieved. *(Courtesy Sherwin-Williams Co.)*

Fig. 17–6. Applying a clear finish, or sealer, over the antique glaze. *(Courtesy Sherwin-Williams Co.)*

the surface. If this is not done, the finishing material used in the antiquing process will not adhere properly. Lifting of the finish will most probably result. Do not use a cleaning preparation that will dissolve the old finish, or you will have to completely remove it. (See the appropriate sections in Chapter 7, *Repairing and Restoring.*) If the old finish is subject to severe lifting, and there are other indications that it is no longer adhering properly to the surface, it will have to be removed.

Top coats are generally not required over an antique finish, although it is a good idea if the surface is expected to receive more than the average amount of wear. A satin-sheen varnish or a wax will provide adequate protection under most conditions. Allow the glaze at least four days to dry before applying the topcoat.

Antiquing should never be done when the weather is excessively humid. Low temperatures (especially those below 50°F) will also have a harmful effect on the finish. Ideal conditions exist when the temperature ranges from 65° to 75°F, and the humidity is relatively low.

Removing the glaze from the surface can be done in a number of different ways, each with its own interesting effect. The two principal means of removing the glaze are a pad of cheesecloth and a dry brush. The cheesecloth pad is used for wiping the larger (and generally flat) surface areas. A brush is used for carvings, trim, and other difficult-to-reach sections of the surface.

Wiping is done in long, straight strokes, always in the same direction. The pad of cheesecloth should be occasionally refolded to expose a clean, unsaturated surface. The brush is inserted into carvings and other recessed areas and dragged out, removing portions of the glaze. Clean the brush frequently with a suitable solvent, or you will find that you are simply transferring glaze from one spot to another.

Never allow the glaze to dry completely before you start to wipe it; you cannot do anything with it once it is dry. The sooner you wipe it, the lighter the effect will be. Wipe from the center of an area out toward its edges, and try to create gradual shadings. Abrupt changes from light to dark indicate poor technique.

Apply the glaze over transfers (decalcomania), striping, and other decorating techniques. Do not attempt to add them to the glaze. If varnish or lacquer is used as a protective top coat, dull rub it or apply a polish. The former approach results in a more "antique" effect.

Antiquing with Gold

The white and gold finishes of much French Provincial furniture can be imitated by antiquing the surface with a gold enamel applied over a white enamel base coat. Other interesting effects can be obtained by using black, red, brown, or dark green as the base coat.

Apply the white enamel base coat (an eggshell or gloss enamel is recommended) in the same manner as described earlier in this chapter (see THE ANTIQUING PROCEDURE. Additional information on enameling is found in Chapter 14). Give the enamel sufficient time to dry thoroughly before proceeding any further. If the surface is glossy, sand it lightly with a very fine grade of sandpaper and remove the dust with a tack rag or clean cloth. Do not sand the base coat until you are certain it is dry.

The gold enamel can be applied by:

1. Dry brushing,
2. Spattering,
3. Brushing and wiping.

In the dry-brushing method, the brush is dipped into the enamel and wiped almost dry before it is applied. The tip of the brush is then gently dragged nearly parallel to the surface and manipulated with an irregular, flicking movement, Never apply any great pressure, or you will deposit concentrations of gold enamel. If properly applied, you will obtain an interesting streaked effect.

The base coat can also be spattered with gold by striking or flicking a brush dipped in enamel with a table knife or wood stick (a piece of wood dowel will do nicely). A toothbrush or small varnish brush can be used, but the latter should be cut shorter to make the bristles stiffer. You can also flick the brush with your finger, if you do not mind messy fingers. The gold spatters will form irregular patterns on the surface, and this is exactly the effect you are seeking with this technique.

Gold enamel dries too quickly for the brushing and wiping method of application, so a substitute must be used. Try mixing gold bronzing powder with a clear antiquing liquid. The latter can be purchased from most paint supply stores that carry antiquing kits and other finishing materials. You will probably have to experiment a bit until you succeed in obtaining a suitable mixture (see Chapter 18, *Gilding and Bronzing*, for suggestions). Brush the gold mixture onto the surface and wipe it off with a clean piece of cheesecloth.

If you want to apply a clear top coat of varnish for additional protection, you must first seal the enamel with a washcoat of white shellac. Make certain that the washcoat has completely dried before applying the varnish.

Shading

The purpose of *shading* is to darken the edges of certain areas of the furniture. The contrast with the lighter areas gives the effect of the worn, faded surface one finds on old furniture. It differs from highlighting in that it generally involves the addition of a darker color tone to a lighter one, or applying the glaze more thickly on some areas than on others. Highlighting is essentially the opposite procedure, except that in this case the color is lightened by wiping rather than by the addition of a lighter color (see HIGH-LIGHTING in this chapter). Some finishers also refer to this procedure (i.e., wiping the glaze to lighten the color) as shading, but they are technically incorrect. The glaze is applied (most commonly by spraying) thinly in some spots, more thickly in others when shading. It is wiped away if you are highlighting the finish.

Shading can be done so that the lighter and darker color shades blend (i.e., are "feathered") into one another, or so that a somewhat more abrupt and contrasting transition occurs. The choice is yours.

Highlighting

Highlighting (Fig. 17–7) creates an aged, worn appearance by lightening or darkening portions of the surface so that other areas are accentuated (highlighted). The raised portions of carvings, moldings, or borders are most commonly highlighted by rubbing their surfaces lightly with a fine grade of sandpaper or steel wool. You must be careful not to remove too much of the finish, or you may scratch through to the wood. Should this happen, you will have to strip the surface and refinish it.

A good highlighting technique will produce what closely resembles the worn spots and other signs of wear that would take years for the wood to acquire naturally. Therefore, you must rub the surface in those areas that would have received wear under normal conditions. A haphazard removal of the finish must be avoided. Sometimes the corners or edges of a piece of furniture will be sanded with coarse sandpaper to give the appearance of wear. When the finish is applied, these artificially "worn" areas are highlighted.

Highlighting can also be accomplished chemically by darkening the recessed areas of carvings and moldings, or the edge of a border. A dark stain compatible with the previously applied finishing materials can be applied to the areas you want darkened. Wipe the excess off before it dries (see GLAZING STAINS in this chapter).

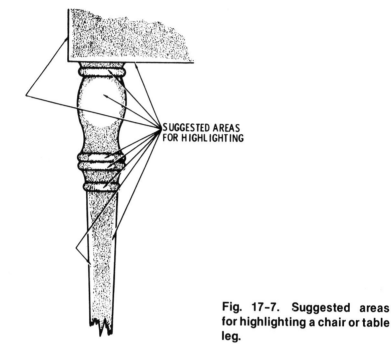

SUGGESTED AREAS
FOR HIGHLIGHTING

Fig. 17-7. Suggested areas for highlighting a chair or table leg.

Spattering

Spattering (Fig. 17–8) is the technique of flicking specks of ink or flat black paint against a glazed surface. Glaze of a different or darker color from the surface can also be used. A brush with the bristles cut off short or a toothbrush is barely dipped into the liquid to be spattered and flicked against the surface by moving a finger, knife blade, or wood dowel across the bristles. The closer the brush is to the surface, the larger the spots will be. A wax or clear varnish can be applied as a protective top coat.

Marbleizing

Materials and Methods

Marbleizing is a painted treatment that imitates the surface of polished marble. There are two approaches to creating the effect:

Fig. 17-8. Spattering a glazed surface with specks of flat black paint.

subtractive and additive. Both begin with a base coat that is allowed to dry. Then the characteristic marble veins are created by brushing, typically with a turkey or goose feather. Other "tools" can be used, such as a folded piece of heavy paper with a torn edge, or old scruffy oil painting brushes. Finally a protective clear finish is applied.

With the subtractive method, a coat of paint is applied and then areas are removed or disturbed in distinctive patterns to expose the contrasting color base beneath. This method is easier to do with solventborne (oil-base) paints, although waterborne (latex) paint can also be used. Solventborne paint used with the subtractive method can result in a more realistic marble appearance than the additive method.

With the additive method veins are painted on the base coat, allowed to dry, and covered with a transparent glaze. Then two or three more layers of veining and glazing are added, creating an appearance of translucent depth within the surface. This method is easier with waterborne (latex) paints because this quick drying paint allows the repeated layers to be done within a reasonable time.

Beginners will find solventborne paints easier to work with at first. The longer drying time of these paints gives you time to work. If you do not get the effect you want, you can just wipe the whole layer off and start over. Practice and experiment on a waste board to try out the whole procedure you intend to use before actually beginning on your furniture.

Additive Method Procedure

1. Prepare the surface according to Chapter 9.
2. Apply a base coat and allow it to dry.
3. Mask off the area of treatment with tape. Use auto-body masking tape which is less sticky than regular masking tape. Press the tape on very lightly. This will keep it from pulling off finish paint beneath when it is removed. Burnish the tape down only at the very edge that will be painted over, to keep the paint from seeping underneath.
4. Veining. To apply the first layer of veins, put a small amount of dark colored paint in a flat dish or can lid. Dip the feather in the paint and apply it to the surface in a characteristic vein-like pattern (Fig. 17–9). Allow the paint to dry.
5. Glazing. To glaze the surface, thin down a small amount of light-colored paint and put it in a flat plate or can lid. Wad up a piece of terry cloth toweling and dip in the paint. Pounce the toweling on a waste board to distribute the paint evenly across the toweling and to test the amount of paint that is applied. You want only a thin transparent coating, so keep pouncing on the waste board until it is thin enough. Then pounce the paint over the veined surface (Fig. 17–10). Go over the whole surface, varying the coverage according to the effect you want. Allow the glazing to dry.

Fig. 17–9. Veining. A feather is used to apply paint imitating marble veins. *(Courtesy Ralff & Sons)*

6. Repeat steps 4 (Veining) and 5 (Glazing) up to three times to get the effect you want (Fig. 17–11). Each additional step increases the effect of depth into the surface.

7. Remove the masking tape as soon as the last coat is dry. Tape left in place longer than necessary may not come off cleanly.

8. Apply a clear protective finish over all. A fast drying alkyd varnish (such as Benwood One Hour Clear Finish) will work over waterborne or solventborne paint. Test first and check with the paint manufacturer to assure compatibility.

Fig. 17–10. Glazing. A transparent coating of paint is applied with a piece of cloth. *(Courtesy Ralff & Sons)*

Veining, Design and General Appearance

Irregular patterns look most natural. Use a more dramatic bold pattern on the first veining so that it shows through subsequent glazings. Make the second veining coat different in character, such as thin and dark (Fig. 17–11).

Study real marble to learn the effect you want to imitate. Tile shops often have samples you can buy for future reference. Fancy

Fig. 17-11. Repeat veining. Here thin dark veins are applied in contrast to the wide, lighter veins applied previously. *(Courtesy Ralff & Sons)*

public buildings often have a variety of marbles as a decorative wall and floor finish. Notice how the marble is divided into smaller sheets that are applied to the walls and floors. Use these same patterns and sizes to divide up the surfaces you want to decorate on your furniture. Veins in real marble are created when the marble cracked and liquid stone flowed into the crack and then hardened. Give your veins this same fractured appearance. Study real marble to determine which colors to use when imitating them. Once you learn to imitate real marble, be bold. You can use other colors that would never appear in nature, but give the striking effect that you want.

Distressing

Distressing refers to the marking of furniture in such a way as to create an antique effect. Marking can be done in any one of the three following ways:

1. Physically scratching, gouging, or denting the wood,
2. Placing random marks on the filler, sealer, or between *finishing* coats with a black or dark brown crayon,
3. Spattering the filler, sealer, or intermediate finishing coats with a dark color.

Wood Graining

Wood graining refers to the creating of simulated grain patterns in a glaze applied over the surface. The purpose of graining is to make a wood with an uninteresting grain look more attractive. This technique is designed to achieve a special decorative effect, not to create an exact reproduction of a wood grain.

Complete wood-graining kits are available through local and mail-order suppliers of wood finishing materials, but the same tools and materials can be found in many home workshops. You will need two brushes to apply the base coat and glaze, a flat base coat, enough glaze for two coats, a tool device for graining, and a clear top coat. A brush, whisk broom, or steel comb can be used in place of the tools found in the commercial kits.

The steps in the wood graining procedure are as follows:

1. Prepare the surface by sanding until it is completely smooth.
2. Remove the dust left by the sanding operation with a tack rag or a clean, lint-free cloth.
3. Apply a base coat of flat paint or enamel, and allow it sufficient time to thoroughly dry.

4. Sand the surface lightly with a very fine grade of sandpaper.
5. Clean off all the dust left by the sanding operation.
6. Quickly brush a coat of glaze over the entire surface.
7. Before the glaze has a chance to dry, draw the graining tool across the surface from one end to the other in parallel, overlapping rows. The simulated grain lines must be continuous and unbroken. The grain lines may slant, weave, or wiggle. They should not be drawn in a straight line across the surface, because this does not reflect the natural effect of real wood grain. Draw the graining tool so that the lines move around knots in the wood.
8. Allow the glaze sufficient time to dry thoroughly.
9. Apply a top coat of clear varnish or wax to protect the wood graining.

The bristles or teeth of a typical wood graining tool are flexible. By putting pressure on the tool, you can give the simulated grain lines the same irregular spacing as the natural ones.

Varnish can be used as both the base coat and the glaze (see Steps 3 and 6) instead of the ones described above. The varnish base coat should be a lighter color or shade than the glaze. If you are more interested in a decorative effect that imitating wood grain, try experimenting with colors not natural to wood, such as gold, silver, bronze, or bright red.

Glazing Stains

Highlighting a finish is often done with a *glazing stain.* These are secondary or additive stains. In other words, they are added to the surface for decorative purposes, and not for such primary functions as filling, sealing, or staining (see SHADING STAINS).

Glazing stains may be applied by either brushing or spraying, and generally require about 24 hours to dry. Faster-drying glazing stains are available, but these are usually not of the same quality as the slower-drying oil-base types.

A cloth, camel's hair brush, or other suitable blending device can be used to remove the glazing stain before it dries. The brush is recommended for the slower-drying glazing stains.

Shading Stains

Shading stains are used principally to equalize the color of previously stained furniture. These are primary stains that have a definite and important function in finishing schedules that require their use. However, shading stains can also be used to create a highlighted effect, which gives them a secondary or decorative function as well.

The composition of a shading stain is equivalent to that of a thinned colored lacquer. As a result, it dries very rapidly and sets fast. It should be applied by spraying.

Shading stains are usually applied directly over pigment stain, non-grain-raising stain, or lacquer sealer. Applying these stains over the sealer is the method most commonly used, especially in the furniture industry. Its one major disadvantage is that chipping or other forms of impact may cause part of the finish to be removed, carrying with it some of the color. This can be avoided by applying the shading stain directly over the base stain rather than the sealer.

CHAPTER 18

Gilding and Bronzing

Gilding and *bronzing* are special decorating techniques involving the application of metal in extremely thin sheets or powder to the finish. Gilding is the older of the two techniques, dating back to as early as the Egyptian pharaohs. The use of bronzing powders is a comparatively recent development and has largely replaced gilding. The former is easier to apply, but lacks the durability of gilding.

Tools and Materials

Many of the tools and materials used in gilding and bronzing have already been described in other chapters. However, a few others are used specifically for these two decorating techniques. A brief description of their nature and use will be covered in this section.

A home workshop completely equipped to do any type of gilding or bronzing should have the following tools and supplies:

1. Sharp scissors or a knife for cutting the metal leaf.
2. Metal leaf or bronzing powder in the desired color.

3. Agate burnisher or velvet pad for burnishing (polishing) the gilded surface.
4. A sealer (shellac washcoat or a sanding sealer) to cover a wood surface.
5. Gold size to serve as a base for the metal leaf (a clear coat of varnish will be adequate).
6. Red or black acrylic paint to serve as a contrast for the gilding.
7. A camel's hair brush to smooth wrinkles out of the metal leaf.
8. Suitable brushes for applying the various finishing materials (sealer, size, etc.). (See Chapter 2, *Finishing Tools and Supplies.*)
9. A gilder's brush (or tip) for picking up the gold leaf. A thin piece of cardboard also works well.

Gilding

Gilding is the technique of applying leaf metals (extremely thin sheets of metal) to the finish for a special decorative effect (Fig. 18–1). Gold leaf or metal leaf made to imitate gold (particu-

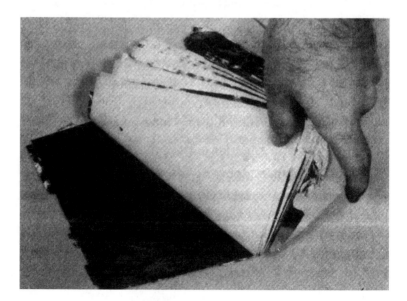

Fig. 18–1. Examples of metal leaf.

larly in contrast with a red or black finish) was, for a long time, a popular favorite, but others, such as silver leaf and aluminum leaf, were also used. Because of the popularity of gold as a color, gilding is frequently referred to as *gold leafing*.

Gilding can be applied to varnish, lacquer, paint, or enamel finishes. It can also be applied *under* varnish. Gilding can be used as the final step in the finishing schedule, or it can be used to decorate previously finished furniture. In the latter case, all wax and polish must be removed from the surface before the gilding procedure begins. Otherwise, the metal leaf will not adhere well to the surface.

Gold leaf is sold in books of 25 leaves. Each leaf is tissue-thin, and about four inches square. Sheets of tissue paper are placed between each gold leaf to provide easier handling. Gold leaf is also sold in ribbons or rolls for use as borders.

Gilding (Gold Leafing) Procedure

Gilding (gold leafing) may be applied to either plaster of paris (usually the "carved wood" border on many ornate picture frames), a bare wood surface, or a finish (e.g., paint, enamel, varnish, or lacquer).

As already mentioned, gold leafing is an older decorating technique than bronzing and dates back at least to the Ancient Egyptian period. It is far more durable than bronzing (we still have excellent examples of this technique taken from Egyptian tombs), but it takes much longer to apply. Because of this and a mistaken belief that it requires great skill, most people avoid gold leafing and choose bronzing.

Gilding may be applied to either plaster of paris or a wood surface. In either case, the surface will have to be properly prepared so that it will serve as a suitable base for the finishing materials and gold leaf. The procedure for preparing plaster and wood surfaces for gilding is as follows (Fig. 18–2):

1. A wood surface should be prepared according to the instructions suggested in Chapter 9. Plaster of paris moldings should be inspected for damage and repaired before proceeding any further (see REPAIRING MOLDINGS in this chapter).

STEP 1 PREPARE THE WOOD SURFACE
SO THAT IT IS SMOOTH AND EVEN.

STEP 2 BRUSH ON A WASHCOAT SEALER
(LIGHTLY SAND AND REMOVE
DUST IN STEP 3 AND 4).

STEP 5 BRUSH ON A COAT OF RED
ACRYLIC PAINT.

STEP 6 BRUSH ON A COAT OF THIN
VARNISH (= GOLD SIZE).

STEPS 7–12 APPLY GOLD LEAF

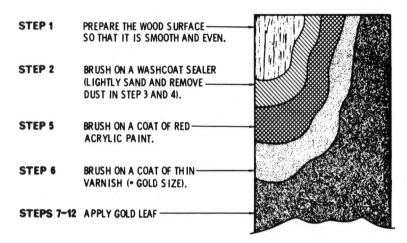

Fig. 18-2. The gold leafing procedure.

2. Seal the wood surface with a washcoat of shellac, and allow it
   sufficient time to dry.
3. Lightly sand the undercoat with a very fine sandpaper.
4. Remove all dust left by the sanding operation with a tack rag
   or a clean, lint-free cloth.
5. Apply a coat of red acrylic paint over the shellac washcoat, and
   allow it sufficient time to thoroughly dry.
6. Brush on a thinned coat of varnish. Follow the manufacturer's
   recommendations for thinning or read the appropriate sections
   in Chapter 12. Mineral spirits can be used in a one-to-one
   formula. The surface is now ready for application of the gold
   leaf.
7. Before the varnish dries completely and while it is still tacky,
   apply the gold leaf to the surface. Press the gold leaf down and
   smooth out wrinkles with a soft camel's hair brush or ball of
   cotton.
8. Apply the next gold leaf so that there is a slight overlap (⅛ to
   ¼ inch) with the first one. Smooth the second leaf down so that
   your movements are always in the direction of the first one
   (Fig. 18–3). This eliminates the problem of tearing up the edge
   of a leaf.

1. SLIP A THIN PIECE OF CARDBOARD UNDER THE METAL LEAF AND REMOVE IT FROM THE BOOK.

2. POSITION THE METAL LEAF.

3. SLIP OUT THE CARDBOARD.

SLIGHT OVERLAP

4. PLACE THE NEXT LEAF SO THAT IT SLIGHTLY OVERLAPS THE ONE BEFORE.

Fig. 18-3. Applying the gold (or metal) leaf.

9. Breaks, holes, or tears in the gold leaf can be repaired with a second leaf applied over the damaged area.
10. Let the gilding dry for 24 to 48 hours. You will want to be absolutely certain that the surface is completely dry, or the gold leaf will not adhere properly.
11. After the surface has thoroughly dried, lightly smooth the

gilded areas with a ball of cotton. This will break off all loose
and ragged ends.
12. Polish (burnish) the gilding by rubbing it lightly with an agate
burnisher or a velvet pad. Burnish only the high points of the
moldings.

There are several suitable variations of this finishing schedule
that you might like to consider. For example, a flat enamel (also
red) can be substituted for the acrylic paint in Step 5. A black
enamel or acrylic paint will also give an interesting effect. Some
finishers like to use two or three undercoats of gesso (a mixture of
glue or size, white zinc, and gypsum) over the shellac washcoat.
Gesso was originally developed as a sealer for French and Italian
furniture of the eighteenth and early nineteenth centuries, and was
usually made by mixing glue and plaster or whiting. Gesso can be
purchased in most local paint supply stores. Each gesso coat is
sanded and all the dust removed before the next coat of finishing
materials is applied. The gesso coat, properly sanded, gives an extremely smooth surface for the rest of the finishing materials. An
abbreviated finishing schedule in which gesso undercoats are used
is as follows:

1. Wood preparation,
2. Shellac washcoat,
3. First gesso undercoat,
4. Light sanding,
5. Removal of dust,
6. Second gesso coat,
7. Light sanding,
8. Removal of dust,
9. Continue with Steps 5 through 12 of the basic finishing schedule for gilding.

A sanding sealer can be substituted for the shellac washcoat in
Step 2 of the finishing schedule. This would make a gesso undercoating unnecessary, since a sanding sealer will also produce a
smooth and uniform surface when properly sanded. The consistency of an acrylic paint is such that you could probably do away
with any type of sealing step. Consequently, some finishers try to
reduce the application time by working with an acrylic paint and

no sealer. This would eliminate Steps 2 through 4 of the finishing schedule for gilding.

The varnish added to the surface in Step 6 is referred to as *size* or *gold size*. The size need not be limited to varnish. Shellac, lacquer, glue and water, and others have also been used with varying degrees of success. The important thing to remember is that whatever size is used *must* be chemically compatible with the topcoat, should you decide to apply one. Gold leaf does not need to be protected, but some of the other metals may tarnish slightly. Spraying the surface with a light topcoat of shellac, lacquer, or clear varnish should give adequate protection.

Repairing Moldings

The carvings on gilt picture or mirror frames are often made of plaster of paris. If they are broken, they can be repaired by molding a replacement piece from one of the carvings on a different corner. Liquid latex-base molding compounds can be used to make the mold and are available in most paint and hardware stores.

The procedure for repairing plaster moldings is as follows:

1. Clean the surface of the break so that no dirt, grease, or other contaminants will prevent the glue from sticking properly.
2. Coat the carving you wish to use as a replacement piece with latex. Coat it thickly, with two to three coats. Allow enough time for the latex to completely dry.
3. Remove the latex mold, place it in a supporting box (containing dirt or sand), and adjust it. That is to say, push it into the dirt or sand so that the mold will retain its shape when the plaster of paris is poured into it. Wet plaster can also be used in the box. It should be allowed to set before it is used as a support for the mold.
4. Pour the plaster into the mold and allow it sufficient time to set.
5. Remove the mold and fit the replacement piece to the broken carving. Some trimming may be necessary.
6. Glue the replacement piece in position and fill any cracks with a suitable filler material.

7. Finish the new surface in the same manner as the rest of the surface (see GILDING PROCEDURE or BRONZING PROCEDURE in this chapter).

Bronzing

Bronzing (or *powder gilding*) is the process of covering, or overlaying, a surface with a metal powder. Bronzing powder is available in a much greater variety of colors than gold leaf, which gives it a certain advantage over the latter. However, the bronzing powder does not hold its color as well because it is subject to tarnishing after a period of time.

The bronzing powder may be rolled onto a surface after a coating of bronzing liquid has been applied, or it may be mixed with the bronzing liquid before application and the solution then brushed onto the surface. Both methods give good results. The manufacturer's instructions should suggest an appropriate formula for mixing the bronzing powder and bronzing liquid.

Bronzing powder is made by grinding metal leaf into a powder form. The grinding is done in several grades, ranging from fine to coarse. Bronzing liquids are of several types, depending largely upon the type of top coat that will be used. For example, a lacquer-base bronzing liquid is designed specifically for use with a clear lacquer top coat. If the bronzing liquid is chemically incompatible with the top coat, it will cause it to dissolve and lift.

Bronzing Procedure

The procedure for bronzing is similar to the one described for gilding (gold leafing) in the initial stages of the finishing schedule. As a convenience to the reader and for purposes of review, they will be repeated here.

The procedure for bronzing a surface is as follows (Fig. 18–4):

1. Read the instructions for preparing a wood surface suggested in Chapter 9. If you are dealing with moldings, examine them for damage. Methods for repairing damaged moldings are covered in this chapter (see REPAIRING MOLDINGS).

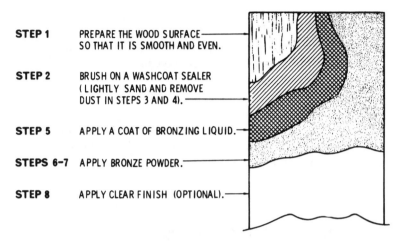

STEP 1 PREPARE THE WOOD SURFACE
SO THAT IT IS SMOOTH AND EVEN.

STEP 2 BRUSH ON A WASHCOAT SEALER
(LIGHTLY SAND AND REMOVE
DUST IN STEPS 3 AND 4).

STEP 5 APPLY A COAT OF BRONZING LIQUID.

STEPS 6-7 APPLY BRONZE POWDER.

STEP 8 APPLY CLEAR FINISH (OPTIONAL).

Fig. 18-4. The bronzing procedure.

2. Seal the surface with a washcoat of shellac, and allow it sufficient time to dry thoroughly. A sanding sealer may be used instead.
3. Sand the sealer coat lightly with a fine grade of sandpaper. Always sand in the direction of the grain.
4. Remove the dust left by the sanding operation with a tack rag or a clean, lint-free cloth.
5. Apply a coat of bronzing liquid (varnish with a japan drier added) to the surface. This serves the same purpose as does gold size in the gold leafing procedure (i.e., provides the sticky surface to which the bronzing powder adheres). A thinned coat of varnish, shellac, or lacquer will serve as an excellent substitute for the bronzing liquid.
6. Before the bronzing liquid or clear finish dries completely and while it is still tacky, apply the bronzing powder to the surface. This is commonly and most effectively done by wrapping a piece of velvet (the pile facing out) around the finger, and using this as the "brush." The finger is dipped into the bronzing powder and gently tapped onto the surface.
7. Allow the bronzing liquid or clear finish sufficient time to dry thoroughly before attempting to remove any excess powder.

This can easily be done by placing a vacuum hose near (but *not* touching) the bronzed surface.

8. The bronzed surface may be coated with a clear finish (varnish, shellac, or lacquer), or left uncoated.

Step 6 can be eliminated by mixing the bronzing powder with the bronzing liquid or clear finish before applying it. This is done on a one-to-one basis, and the resulting mixture is then thinned to brushing consistency with an appropriate solvent, such as denatured alcohol for shellac, turpentine for varnish, and lacquer thinner for lacquer.

Stenciling with Bronzing Powder

Stenciled designs can also be added to finishes with bronzing powders. This technique is somewhat more complicated than stenciling with paint, but should offer no difficulty if the instructions are carefully followed.

The procedure for stenciling with bronzing powder is as follows:

1. Follow Steps 1 through 5 in the finishing schedule for bronzing (see BRONZING PROCEDURE in this chapter).
2. Apply the stencil to the tacky surface. Gently press the stencil down until all the edges of the design are tight against the surface.
3. Apply the bronzing powder with a piece of velvet (see Step 6 in the basic finishing schedule for bronzing).
4. Work inward from the edges of the stencil. The greatest concentration of bronzing powder should be along the outer edges of the stencil design; the smallest, toward the center point. This shading effect creates the appearance of depth.
5. The bronzing powder is applied either with a circular movement or in the natural direction of the design.
6. After having allowed the bronzing liquid 24 hours to dry, remove any excess bronzing powder by first vacuuming (do not let the nozzle touch the surface) and then rinsing with luke-

warm water. Another method is to press the surface lightly with a damp cloth.

7. Remove the stencil, and apply a clear finish compatible with the underlying finishing materials.

Imitation Gold Coatings

Metallic colored enamels and lacquers in various shades of bronze and gold can be brushed or sprayed onto the surface. Both the enamel and lacquer must be stirred constantly to prevent the metallic colored pigments from settling to the bottom of the can. If you are using a spray can, shake the can often to keep the nozzle clean.

The surface must be properly prepared and sealed before applying the enamel or lacquer. The procedures are described in Chapter 13, *Lacquer Finishes*, and Chapter 14, *Paint and Enamel Finishes*.

Special Effects

The finishing schedules for gilding (gold leafing) described earlier in this chapter may be extended by several more steps to give an interesting antiquing effect. The gilding finishing schedule ended with the burnishing (polishing) of the gold leaf (see Step 12). This can be extended as follows:

1. Cover the entire surface (including the gold leaf) with a coat of white enamel. A white water- or oil-base paint may also be used.

2. Before the coat has dried, take a soft, clean, lint-free cloth and wipe the enamel (or paint) from the high points of the gilding.

3. Allow sufficient time for the surface to dry completely.

4. Apply a glaze (raw umber mixed with varnish) to the entire surface. Wipe away portions of the glaze to obtain a shaded effect.

5. After the glaze is completely dry, smooth it with a very fine steel wool.

6. Apply a wax and rub the surface gently with a clean, lint-free cloth.

Gold leaf (as well as silver and other types of metal leaf) may be antiqued or given a marbleizing effect. For more information, read the appropriate sections in Chapter 17, *Antiquing and Related Techniques.*

CHAPTER 19

Decorating Furniture

A variety of techniques for decorating furniture have been developed over the years. Those that will be considered in this chapter are primarily the type that involve adding or attaching a decorating material to the surface of the finish.

This chapter concerns itself with a description of the following furniture decorating techniques:

1. Decoupage,
2. Flocking,
3. Decorating with fabric,
4. Decorating with wallpaper,
5. Stenciling,
6. Using decalcomania transfers,
7. Attaching relief carvings.

All of these furniture-decorating techniques involve the addition of some sort of decorative material to the finish. Some, such as decoupage and flocking, require a slight modification of the finish.

Decoupage

Decoupage is the decorative process of pasting or gluing pictures, fabrics, photographs, or any suitable flat material to a base (in this case, the surface of the furniture) and covering it with a clear finish. It is easy, enjoyable, and satisfying.

Decoupage is a decorating technique that dates from the late seventeenth and early eighteenth centuries. It represents the attempts of European cabinetmakers to imitate the beautiful lacquer furniture being imported at that time from Japan and China. Although originating in Italy, it quickly spread to France, Germany, England, and other European countries, where it resulted in the creation of unique forms and styles. Its great popularity in eighteenth-century France earned it its name, *découpage* (a noun derived from the French verb *découper*, "to cut out, cut up").

The subjects and designs are practically limitless, and are found everywhere in your daily life. For example, magazines provide excellent colored illustrations for decoupage subjects. Other good sources are postcards and greeting cards. Arts and crafts stores also carry prints suitable for decoupage. Original artwork such as pen and ink drawings on parchment paper is also suitable.

Perhaps the only real limitation is the size of the design. The size should be such that it is in scale to the surface area for which it is intended. That is to say, it should not destroy the balance of the overall design.

Decoupage Materials

The materials required for decoupage are as follows:

1. The illustrations or materials (photographs, sketches, pictures, fabrics, etc.) to be done with decoupage.
2. Two pairs of small scissors for trimming the illustration or material. One pair should be straight, the other pair curved.
3. Tweezers for handling small objects.
4. A lint-free cloth or tack rag for removing the dust and residue of any sanding operations from the surface.
5. A supply of very fine to fine sandpaper is recommended for the surface preparation.

6. A sealer. This will be a thinned version of the top coat or a thinned shellac. A shellac sealer can be used under most lacquers and varnishes.
7. Glue or paste for attaching the design to the surface.
8. An undercoating. These are usually paints or enamels and provide a flat, opaque background to the design.
9. A clear top coat.

A word of caution: the sealer, undercoating, and top coat *must all be compatible with one another*. Remember that the various manufacturers use different formulas for the production of their materials. Moreover, certain finishing materials are by their very nature incompatible with others. The results of combining incompatible finishing materials are very discouraging. Sometimes the top coat will never completely dry, retaining a permanent tacky condition. Or the sealer or undercoating may bleed through into the top coat, causing the finish to lift or bulge. The only solution to the problem is the time-consuming one of completely stripping off the finish and starting all over. It would be better to select the finishing materials with care and avoid this problem altogether. If you have any doubts, follow the manufacturer's recommendations.

The Decoupage Procedure

The procedure for applying a decoupage design to a wood surface is as follows (Fig. 19–1):

1. Sand the surface with a fine grade of sandpaper (6/0). The surface must be smooth and clean. Remove all dust resulting from the sanding with a tack rag or other appropriate means.
2. Apply a sealer over the old finish. The type of sealer you use will depend upon the type of top coat already on the surface. If you applied the original top coat and you still have the finishing materials, look at the instructions, where the manufacturer will most likely have suggested a suitable sealer. If you did not apply the original top coat, it would be wise to test a small portion of it (preferably on the bottom or some other area not usually in view). A sealer of thinned shellac will probably be your best bet. A shellac sealer can be applied over paint, wax, and

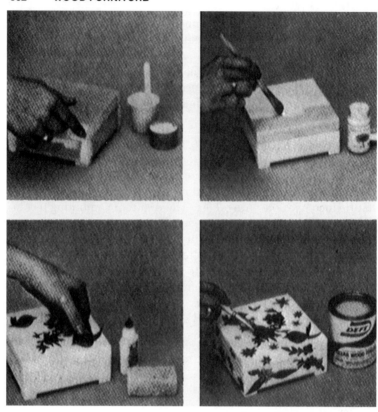

Fig. 19-1. The decoupage procedure. *(Courtesy Deft, Inc.)*

many other types of surfaces without causing the old top coat to lift and combine with the new finishing materials.

3. Allow the sealer coat enough time to dry thoroughly. Sand it lightly with a fine grade of sandpaper (6/0), removing all dust resulting from the sanding. Apply the desired undercoating. Remember that it must be chemically compatible with the sealer and top coat you have selected. Allow the undercoating enough time to dry thoroughly.

4. Choose a suitable design and trim it to the desired size. Careless cutting will detract from the final overall appearance, so a

certain amount of care must be taken with this step. The beginner should not expect to obtain excellent results on the first attempt. Cutting is much more difficult than it looks, and requires some degree of practice.

5. Apply water paste or white glue to the back of the design and to the area it will cover. The paste or glue should be diluted so that lumps will not form between the surface and the design.

6. Press the design onto the surface and smooth out all wrinkles and any excess paste or glue. Wipe away the excess paste or glue with a damp cloth, and allow sufficient time for it to dry completely. Both water paste and white glue clean up very easily.

7. A clear lacquer or varnish or the specially prepared coatings provided with decoupage kits can now be applied to the entire surface area as the top coat. The number of coatings applied will depend upon the desired effect. For example, a varnish top coat could have as many as 15 to 20 coats. Allow each coat sufficient time to dry. After having applied the first 9 or 10 coats, wet sand the surface with a find grade of waterproof sandpaper.

8. Apply the remaining coats, allowing each to dry thoroughly before applying the next one. The maximum number of top coats one should use is really an individual decision. However, the minimum number is governed by the amount of top coat required to cover the design without any noticeable transition between it and the surrounding area. After each coat has dried, test it lightly by running your finger across the surface. When the surface is smooth and even, you have reached the minimum number of top coats.

9. As soon as the final coat has dried, it should be lightly but thoroughly rubbed with a fine grade of sandpaper. This will be a wet rubbing, and is designed to produce a uniformly smooth surface that imparts a soft, satiny glow. A find grade of steel wool or pumice and rottenstone (oil may be used as a lubricant instead of water) may be substituted for the sandpaper.

10. Remove any residue left by Step 9, make certain that the surface is completely dry, and apply several coats of a paste wax. Polish the surface with a soft, lint-free cloth.

Some finishers prefer to sand after each top coat application, rather than once after nine or ten have been applied (see Step 7 above). This will take longer, but it will probably increase the smoothness of the surface. Surface uniformity and smoothness are the primary reasons for sanding. Take particular care not to sand through the top coat and damage the illustration or object used in the decoupage. Always sand lightly, and work slowly. Haste not only makes waste in this case, it also causes disasters.

If there is any printing on the reverse side of an illustration to be used in decoupage, it should be sealed so that it will not bleed through the illustration. A diluted solution of white glue is ideal for this purpose. Make certain that the glue sealer has dried before proceeding to the next step. The same results can be obtained by lightly spraying the surface with clear lacquer. This also reduces the tendency of the paper to wrinkle.

The coloring on the surface of the illustration or object used in the decoupage can also bleed through into the top coat. This too may be prevented by sealing the surface. A clear lacquer spray or a thin washcoat of thinned shellac is recommended for this purpose, subject always, of course, to chemical compatibility with the top coat as well as the coloring composition of the illustration or object being covered.

Flocking

Flocking (Fig. 19–2) is a procedure for creating a soft, feltlike surface by spraying material fibers onto a background coating of enamel, lacquer, varnish, or water-soluble glue. It was originally a novelty finish, but it has become so widely used that it is now regarded as one of the standard finishing procedures. It is employed not only for its decorative effect, but also quite commonly for such utilitarian uses as drawer linings, table tops, and similar items.

All the equipment and supplies necessary for preparing the surface up to (but not including) the application of the flock are the same as those listed for other finishing processes. However, two items unique to flocking are the sprayer and the supply of flock fibers.

The sprayer is a simple, hand-operated insecticide sprayer that can be purchased at any hardware store, garden supply store, or

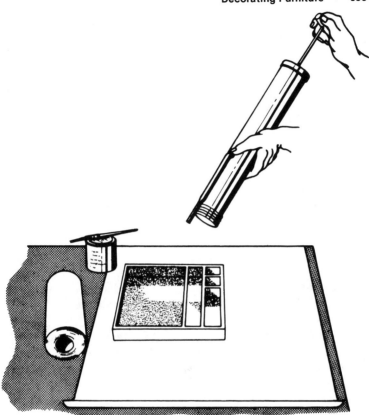

Fig. 19-2. Process of flocking.

nursery. *Never* use a sprayer that has already been used to spray an insecticide. Sprayers are so relatively inexpensive that it is simply not worth the trouble worrying about whether or not you got it clean enough to use in the flocking operation. Special flock-spraying guns, both powered and hand-operated, are available from the manufacturers of flocking supplies, but these do not do the job any better than the simple insecticide sprayer.

Flock is commercially available in many different types of fibers (e.g., wool, cotton, rayon, etc.) and fiber colors. Fiber sizes range up to ¼ inch in length, and are produced so that all fibers in a specific size are of the same length. By selecting a particular type and length of fiber, various materials can be simulated. For example, cotton flock will produce a finish having the appearance of suede, and rayon flock produces the texture and characteristics of velvet or velour.

Flocking is a relatively easy decorative technique for the beginner to learn, and the results can be quite satisfying.

The steps in the flocking procedure are as follows:

1. Prepare the surface according to the instructions given in Chapter 9. As always, the surface must be clean and smooth.
2. Seal the surface. The sealer selected should be compatible with the flock undercoating. This is particularly true if lacquer is selected for the undercoating. The safest procedure is to follow the manufacturer's recommendations.
3. Apply the undercoating. This can be done by brushing or spraying, although the latter method is especially recommended for lacquer. Generally the manufacturer of the flocking material will recommend his own undercoating. If enamels, varnishes, or lacquers are used, they should be thinned before application.
4. Allow the undercoating to dry until it is tacky to the touch.
5. Spray the flocking material onto the tacky surface. Try to cover the surface with a uniform layer of flock. Avoid leaving thin spots.
6. Allow the surface about 24 hours to become completely dry. Blow or shake off the excess flock. Vacuuming is also recommended, so long as the nozzle of the hose or attachment (the brush type) does not touch the surface. Do *not* brush off the excess flock. Brushing could result in removing part of the flock attached to the finish.

Flock designs (flowers, symbols, etc.) can be created by using a stencil. The stencil should be cut from oiled stencil paper. When using the stencil, take particular care not to allow any of the undercoating for the flock to get under the edges of the stencil.

Fabric Finishes

Fabrics are also used for decorative finishes. They are cut to fit panels and other surface areas of furniture. Because of the relative thickness of a piece of fabric, it is best to use it on a portion of the surface bordered by a raised trim. In this respect, pieces of colored burlap provide an interesting decorative effect on a child's dresser or playroom furniture.

Fabric can be attached with white glue or paste. Coat both the back of the fabric and the area to which it is to be attached. Press down on the fabric and smooth from the center out toward the edges until all the excess glue or paste is squeezed out at the edges. Wipe away the excess paste with a damp, clean cloth.

Wallpaper Finishes

Wallpaper can be used in the same way as fabrics to decorate the larger surfaces areas of furniture. Wallpapers come in an almost unlimited variety of designs, colors, and textures, so the finisher is provided with a great deal of latitude in selection.

The same white glues or pastes used to attach fabrics can also be used for wallpaper. The method of attachment is also the same. Coat both the back of the wallpaper and the area of the surface to which it is to be attached with the glue or paste. Position the wallpaper, cover it with a piece of transparent plastic to protect it from fingerprints, and press out the excess glue by smoothing from the center out toward the edges. Wipe away the excess glue or paste with a clean, damp cloth.

Stenciling

Stenciling is a decorating technique in which designs are added to surfaces by means of precut patterns (stencils). Stenciling can be done with paint or with bronzing powders. Both techniques use the same kind of stencil.

A *stencil* is a pattern (design, letters, or numbers) cut into a sheet of stencil paper (although other materials can be used) that is affixed to the surface of a piece of furniture. The cut-out areas of the stencil expose the surface that is to be decorated.

Stenciling with paint requires a special brush. The brush strokes are almost vertical, with an up and down motion. The paint is applied in a direction away from the edges of the stencil and toward the center. This prevents paint from working up under the edges of the stencil and marring the outline of the design.

Instead of using paint, you might want to try applying flock material to the open areas of the stencil (see FLOCKING in this chapter).

The stencil should be stiffened with a thin coat of shellac (even if you are using stencil paper). Particular care must be taken when attaching the stencil to the surface of the furniture. Every edge of the stencil must be tight against the surface, or paint will seep through.

The stencil can be affixed to the surface with tape or by pressing it into the tacky surface of a coat of varnish. Complicated designs have narrow ties between sections that "float" free within major cut-out areas. These can be painted out after the stencil paper is removed from the surface.

Another method of stenciling is to make a separate stencil for each part of a design. A variation is to mark out certain portions of the design in order to add other colors. Both these methods require considerable time and patience. A fine sable brush is used for touching up the stencil.

Decalcomania Transfers (Decals)

Decalcomania transfers (decals) are colorful designs and pictures that can be affixed to a surface for an additional decorative touch.

These decals consist of a specially coated paper that is covered with a clear varnish or lacquer. A design or picture is superimposed over this clear finish. This is done by painting, hand drawing, or printing.

The decal is first soaked in warm water until the varnish or lacquer film (with the design or picture imprinted on its surface) frees itself from the paper backing. It is then placed on the surface to be decorated.

It is becoming increasingly difficult to find good decals in stores. Some of the smaller arts and crafts stores may still carry them, but they are no longer as popular as they once were.

Fig. 19-3. Examples of wood carvings.

Attaching Relief Carvings

Another method of decorating furniture is by attaching relief carvings and applying a finish that matches the rest of the surface (or one that creates a contrast between the carving and the background). Fig. 19–3 illustrates some typical examples of relief carvings. They are available unfinished through mail-order firms specializing in wood-finishing materials, and many local retail outlets.

CHAPTER 20

Safety: Fire, Health, and the Environment

Introduction

Many people think that a product is safe to use if it is sitting on a shelf at the local store. After all, how bad could it be? The last time you finished a piece of furniture nothing bad happened. You cannot even see or smell any vapors, and you will only be exposed for a few hours. It is not like you are using the stuff all day long for forty years.

The plain fact is that it can be really bad, and even worse. Too many people face life-long impairment and even death by disregarding safety when finishing. You do not have to be afraid of finishing products, just use them with knowledge and care.

Three critical safety issues will be considered here. They are fire, personal health, and environmental contamination. After a few introductory ideas about safety, you will learn how these critical issues relate to the purchase, use, disposal, and storage of finish materials.

This chapter does not include everything you need to know about finishing safety; no single chapter, or even a whole book, could. It does provide you with a way of thinking about safety and shows you how to find the information you need to make the decisions and take the actions to assure your safety. In the end you must assume the responsibility for your own safety and the safety of the people around you.

A basic tactic in preventing tragedy is to give some forethought about your specific situation and how it relates to safety issues. To use finish products safely you will need to have specific information and then put that information into practice to gain the experience needed to become truly knowledgeable.

Action, Cause and Effect

Every action you take causes certain effects. If you spread finish remover out on a piece of furniture, the varnish softens. This is the effect you want. If you do this stripping in a small room without ventilation, you may get dizzy and fall unconscious. This is an effect you do not want. It is important to think through all of the possible effects of your actions.

Immediate effects are easy to recognize. If you spill methylene chloride finish remover on your arm it will give you a burning sensation right away.

Long-term effects are more subtle. If you breathe hazardous fumes once for a few hours it may damage a few of your brain cells. "No big deal," you may think. But, if you breathe them every day for ten years, more and more cells are damaged. The cumulative effect can impair vision or other important brain functions.

Individuals vary in their reactions to chemicals—some are more sensitive to others. Given the large number of chemicals and the limited testing done on them, you can't predict how a chemical will affect you personally. It is foolish to take chances on exposure.

Vectors

Vectors are the pathways these chemicals follow during and after use. A typical vector is from the can of varnish, onto the brush, and then onto the table top. That is the vector you want and would expect. But there are unexpected pathways these hazardous materials can take. For example, some varnish dribbles down the side of the can. When you pick up the can some gets on your fingers. When you are done varnishing, you go outside and smoke a cigarette. A little varnish gets on the cigarette. As the cigarette burns the varnish burns too and you inhale the combustion products. Once in your lungs, the combustion products pass easily to your blood stream and are on their way to your liver.

You have to think of where these materials will end up and what the consequences are once they get there. Here are more examples.

- Heavier-than-air vapors from the solvent in the varnish could flow through a drainage pipe in the cellar floor over to the furnace room and ignite. The fire follows the trail of vapors back to your finishing room and starts a major fire.
- When you are sanding between coats of varnish, the dust rises into the air. Direct exposure like this is obvious so you wear a respirator. Then you take off the respirator and walk into the house. You scoop up your three-year-old daughter for a big hug. She will breathe in the varnish dust that accumulated in your hair and clothes during your sanding.

As you can see, the pathways these chemicals follow can be obscure and insidious. Proper safety practices control chemical vectors to prevent or reduce hazards.

Information

Labels and Instructions

The first and most ready source of safety information is labels and instruction sheets that come with the product. Read and follow all instructions and warnings. Manufacturers know their products are hazardous and would not jeopardize sales with negative warnings unless they were truly necessary.

Material Safety Data Sheets

Manufacturers develop and provide an additional source of safety information called Material Safety Data Sheets (MSDS). Each product has a sheet (usually more than one page) that identifies the product and details fire, health, and environmental safety issues that relate to that specific product.

When you order or buy finishing products ask for the MSDS. If your supplier does not have MSDS, manufacturers are very cooperative in providing them. All it takes is a phone call. Manufacturers' phone numbers are usually on the product label. If not, use telephone information to obtain the number. Safety guidelines and products change frequently so check to be sure MSDS you already have on hand are up to date.

MSDS contain a mixture of technical as well as easy to understand information. In the following example consider a typical MSDS for a product called "Thin-X." This is a fairly common type of paint thinner. As you will learn, even common products like this should be used with caution. This MSDS is made up of ten sections each of which we will look at to see how the information in it can be used.

One of the most important sections is "I. Protection and Precautions." This is the section you do not want to skip.

Note: Keep in mind that this is an example only. Do not use the actual information in this MSDS since it applies only to this product and will probably be out of date by the time you read this.

As you can see, for the ordinary finisher some parts of this MSDS are more readable and usable than others. You have to sift through it all to find the information that applies to your situation. But do not be mistaken that none of it applies to you. Most of it always will (Fig. 20–1).

Guidelines

Following are examples of the potential hazards you face as you purchase, use, store, and dispose of finishing materials. Specific guidelines you can use to prevent or reduce the hazards are listed.

Purchase

When buying finish materials:

- Consider your needs carefully. Buy the least hazardous material that will do the job.
- Read labels and other product literature. This will help you determine if the product will fill your needs and alert you to any special safety equipment you may need.
- Buy only the amount you need. This reduces storage hazards and saves money since many finish products "go bad" over time.

Date Issued 06/01/89
Supersedes date: 11/07/88

THIN-X

SCL STERLING-CLARK-LURTON CORP.

184 COMMERCIAL STREET, BOX J, MALDEN, MASSACHUSETTS 02148   TELEPHONE 617/322-0163

MATERIAL SAFETY DATA SHEET

A. IDENTIFICATION AND EMERGENCY INFORMATION

PRODUCT NAME
Thin-X

PRODUCT CODE
1000

CHEMICAL NAME
Petroleum Solvent

CAS NUMBER
8052-41-3

PRODUCT APPEARANCE AND ODOR
Clear water-white liquid
mild mineral spirits odor

MEDICAL EMERGENCY TELEPHONE NUMBER
SCL (DAYS ONLY MON. - THURS.)   617-322-0163
MASS POISON INFO   617-232-2120
CHEMTREC (TRANSPORTATION)   800-424-9300

Fig. 20-1. (A) Identification and Emergency Information. This section names and describes the product. If you thought a finishing product was incorrectly labeled, you might be able to confirm its identity by this description of its outward appearance and odor. If you call the emergency phone numbers listed, use these names and numbers to identify the product. *(For reference only.) (Courtesy Sterling-Clark-Lurton Corp.)*

```
------------------------------------------------------------------
            B.  COMPONENTS AND HAZARD INFORMATION
------------------------------------------------------------------
```

COMPONENTS	CAS NO. OF COMPONENTS	APPROXIMATE CONCENTRATION

This product can be defined as:
low aromatic stoddard solvent — 8052-41-3 — 100%

It consists predominantly of C7-C0 hydrocarbons

This product contains:

C7-C10 saturated hydrocarbons	Mixture	Approximately 92+%
Toluene	108-88-3	Approximately 0.4%
Xylene	1330-20-7	Approximately 0.5%
Ethylbenzene	100-41-4	Approximately 0.2%
C8+ Aromatics	Mixture	Approximately 6%

See Section E for Health and Hazard Information.

See Section H for additional Environmental information.

HAZARDOUS MATERIALS IDENTIFICATION SYSTEM (HMIS)

HEALTH	FLAMMABILITY	REACTIVITY	BASIS	RECOMMENDED BY SCL
1	2	0		

HAZARD RATING   LEAST - 0
Slight -1   Moderate -2   High - 3
Extreme -4

EXPOSURE LIMIT FOR TOTAL PRODUCT	BASIS
100 ppm (525 mg/m3 for an 8-hour workday)	Recommended by the American Conference of Governmental Industrial Hygienists (ACGIH) for stoddard Solvent
100 ppm 8-hour TWA	OSHA Regulation 29 CFR 1910.1000

Fig. 20-1. (B) Components. The major chemicals that make up the product are listed here. You could compare the names of these chemicals and the exposure limits with those listed on your protective gloves or respirator to assure they are resistant to the chemicals. You can see that this product has a moderate (2) flammability rating and a slight (1) health hazard rating. This tells you to prioritize your precautions giving more emphasis to the fire hazard. *(For reference only.) (Courtesy Sterling-Clark-Lurton Corp.)*

PRIMARY ROUTES OF ENTRY AND EMERGENCY
AND FIRST AID PROCEDURES

EYE CONTACT

If splashed into the eyes, flush with clear water for 15 minutes or until irritation subsides. If irritation persists, call a physician.

SKIN

In case of skin contact, remove any contaminated clothing and wash skin thoroughly with soap and water.

INHALATION

If overcome by vapor, remove from exposure and call a physician immediately. If breathing is irregular or has stopped, start resuscitation, administer oxygen, if available.

INGESTION

If ingested, DO NOT induce vomiting; call a physician immediately.

Fig. 20-1. (C) Primary Routes of Entry and First Aid. This section tells you how the chemicals can enter your body and what to do if you are exposed—easy to read and easy to do. *(For reference only.)* *(Courtesy Sterling-Clark-Lurton Corp.)*

FIRE AND EXPLOSION HAZARD INFORMATION

FLASH POINT (MINIMUM)
Combustible - Per DOT 49 CFR 173.115
38°C (100°F)
ASTM D 56, Tag closed cup

AUTOIGNITION TEMPERATURE
Approximately 255°C (490°F)
ASTM D 2155

NATIONAL FIRE PROTECTION ASSOCIATION (NFPA) - HAZARD IDENTIFICATION

HEALTH	FLAMMABILITY	REACTIVITY	BASIS
0	2	0	Recommended by the National Fire Protection Association

HANDLING PRECAUTIONS
This liquid is volatile and gives off invisible vapors. Either the liquid or vapor may settle in low areas or travel some distance along the ground or surface to ignition sources where they may ignite or explode.

Keep product away from ignition sources, such as heat, sparks, pilot lights, static electricity, and open flames.

FLAMMABLE OR EXPLOSIVE LIMITS (APPROXIMATE PERCENT BY VOLUME IN AIR)
Estimated values: lower flammable limit 0.9%   Upper Flammable limit 7%

EXTINGUISHING MEDIA AND FIRE FIGHTING PROCEDURES
Foam, water spray (fog), dry chemical, carbon dioxide and vaporizing liquid type extinguishing agents may all be suitable for extinguishing fires involving this type of product, depending on size or potential size of fire and circumstances related to the situation. Plan fire protection and response strategy through consultation with local fire protection authorities or appropriate specialists.

The following procedures for this type of product are based on the recommendations in the National Fire Protection Association's "Fire Protection Guide on Hazardous Materials," Eighth Edition (1984):

Use dry chemical, foam or carbon dioxide to extinguish the fire. Water may be ineffective, but water should be used to keep fire-exposed containers cool. If a leak or spill has ignited, use water spray to disperse the vapors and to protect men attempting to stop a leak. Water spray may be used to flush spills away from exposures. Minimize breathing of gases, vapor, fumes or decomposition products. Use supplied-air breathing equipment for enclosed or confined spaces or as otherwise needed.

NOTE: The inclusion of the phrase "water may be ineffective" is to indicate that although water can be used to cool and protect exposed material, water may not extinguish the fire unless used under favorable conditions by experienced fire fighters trained in fighting all types of flammable liquid fires.

DECOMPOSITION PRODUCTS UNDER FIRE CONDITIONS

Fumes, smoke, carbon monoxide, aldehydes and other decomposition products, in the case of incomplete combustion.

"EMPTY" CONTAINER WARNING

"Empty" containers retain residue (liquid and/or vapor) and can be dangerous. DO NOT PRESSURIZE, CUT WELD, BRAZE, SOLDER, DRILL, GRIND OR EXPOSE SUCH CONTAINERS TO HEAT, FLAME, SPARKS, STATIC ELECTRICITY, OR OTHER SOURCES OF IGNITION; THEY MAY EXPLODE AND CAUSE INJURY OR DEATH. Do not attempt to clean since residue is difficult to remove. "Empty" drums should be completely drained, properly bunged and promptly returned to a drum reconditioner. All other containers should be disposed of in an environmentally safe manner and in accordance with governmental regulations. For work on tanks refer to Occupational Safety and Health Administration regulations, ANSI Z49.1, and other governmental and industrial references pertaining to cleaning, repairing, welding, or other contemplated operations.

Fig. 20-1. (D) Fire and Explosion Hazard. There is some technical information here. If you do not understand it, skip over it to the "Handling Precautions" topic. Here you can see that the liquid or invisible vapors can travel to remote locations and be ignited. So you have to keep track of these vapors to avoid an explosion. You will recall from section B. that flammability is the greatest hazard, so this section goes on to describe fire fighting procedures at some length. Here you will find the type of extinguisher to have on hand when using this product. Container disposal information is included here. *(For reference only.) (Courtesy Sterling-Clark-Lurton Corp.)*

E. HEALTH AND HAZARD INFORMATION

VARIABILITY AMONG INDIVIDUALS

Health studies have shown that many petroleum hydrocarbons and synthetic lubricants pose potential human health risks which may vary from person to person. As a precaution, exposure to liquids, vapors, mists or fumes should be minimized.

EFFECTS OF OVEREXPOSURE (SIGNS AND SYMPTOMS OF EXPOSURE)

High vapor concentrations (greater than approximately 1000 ppm) are irritating to the eyes and the respiratory tract, and may cause headaches, dizziness, anesthesia, drowsiness, unconsciousness, and other central nervous system effects, including death.

NATURE OF HAZARD AND TOXICITY INFORMATION

Prolonged or repeated skin contact with this product tends to remove skin oils, possibly leading to irritation and dermatitis; however, based on human experience and available toxicological data, this product is judged to be neither a "corrosive" nor an "irritant" by OSHA criteria.

Product contacting the eyes may cause eye irritation.

Laboratory animal studies have shown that prolonged and repeated inhalation exposure to light hydrocarbon vapors in the same naphtha boiling range as this product can produce adverse kidney effects in male rats. However, these effects were not observed in similar studies with female rats and male and female mice and in limited studies with other animal species. Additionally, in a number of human studies, there was no clinical evidence of such effects at normal occupational levels. It is therefore highly unlikely that the kidney effects observed in male rats have significant implications for humans exposed at or below the recommended vapor limits in the workplace.

Product has a low order or acute oral and dermal toxicity, but minute amounts aspirated into the lungs during ingestion or vomiting may cause mild to severe pulmonary injury and possibly death.

This product is judged to have an acute oral LD50 (rat) greater than 5 g/kg of body weight, and an acute dermal LD50 (rabbit) greater than 3.16 g/kg of body weight.

PRE-EXISTING MEDICAL CONDITIONS WHICH MAY BE AGGRAVATED BY EXPOSURE

Petroleum Solvents/Petroleum Hydrocarbons - skin contact may aggravate an existing dermatitis.

Fig. 20-1. (E) Health. The health section is usually easy to understand and contains specific information on how the product can affect your body. *(For reference only.) (Courtesy Sterling-Clark-Lurton Corp.)*

F. PHYSICAL DATA

THE FOLLOWING DATA ARE APPROXIMATE OR TYPICAL VALUES AND SHOULD NOT BE
USED FOR PRECISE DESIGN PURPOSES.

BOILING RANGE
Approximately 153-202°C
(308-396°F)

VAPOR PRESSURE
Less than 10 mm hg @ 25°C
ASTM D 2879

SPECIFIC GRAVITY (15.6 C/15.6 C)
0.78

VAPOR DENSITY (AIR = 1)
Approximately 5.0

MOLECULAR WEIGHT
145

PERCENT VOLATILE BY VOLUME
100 @ 1 atm. and 25°C (77°F)

PH
Essentially neutral

EVAPORATION RATE @ 1 ATM. AND 25°C
(77°F) (n-BUTYL ACETATE = 1)
0.1

POUR, CONGEALING OR MELTING POINT
Less than − 18°C (0°F)
Pour point by ASTM D 97

SOLUBILITY IN WATER @ 1 ATM. AND 25°C
(77°F)
Negligible; less than 0.1%

VISCOSITY
0.90 cP @ 25°C ASTM D 445

**Fig. 20-1. (F) Physical Data. Technical physical characteristics
are described here. If you have been studying finish technology you
may be able to use this information to gain a detailed understanding for problem solving.** *(For reference only.) (Courtesy Sterling-
Clark-Lurton Corp.)*

G. REACTIVITY

This product is stable and will not react violently with water. Hazardous
polymerization will not occur. Avoid contact with strong oxidants such
as liquid chlorine, concentrated oxygen, sodium hypochlorite or
calcium hypochlorite.

**Fig. 20-1. (G) Reactivity. This section describes how the product
will react with other materials that are likely to be nearby. For
example, sodium hypochlorite is bleach which is sometimes used
in finishing procedures. You would not want this product to get
mixed up with bleach.** *(For reference only.) (Courtesy Sterling-Clark-
Lurton Corp.)*

H. ENVIRONMENTAL INFORMATION.

STEPS TO BE TAKEN IN CASE MATERIAL IS RELEASED OR SPILLED

Shut off and eliminate all ignition sources. Keep people away. Recover free product. Add sand, earth or other suitable absorbent to spill area. Minimize breathing vapors. Minimize skin contact. Ventilate confined spaces. Open all windows and doors. Keep product out of sewers and watercourses by diking or impounding. Advise authorities if product has entered or may enter sewers, watercourses, or extensive land areas. Assure conformity with applicable governmental regulations. Continue to observe precautions for volatile, combustible vapors from absorbed material.

THE FOLLOWING INFORMATION MAY BE USEFUL IN COMPLYING WITH VARIOUS STATE AND FEDERAL LAWS AND REGULATIONS UNDER VARIOUS ENVIRONMENTAL STATUTES:

REPORTABLE QUANTITY (RQ), EPA REGULATION 40 CFR 302 (CERCLA SECTION 102)

No RQ for product or any constituent greater than 1% or 0.1% (carcinogen).

THRESHOLD PLANNING QUANTITY (TPQ), EPA REGULATION 40 CFR 355
(SARA SECTIONS 301 - 304)

No TPQ for product or any constituent greater than 1% or 0.1% (carcinogen).

TOXIC CHEMICAL RELEASE REPORTING, EPA REGULATION 40 CFR 372
(SARA SECTION 313)

This product contains approximately 2% 1,2,4-Trimethyl benzene.

HAZARDOUS CHEMICAL REPORTING, EPA REGULATION 40 CFR 370
(SARA SECTIONS 311-312)

EPA HAZARD CLASSIFICATION CODE:	ACUTE HAZARD	CHRONIC HAZARD	FIRE HAZARD	PRESSURE HAZARD	REACTIVE HAZARD	NOT APPLICABLE
	XXX		XXX			

Fig. 20-1. (H) Environmental. If this product is released or spilled into the environment the measures to take are described here. (*For reference only.) (Courtesy Sterling-Clark-Lurton Corp.*)

I. PROTECTION AND PRECAUTIONS

VENTILATION
Use only with ventilation sufficient to prevent exceeding recommended exposure limit or buildup of explosive concentrations of vapor in air. No smoking, flame or other ignition sources.

RESPIRATORY PROTECTION
Use supplied-air respiratory protection in confined or enclosed spaces, if needed.

PROTECTIVE GLOVES
Use chemical-resistant gloves, if needed, to avoid prolonged or repeated skin contact.

EYE PROTECTION
Use splash goggles or face shield when eye contact may occur.

OTHER PROTECTIVE EQUIPMENT
Use chemical-resistant apron or other impervious clothing, if needed, to avoid contaminating regular clothing, which could result in prolonged or repeated skin contact.

WORK PRACTICES / ENGINEERING CONTROLS
Keep containers closed when not in use. Do not store near heat, sparks, flame or strong oxidants. To prevent fire or explosion risk from static accumulation and discharge, effectively ground product transfer system in accordance with the National Fire Protection Association standard for petroleum products.

In order to prevent fire or explosion hazards, use appropriate equipment.

Information on electrical equipment appropriate for use with this product may be found in the latest edition of the National Electrical Code (NFPA-70). This document is available from the National Fire Protection Association, Batterymarch Park, Quincy, Massachusetts 02269.

PERSONAL HYGIENE
Minimize breathing vapor or mist. Avoid prolonged or repeated contact with skin. Remove contaminated clothing; launder or dry-clean before re-use. Remove contaminated shoes and thoroughly clean and dry before re-use. Cleanse skin thoroughly after contact, before breaks and meals, and at end of work period. Product is readily removed from skin by waterless hand cleaners followed by washing thoroughly with soap and water.

Fig. 20–1. (I) Protection and Precautions. This is one of the most important sections. Here key protective measures are summarized in clearly laid out and concise guidelines. Follow these guidelines to use the product safely. Under the Personal Hygiene topic are precautions that you can use as a last defense to protect your body from the ill effects of this product. *(For reference only.) (Courtesy Sterling-Clark-Lurton Corp.)*

J. TRANSPORTATION AND OSHA RELATED LABEL INFORMATION

TRANSPORTATION INCIDENT INFORMATION

For further information relative to spills resulting from transportation incidents, refer to latest Department of Transportation Emergency Response Guidebook for Hazardous Materials Incidents, DOT P 5800.3.

DOT IDENTIFICATION NUMBER

UN   1255

OSHA REQUIRED LABEL INFORMATION

In compliance with hazard and right-to-know requirements, the following OSHA Hazard Warnings should be found on a label, bill of lading or invoice accompanying this shipment.

DANGER!

COMBUSTIBLE

Note: Product label will contain additional non-OSHA related information.

THE INFORMATION AND RECOMMENDATIONS CONTAINED HEREIN ARE, TO THE BEST OF SCL KNOWLEDGE AND BELIEF, ACCURATE AND RELIABLE AS OF THE DATE ISSUED. SCL DOES NOT WARRANT OR GUARANTEE THEIR ACCURACY OR RELIABILITY, AND SCL SHALL NOT BE LIABLE FOR ANY LOSS OR DAMAGE ARISING OUT OF THE USE THEREOF.

THE INFORMATION AND RECOMMENDATIONS ARE OFFERED FOR THE USER'S CONSIDERATION AND EXAMINATION, AND IT IS THE USER'S RESPONSIBILITY TO SATISFY ITSELF THAT THEY ARE SUITABLE AND COMPLETE FOR ITS PARTICULAR USE. IF BUYER REPACKAGES THIS PRODUCT, LEGAL COUNCIL SHOULD BE CONSULTED TO INSURE PROPER HEALTH, SAFETY AND OTHER NECESSARY INFORMATION IS INCLUDED ON THE CONTAINER.

THE ENVIRONMENTAL INFORMATION INCLUDED UNDER SECTION H HEREOF AS WELL AS THE HAZARDOUS MATERIALS IDENTIFICATION SYSTEM (HMIS) AND NATIONAL FIRE PROTECTION ASSOCIATION (NFPA) RATINGS HAVE BEEN INCLUDED BY SCL, U.S.A. IN ORDER TO PROVIDE ADDITIONAL HEALTH AND HAZARD CLASSIFICATION INFORMATION. THE RATINGS RECOMMENDED ARE BASED UPON THE CRITERIA SUPPLIED BY THE DEVELOPERS OF THESE RATING SYSTEMS, TOGETHER WITH SCL INTERPRETATION OF THE AVAILABLE DATA.

Fig. 20–1. (J) Transportation and Labels. If you put this product into another container, label it according to these guidelines. In the disclaimer you will notice the manufacturer also recommends that you think about what you are doing and consider the consequences of your actions. *(For reference only.) (Courtesy Sterling-Clark-Lurton Corp.)*

Use

The three main hazards that can occur during the application of finishing materials are that they will get into your body and cause health problems, that flammable vapors and liquids will cause a fire, and that the materials will contaminate the environment. The hazards are especially critical when sprayers and aerosol cans produce a fine mist of solvents and excessive vapors.

Here are some examples of how the three critical safety issues of fire, health, and environment relate to these potential hazards during the application of finish materials.

A fire hazard develops as vapors, mists, or dust build up to excessive levels. Sparks or flames can easily ignite the flammable or explosive materials.

A health hazard can occur when vapors and mists are breathed in. The hazardous materials settle deep in the lungs and may be absorbed into the blood and quickly distributed throughout the body. Some chemicals can even be absorbed directly through the skin. Once chemicals are in the body, they can damage sensitive tissues and systems.

An environmental hazard is created if you pour leftover thinner on the ground. Rain could wash it into the ground water, where it can flow into a shallow dug well that is someone's water supply.

Following are guidelines you can use to mitigate the hazards.

Limit exposure
- Take frequent breaks.
- Use only the recommended amount. More is not necessarily better and may add to the hazard.
- If pregnant, avoid exposure to toxic materials.
- Keep children, pets, and wildlife out of the finishing area.
- Always label containers to show their contents and hazards. If you expect to use the container beyond the current work session, add a label. A temporary container without a label often becomes a permanent one without a label.
- Keep the work area clean and organized.

Ventilate
- Ventilation is a basic precaution to prevent the buildup of harmful vapors, mist, and dust when working indoors.
- Set up cross ventilation so that fresh air is coming into the

work area from one side and exhausting out the other side. There should be enough air movement so you can feel at least a slight draft or breeze.

- Fans can be used to set up forced air movement. Ordinary household window fans can create sparks that would ignite heavy vapor, mist, and dust concentrations. Explosion-proof fans and electrical equipment should be used in the finishing area. Check with your equipment supplier or manufacturer to determine if it is explosion-proof.

- Set up a negative air pressure in the finishing area by using exhaust fans in a window or an exterior wall to pull air directly from the finishing area to the outdoors. If you set a fan anywhere inside to blow air out of the finishing room, you may force contaminated air into other parts of the building. The positive air pressure could force vapors through small openings to other parts of the building.

- Consider what happens to vapors and mist once exhausted. You would not want to blow these harmful chemicals over to the nursery school next door, or ruin the finish on your car in the parking lot.

- Work outdoors if possible.

Eliminate sources of ignition
- Put out stove or furnace pilot lights.
- Turn off electric equipment, such as motors, thermostats and heaters that may produce sparks.
- Control humidity to reduce static electricity sparking caused by dry air.
- Steel tools dropped on a concrete floor can produce a spark.

Wear respirator
- Do not breathe vapors, mist, and dust.
- Wear a respirator rated for the chemicals you are exposed to.
- Take frequent breaks.

Wear eye protection
- Use safety glasses or goggles with splash protection.
- Contact lenses of the soft lens type are permeable to solvent vapors due to their high water content and can thus trap

solvents against the eye. Symptoms are chronic watering, redness, and burning during and after use of solvents while wearing soft lens contacts. Check with your eye care specialist before working with volatile solvents.

Keep materials off your body
- Have washing facilities at hand in case materials get on your skin.
- Wear protective clothing, gloves and goggles.
- If clothing becomes contaminated, change into clean clothes.
- Launder contaminated clothes separately from the rest of the wash.

Mixing products
- Products can react to each other with unexpected results.
- Only mix products when you know what you are doing.
- Never add water to a chemical. Add the chemical to the water. This is easy to remember because in the alphabet the "C" in "Chemical" is before the "W" in "Water."
- Bleach and Ammonia. Do not mix bleach with ammonia or with any detergents or cleansers containing ammonia. Mixed together the two are a lethal combination. In several cases people have died from breathing the fumes from a bleach and ammonia mixture. Many household cleaners contain ammonia.
- Do not contaminate containers holding stock supplies. Keep lids and caps with original containers. Do not put unused materials back into stock containers.

Disposal
- Do not incinerate aerosol cans. They may explode.
- Use up product so there is nothing to dispose.
- Never put harmful chemicals down the drain or on the ground.
- Some cities and states have programs to collect small amounts of hazardous materials from households. Check with your local and state officials.

- If you are setting up a commercial operation, you must abide by local, state, and federal regulations regarding the use of hazardous chemicals. Contact the appropriate authorities for more information.

Storage

- Store all finish materials securely in locked cabinets away from children and animals.
- Close containers securely. Some materials can evaporate through loose lids over a long period.
- For long term storage (more than a week) keep finish materials in a shed or garage separate from living spaces.
- Check containers for damage at least once a year. Many finish products can expand or shrink in volume enough to burst or crush containers. Dispose of any containers showing signs of rust.
- Do not store aerosol cans near heat sources such as heaters and furnaces. They may explode.
- Keep materials in original containers.

Of course it takes a lot of time and a certain expense to follow the appropriate guidelines. And a typical finishing procedure requires the use of a few or even several different products. Often the actions needed to follow safety guidelines will overlap from one product to the next resulting in economies. It definitely costs more than the purchase price to use a finishing product safely. Can it possibly be worth it? Common sense says yes.

Low VOC (Volatile Organic Compounds) Coatings

VOC are the solvents in paints and other coatings that combine with oxygen in the air to create low-level ozone, the main ingredient of smog. A few states have set VOC limits to protect the environment. Many more will within the next few years. Low VOC products also reduce fire and health hazards.

Finish manufacturers have dealt with the new regulations in two ways. They are expanding and heavily promoting their lines of waterborne coatings. And they are changing the formulations of their solvent-base coatings in three important ways.

Application methods and performance of these paints are substantially different than the common solventborne paints. Wet paint films may skin over and feel dry but still be liquid enough underneath to slide right off the wall if you lean against it.

Emulsion-based coatings usually take more time to achieve top quality appearance and performance. Surface preparation is particularly important because of poor penetration and adhesion.

It is a period of great change in the paint industry. Formulations can change from month to month. Major manufacturers are pulling out of whole states at a time or dropping whole lines of products, so you cannot depend on having tried-and-true products to use. So what can you do to prepare? Begin experimenting with the new formulations now so it is not a sudden shock when you are forced to switch. Set up your own test panels and evaluate performance over extended periods like a year or two. Use the new finishes on smaller jobs, so if there are problems at least they will be small ones. By the time changes are mandatory you will have the experience and knowledge to make the shift.

Glossary

Alkyd resin-base paints—Paints using a synthetic alkyd resin as a binder.

Alligatoring—intersecting cracks and ridges on furniture finish, usually the result of overexposure to sunlight.

Aniline—pigments derived from petroleum distillation.

Antiquing—a furniture-finishing process in which a glaze is applied and then wiped off to suggest an aged appearance.

Blonding—applying a very light tinted or white pigmented stain to wood to make it look lighter.

Bronzing—covering or overlaying a surface with the metal powder.

Crazing—irregular patterns of minute cracks on a furniture finish.

Decalcomania transfers (decals)—pictures or designs on specially coated paper that is covered with clear varnish or lacquer.

Decoupage—decorating objects or furniture with pasted paper, fabric, or photographs and sealing with a clear finish.

Distressing—scratching, gouging, denting, or marking a piece of furniture or its finish to give the impression of age or use.

Dry rot—a crumbling or powdery condition of wood resulting from a fungus that consumes the wood in moist areas.

Enamel—an opaque, hard finish consisting of pigments in an alkyd or urethane base. Enamels are slower drying, have a higher gloss and a tougher surface than paints.

Face veneer—a very thin sheet of high-quality wood selected for particularly attractive appearance.

Fillers—pastes or liquids used to fill the pores in open-grain woods before applying finishes.

Flitch—a squared longitudinal section of a log which is cut into thin slices for veneer.

Flocking—creating a soft, feltlike surface by spraying material fibers onto a background coating of enamel, lacquer, varnish, or water-soluble glue.

French polish—a tough transparent finish produced by applying many thin coats of shellac over a linseed oil base.

Gilding—applying leaf metals to a finish to imitate gold.

Glazing—see *Antiquing.*

Gold leaf—very thin ribbons or squares of gold applied to a surface with varnish.

Grain-raising—a rough, uneven surface on wood caused when water makes some of the wood fibers swell and rise above the wood surface.

Hardwood—wood from a deciduous or broad-leafed tree. These trees shed their leaves every year.

Heartwood—wood cut from the center of the tree where the cells were no longer living when the tree was harvested. Heartwood is usually darker, denser, and harder than sapwood from the exterior of the tree.

Inlay—inserting wood of contrasting color or texture into a surface for decoration.

Intarsia—inlay; inserting decorative wood into grooves and recesses cut into the background wood to form decoration.

Lacquer—a very fast drying finish combining nitrocellulose, resins, plasticizers, and a solvent containing acetone. The most widely used top coat in production furniture finishing.

Latex paint—waterborne paint used primarily for interior and exterior house painting.

Linseed oil finish—a penetrating, slow-drying finish made from flax seed and often combined with driers, turpentine, or mineral spirits when used on furniture.

Low VOC varnishes and paints—finishing products with low Volatile Organic Compounds, to reduce health and environmental hazards.

Marbleizing—wiping a wet painted surface or dribbling paint onto it to make it look like marble.

Mercator—cutting a pattern out of a veneer and inserting a decorative design of other veneers to form a decorative panel.

Milk paint—an early method for making paints by mixing natural pigments such as clay or brick dust with milk.

Mosaic—inlaying small pieces of tile, glass, stone, or other materials into a surface to form a design or decoration.

Non-grain-raising (NGR) stains—the most commonly used stains in furniture finishing, consisting of solvents, coal tar dilutants, and aniline dyes.

Oil-base paints—(solventborne) paints made of solvent, binders, and pigments.

Oleoresinous varnish—see *Varnish (oil-base)*

Penetrating finishes—a finish that soaks into the wood surface and then hardens.

Piano finish—a high-gloss finish produced by repeatedly rubbing a clear or pigmented shellac finish.

Plastic laminate—thin sheets applied like veneer to table tops and formed of layers of paper impregnated with resin and bonded together with heat and pressure.

Pumice stone—a white powder available in different grades and used for polishing and buffing a surface after the final sanding or finish coat.

Reamalgamation—repairing damaged finishes by dissolving the finish and allowing it to reform.

Rottenstone—a very fine powdered abrasive, often used after pumice stone to obtain a very high polish.

Sanding blocks—pieces of wood, rubber, or felt used as backings for sandpaper.

Satin finish—a dulled finish made by rubbing with pumice stone.

Scraper—a piece of sharp-edged steel used to smooth a wood surface or remove a finish coat.

Sealer—a coating that functions as a barrier between two incompatible substances.

Shellac—a furniture finish made from a sticky resinous substance secreted by the lac insect

Softwood—wood for a coniferous tree.

Solventborne—a finish with a vehicle made up of solvents.

Spirit stains—alcohol-soluble stains formed by dissolving aniline dye powders in alcohol.

Spiriting-off—a technique that uses alcohol and a mineral oil-base polish to create a high luster on a varnish finish.

Stenciling—a decorating technique in which designs are added to surfaces by means of precut patterns.

Tack rags—cloths impregnated with a sticky substance and used to remove dust or sanding debris from a surface before finishes are applied.

Varnish (oil-base, or solventborne)—a finish made up of resins and drying oils with solvents.

Varnish (synthetic resin)—a fast-drying varnish in which natural resins have been replaced by urethane, alkyd, phenolic, or vinyl resins.

Varnish (water-base)—combines resins with water to produce a varnish that dries faster and is safer to use and easier to clean up than solvent-borne varnishes.

Veneers—any thin layer of wood laminated to a base wood for decorative effect of grain or contrasting color.

Washcoating—applying a thin, fast-drying material over a stain, toner, or the bare wood prior to filling or using a pigment stain.

Waterborne—a finish with a water vehicle. Typically oils and resins are dispersed in the water as an emulsion.

Water stains—water-soluble or latex stains produced by dissolving powdered aniline dye in hot water.

Wood graining—creating simulated grain patterns in a glaze applied to a wood surface.

References

Publications

If you have trouble finding these publications at your local bookstore, they may be out of print. Check at your local library or the library in the nearest larger city. Ask if the publication is available on interlibrary loan or a similar program that obtains books from other libraries. Some magazines listed here are distributed to local newstands. Other trade journals are only available directly from the publisher.

American Woodworker

Rodale Press Inc.
33 E. Minor St.
Emmaus, PA 18098
215 967–5171

This bimonthly magazine often carries articles on finishing methods and materials.

Workbench

> PO Box 7502
> Redoak, IA 51591–0502
> 800 444–1009

> This bimonthly magazine carries a regular column, *Flexner on Finishing*, that covers a wide range of finishing topics. For a sample of Bob Flexner's writing see Chapter 8, *Stripping Finishes*.

The Complete Book of Furniture Restoration

> Tristan Salazar, St. Martin's Press, NY, 1982, 160 pages

> This book covers furniture frame and structural repairs.

Furniture Making Plain & Simple

> Aldren A. Watson and Theodra A Poulos, W. W. Norton & Company, NY, 1984, 328 pages.

> If you want to make your own furniture from scratch with hand tools, or learn how traditional furniture is built, this book is a good place to start.

Marbleizing

> Stuart Spencer, Harmony Books, 1988

> How-to techniques with plenty of examples.

The Art of the Painted Finish for Furniture & Decoration

> Isabel O'Neil, William Morrow & Co., NY, 1971

> Covers antiquing, laquering and gilding.

Recipes for Surfaces

Mindy Drucker and Pierre Finkelstein, Fireside, 1990
A complete step-by-step guide to more than 40 techniques,
many of which are suitable for furniture.

Paint Magic

Jocasta Innes, Pantheon Books, NY, 1981.

Suppliers and Manufacturers

Tremont Nail Company

Elm Street at Rt 28
Box 111
Wareham, MA 02571
508 295–0038

Old-fashioned square-cut nails and early American design
hardware.

Liberon Waxes, Inc.

P.O. Box 86
Mendocino, CA 95460
707 937–0375 or 800 245–5611

Complete line of finishing products.

Star Finishing Products, Inc.

360 Shore Drive
Hinsdale, Ill 60521
708 654–8650; orders only 800 323–5390

Offers complete line of finishing products not sold in stores
for antiques trade, furniture manufacturers, and ama-

teurs. Aerosols, touch-up sticks, furniture surface repair kits. Also offers workshops around the country through colleges for credit hours.

Lex-Aire Products, Inc.

34–2 Sullivan Road
North Billerica, MA 01862
508 663–7202

Turbine-type spray systems.

Mover's Supply House, Inc.

1476 E. 222 Street
Bronx, NY 10469
800 221–8032

Furniture blankets, dollies, hand trucks and other equipment to move your furniture carefully after you have finished it.

Mohawk Finishing Products, Inc.

Rt 30N
Amsterdam, NY 12010
518 843–1380

Complete line of finishing products. Also markets Behlen brand products.

Wood Shed

1807 Elmwood Avenue
Buffalo, NY 14207
716 876–4719

Large selection of exotic veneers, only supplier of Cuban mahogany.

Associations and Organizations

Forest Products Laboratory

USDA Forest Service
One Gifford Pinchot Drive
Madison, WI 53705
608 231–9200

The Forest Products Laboratory researches practically
every aspect of wood products and their uses. Milling, fab-
rication, finishing and painting, fire retarding treatments
and sawdust are just a few of the topics covered. The published results of their work is available to the public. Call
or write with questions. Typically, a report or publication
with an answer will be sent. Unusual questions are wel-
come but may require time to research.

Unfinished Furniture Association

36 S. State St.
1806 Chicago IL 60603
800 487–8321

Several regional groups combined to form this national
association that includes 500 retail outlets, over 100 manufacturers and sales representatives. Call to find your local
unfinished furniture dealers and to request the brochure
"How to Buy Unfinished Furniture."

Training Programs and Workshops

Finishing skills and knowledge are developed by most people
through the actual experience of doing finishing work. Listed here
are a few more formal educational opportunities that focus on finishing. It is important to understand the two kinds of education
available.

Independent educational organizations such as universities and technical colleges draw on a wide array of information and experienced teachers. This type of education depends partly on the reputation of the institution, but mostly on the individual teacher. These programs usually take a knowledge-based skill development approach.

Manufacturers and suppliers offer workshops in how to use their own products. You may get a good training in how to best use their products, but you cannot expect to get an objective view and comparison of different manufacturers' products. These workshops usually take a materials and products approach.

DCTC Wood Finishing Program

> Dakota County Technical College
> 1300 East 145th Street
> Rosemont, MN 55068
> 612 423–8301
> 800 548–5502 (MN only)

> This program provides practical instruction and experience to meet the needs of the wood finishing professional. The course provides a foundation for entry into self-employment or employment with a company. The main areas covered are furniture touch-up and refurbishing, furniture restoration, and woodworking. This is a full time one-year course of study, although part-time study is possible with segmented courses based on the student's own time schedule.

Mohawk Workshops

> Mohawk Finishing Products, Inc.
> Rt 30N
> Amsterdam, NY 12010
> 518 843–1380

> These specialized training sessions on spot refinishing cover the latest techniques and products for repair of dam-

aged finishes on wood and leather/vinyl. The one- to three-day workshops are held at various locations around the country.

Brookfield Craft Center
PO Box 122, Route 25
Brookfield, CT 06804
203 775–4526

Offers a variety of short term workshops that sometimes include finishing topics.

Furniture Conservation Training Program

Training Secretary
CAL/MSC Smithsonian Institution
Washington, DC 20560
301 238–3700

A three-year graduate level program covers restoration, preservation, and stabilization of historic furniture and wood artifacts. Students are selected from applicants on a competitive basis. Applicants must have woodworking skills and a bachelor's degree with courses in drawing, art history, and chemistry. If you are already a professional woodworker or finisher, this program will help you move into the specialized field of furniture conservation and museum-level work.

Index

**Over a Century of Excellence
for the Professional
and
Vocational Trades and the Crafts**

Order now from your local bookstore
or use the convenient order form
at the back of this book.

CONTENTS

ELECTRICAL

House Wiring (Seventh Edition)

ROLAND E. PALMQUIST;
revised by PAUL ROSENBERG

5 1/2 x 8 1/4 Hardcover 248 pp. 150 Illus.
ISBN: 0-02-594692-7 $22.95

Rules and regulations of the current 1990 National Electrical Code for residential wiring fully explained and illustrated.

Practical Electricity
(Fifth Edition)

ROBERT G. MIDDLETON;
revised by L. DONALD MEYERS

5 1/2 x 8 1/4 Hardcover 512 pp. 335 Illus.
ISBN: 0-02-584561-6 $19.95

The fundamentals of electricity for electrical workers, apprentices, and others requiring concise information about electric principles and their practical applications.

Guide to the 1990 National Electrical Code

ROLAND E. PALMQUIST;
revised by PAUL ROSENBERG

5 1/2 x 8 1/4 Hardcover 664 pp. 230 Illus.
ISBN: 0-02-594565-3 $24.95

The most authoritative guide available to interpreting the National Electrical Code for electricians, contractors, electrical inspectors, and homeowners. Examples and illustrations.

Installation Requirements of the 1990 National Electrical Code

PAUL ROSENBERG

5 1/2 × 8 1/4 Hardcover 240 pp.
ISBN: 0-02-604941-4 $24.95

Field guide for installation requirement makes understanding the 1990 Electrica Code simple while on the job. Application and easy-to-understand tables make this th perfect working companion.

Mathematics for Electricians and Electronics Technicians

REX MILLER

5 1/2 x 8 1/4 Hardcover 312 pp. 115 Illu.
ISBN: 0-8161-1700-4 $14.95

Mathematical concepts, formulas, and prob lem-solving techniques utilized on-the-job b electricians and those in electronics and re lated fields.

Fractional-Horsepower Electric Motors

REX MILLER and
MARK RICHARD MILLER

5 1/2 x 8 1/4 Hardcover 436 pp. 285 Illu
ISBN: 0-672-23410-6 $15.95

The installation, operation, maintenance, re pair, and replacement of the small-to-mode ate-size electric motors that power hom appliances and industrial equipment.

lectric Motors (Fifth Edition)

)WIN P. ANDERSON
d REX MILLER

1/2 x 8 1/4   Hardcover   696 pp.
otos/line art
BN: 0-02-501920-1 $35.00

omplete reference guide for electricians, in-
istrial maintenance personnel, and install-
s. Contains both theoretical and practical
scriptions.

ome Appliance Servicing
ourth Edition)

)WIN P. ANDERSON;
vised by REX MILLER

1/2 x 8 1/4   Hardcover   640 pp.   345 Illus.
BN: 0-672-23379-7 $22.50

e essentials of testing, maintaining, and
pairing all types of home appliances.

elevision Service Manual
ifth Edition)

)BERT G. MIDDLETON;
vised by JOSEPH G. BARRILE

1/2 x 8 1/4   Hardcover   512 pp.   395 Illus.
BN: 0-672-23395-9 $16.95

guide to all aspects of television transmis-
n and reception, including the operating
inciples of black and white and color re-
ivers. Step-by-step maintenance and re-
ir procedures.

lectrical Course for
pprentices and Journeymen
hird Edition)

)LAND E. PALMQUIST

1/2 x 8 1/4   Hardcover   478 pp.   290 Illus.
BN: 0-02-594550-5 $19.95

is practical course in electricity for those
formal training programs or learning on
eir own provides a thorough understanding
operational theory and its applications on
e job.

uestions and Answers for
lectricians Examinations
enth Edition)

vised by PAUL ROSENBERG

1/2 x 8 1/4   Hardcover   316 pp.   110 Illus.
BN: 0-02-604955-4 $22.95

ased on the 1990 National Electrical Code,
is book reviews the subjects included in the
rious electricians examinations—appren-
e, journeyman, and master.

MACHINE SHOP AND
MECHANICAL TRADES

Machinists Library
(Fourth Edition, 3 Vols.)

REX MILLER

5 1/2 x 8 1/4 Hardcover 1,352 pp. 1120 Illus.
ISBN: 0-672-23380-0 $52.95

An indispensable three-volume reference set
for machinists, tool and die makers, machine
operators, metal workers, and those with
home workshops. The principles and methods of the entire field are covered in an up-
to-date text, photographs, diagrams, and tables.

Volume I: Basic Machine Shop

REX MILLER

5 1/2 x 8 1/4   Hardcover   392 pp.   375 Illus.
ISBN: 0-672-23381-9 $17.95

Volume II: Machine Shop

REX MILLER

5 1/2 x 8 1/4   Hardcover   528 pp.   445 Illus.
ISBN: 0-672-23382-7 $19.95

Volume III: Toolmakers Handy Book

REX MILLER

5 1/2 x 8 1/4   Hardcover   432 pp.   300 Illus.
ISBN: 0-672-23383-5 $14.95

Mathematics for Mechanical
Technicians and Technologists

JOHN D. BIES

5 1/2 x 8 1/4   Hardcover   342 pp.   190 Illus.
ISBN: 0-02-510620-1 $17.95

The mathematical concepts, formulas, and
problem-solving techniques utilized on the
job by engineers, technicians, and other
workers in industrial and mechanical technology and related fields.

Millwrights and Mechanics
Guide (Fourth Edition)

CARL A. NELSON

5 1/2 x 8 1/4   Hardcover   1,040 pp.   880 Illus.
ISBN: 0-02-588591-x $29.95

The most comprehensive and authoritative
guide available for millwrights, mechanics,
maintenance workers, riggers, shop workers, foremen, inspectors, and superinten-
dents on plant installation, operation, and
maintenance.

Welders Guide (Third Edition)
JAMES E. BRUMBAUGH

5 1/2 x 8 1/4   Hardcover   960 pp.   615 Illus.
ISBN: 0-672-23374-6 $23.95

The theory, operation, and maintenance of all welding machines. Covers gas welding equipment, supplies, and process; arc welding equipment, supplies, and process; TIG and MIG welding; and much more.

Welders/Fitters Guide
HARRY L. STEWART

8 1/2 x 11   Paperback   160 pp.   195 Illus.
ISBN: 0-672-23325-8 $7.95

Step-by-step instruction for those training to become welders/fitters who have some knowledge of welding and the ability to read blueprints.

Sheet Metal Work
JOHN D. BIES

5 1/2 x 8 1/4   Hardcover   456 pp.   215 Illus.
ISBN: 0-8161-1706-3 $19.95

An on-the-job guide for workers in the manufacturing and construction industries and for those with home workshops. All facets of sheet metal work detailed and illustrated by drawings, photographs, and tables.

Power Plant Engineers Guide
(Third Edition)
FRANK D. GRAHAM;
revised by CHARLIE BUFFINGTON

5 1/2 x 8 1/4   Hardcover   960 pp.   530 Illus.
ISBN: 0-672-23329-0 $27.50

This all-inclusive, one-volume guide is perfect for engineers, firemen, water tenders, oilers, operators of steam and diesel-power engines, and those applying for engineer's and firemen's licenses.

Mechanical Trades Pocket Manual (Third Edition)
CARL A. NELSON

4 x 6   Paperback   364 pp.   255 Illus.
ISBN: 0-02-588665-7 $14.95

A handbook for workers in the industrial and mechanical trades on methods, tools, equipment, and procedures. Pocket-sized for easy reference and fully illustrated.

PLUMBING

Plumbers and Pipe Fitters Library (Fourth Edition, 3 Vols.)
CHARLES N. McCONNELL

5 1/2 x 8 1/4   Hardcover   952 pp.   560 Illu
ISBN: 0-02-582914-9 $68.45

This comprehensive three-volume set contains the most up-to-date information available for master plumbers, journeymen apprentices, engineers, and those in the building trades. A detailed text and clear diagrams, photographs, and charts and tables treat all aspects of the plumbing, heating and air conditioning trades.

Volume I: Materials, Tools, Roughing-In
CHARLES N. McCONNELL;
revised by TOM PHILBIN

5 1/2 x 8 1/4   Hardcover   304 pp.   240 Illu
ISBN: 0-02-582911-4 $20.95

Volume II: Welding, Heating, Air Conditioning
CHARLES N. McCONNELL;
revised by TOM PHILBIN

5 1/2 x 8 1/4   Hardcover   384 pp.   220 Illu
ISBN: 0-02-582912-2 $22.95

Volume III: Water Supply, Drainage, Calculations
CHARLES N. McCONNELL;
revised by TOM PHILBIN

5 1/2 x 8 1/4   Hardcover   264 pp.   100 Illu
ISBN: 0-02-582913-0 $20.95

Home Plumbing Handbook
(Third Edition)
CHARLES N. McCONNELL

8 1/2 x 11   Paperback   200 pp.   100 Illus.
ISBN: 0-672-23413-0 $14.95

An up-to-date guide to home plumbing installation and repair.

The Plumbers Handbook
(Eighth Edition)
JOSEPH P. ALMOND, SR.;
revised by REX MILLER

4 × 6   Paperback   368 pp.   170 Illus
ISBN: 0-02-501570-2 $19.95

Comprehensive and handy guide for plumbers and pipefitters—fits in the toolbox or pocket. For apprentices, journeymen, or experts.

Questions and Answers for Plumbers' Examinations (Third Edition)

JULES ORAVETZ;
revised by REX MILLER

5 1/2 x 8 1/4 Paperback 288 pp. 145 Illus.
ISBN: 0-02-593510-0 $14.95

Complete guide to preparation for the plumbers' exams given by local licensing authorities. Includes requirements of the National Bureau of Standards.

HVAC

Air Conditioning: Home and Commercial (Fourth Edition)

EDWIN P. ANDERSON;
revised by REX MILLER

5 1/2 x 8 1/4 Hardcover 528 pp. 180 Illus.
ISBN: 0-02-584885-2 $29.95

A guide to the construction, installation, operation, maintenance, and repair of home, commercial, and industrial air conditioning systems.

Heating, Ventilating, and Air Conditioning Library (Second Edition, 3 Vols.)

JAMES E. BRUMBAUGH

5 1/2 x 8 1/4 Hardcover 1,840 pp. 1,275 Illus.
ISBN: 0-672-23388-6 $53.85

An authoritative three-volume reference library for those who install, operate, maintain, and repair HVAC equipment commercially, industrially, or at home.

Volume I: Heating Fundamentals, Furnaces, Boilers, Boiler Conversions

JAMES E. BRUMBAUGH

5 1/2 x 8 1/4 Hardcover 656 pp. 405 Illus.
ISBN: 0-672-23389-4 $17.95

Volume II: Oil, Gas and Coal Burners, Controls, Ducts, Piping, Valves

JAMES E. BRUMBAUGH

5 1/2 x 8 1/4 Hardcover 592 pp. 455 Illus.
ISBN: 0-672-23390-8 $17.95

Volume III: Radiant Heating, Water Heaters, Ventilation, Air Conditioning, Heat Pumps, Air Cleaners

JAMES E. BRUMBAUGH

5 1/2 x 8 1/4 Hardcover 592 pp. 415 Illus.
ISBN: 0-672-23391-6 $17.95

Oil Burners (Fifth Edition)

EDWIN M. FIELD

5 1/2 x 8 1/4 Hardcover 360 pp. 170 Illus.
ISBN: 0-02-537745-0 $29.95

An up-to-date sourcebook on the construction, installation, operation, testing, servicing, and repair of all types of oil burners, both industrial and domestic.

Refrigeration: Home and Commercial (Fourth Edition)

EDWIN P. ANDERSON;
revised by REX MILLER

5 1/2 x 8 1/4 Hardcover 768 pp. 285 Illus.
ISBN: 0-02-584875-5 $34.95

A reference for technicians, plant engineers, and the homeowner on the installation, operation, servicing, and repair of everything from single refrigeration units to commercial and industrial systems.

PNEUMATICS AND HYDRAULICS

Hydraulics for Off-the-Road Equipment (Second Edition)

HARRY L. STEWART;
revised by TOM PHILBIN

5 1/2 x 8 1/4 Hardcover 256 pp. 175 Illus.
ISBN: 0-8161-1701-2 $13.95

This complete reference manual on heavy equipment covers hydraulic pumps, accumulators, and motors; force components; hydraulic control components; filters and filtration, lines and fittings, and fluids; hydrostatic transmissions; maintenance; and troubleshooting.

Pneumatics and Hydraulics (Fourth Edition)

HARRY L. STEWART;
revised by TOM STEWART

5 1/2 x 8 1/4 Hardcover 512 pp. 315 Illus.
ISBN: 0-672-23412-2 $19.95

The principles and applications of fluid power. Covers pressure, work, and power; general features of machines; hydraulic and pneumatic symbols; pressure boosters; air compressors and accessories; and much more.

Pumps (Fifth Edition)
HARRY L. STEWART;
revised by REX MILLER

5 1/2 x 8 1/4 Hardcover 552 pp. 360 Illus.
ISBN: 0-02-614725-4 $35.00

The practical guide to operating principles of pumps, controls, and hydraulics. Covers installation and day-to-day service.

CARPENTRY AND CONSTRUCTION

Carpenters and Builders Library
(Sixth Edition, 4 Vols.)
JOHN E. BALL;
revised by JOHN LEEKE

5 1/2 x 8 1/4 Hardcover 1,300 pp. 988 Illus.
ISBN: 0-02-506455-4 $89.95

This comprehensive four-volume library has set the professional standard for decades for carpenters, joiners, and woodworkers.

Volume 1: Tools, Steel Square, Joinery
JOHN E. BALL;
revised by JOHN LEEKE

5 1/2 x 8 1/4 Hardcover 377 pp. 340 Illus.
ISBN: 0-02-506451-7 $21.95

Volume 2: Builders Math, Plans, Specifications
JOHN E. BALL;
revised by JOHN LEEKE

5 1/2 x 8 1/4 Hardcover 319 pp. 200 Illus.
ISBN: 0-02-506452-5 $21.95

Volume 3: Layouts, Foundation, Framing
JOHN E. BALL;
revised by JOHN LEEKE

5 1/2 x 8 1/4 Hardcover 269 pp. 204 Illus.
ISBN: 0-02-506453-3 $21.95

Volume 4: Millwork, Power Tools, Painting
JOHN E. BALL;
revised by JOHN LEEKE

5 1/2 x 8 1/4 Hardcover 335 pp. 244 Illus.
ISBN: 0-02-506454-1 $21.95

Complete Building Construction
(Second Edition)
JOHN PHELPS;
revised by TOM PHILBIN

5 1/2 x 8 1/4 Hardcover 744 pp. 645 Illus.
ISBN: 0-672-23377-0 $22.50

Constructing a frame or brick building from the footings to the ridge. Whether the building project is a tool shed, garage, or a complete home, this single fully illustrated volume provides all the necessary information.

Complete Roofing Handbook
JAMES E. BRUMBAUGH

5 1/2 x 8 1/4 Hardcov ____ ____ Illu
ISBN: 0-02-51____

Cov ____ ____ ____ ____ ____fing
ro ____ NEW EDITION ____ ntilation; sky
lig ____ FOR 1992 ____ ngs; dormer constru
tio ____ ____ oning details; and much more.

Complete Siding Handbook
JAMES E. BRUMBAUGH

5 1/2 x 8 1/4 Hardcover 512 pp. ____ 0 Illu
ISBN: 0-02-517880-6 $24.__

This compan ____ ____ ____ plet
 ____ NEW EDITION ____ nsiv
s ____ FOR 1992 ____ panyin
li ____ ____ ____ y aspect of siding
b ____

Masons and Builders Library
(Second Edition, 2 Vols.)
LOUIS M. DEZETTEL;
revised by TOM PHILBIN

5 1/2 x 8 1/4 Hardcover 688 pp. 500 Illu
ISBN: 0-672-23401-7 $27.95

This two-volume set provides practical instruction in bricklaying and masonry. Cover brick; mortar; tools; bonding; corners, openings, and arches; chimneys and fireplaces structural clay tile and glass block; bric walls; and much more.

Volume 1: Concrete, Block, Tile, Terrazzo
LOUIS M. DEZETTEL;
revised by TOM PHILBIN

5 1/2 x 8 1/4 Hardcover 304 pp. 190 Illu
ISBN: 0-672-23402-5 $14.95

Volume 2: Bricklaying, Plastering, Rock Masonry, Clay Tile
LOUIS M. DEZETTEL;
revised by TOM PHILBIN

5 1/2 x 8 1/4 Hardcover 384 pp. 310 Illu
ISBN: 0-672-23403-3 $14.95

WOODWORKING

Wood Furniture: Finishing, Refinishing, Repairing
(Second Edition)
JAMES E. BRU____

NEW EDITION
FOR 1992
____ 5 Illu

ully illustrated guide to repairing furniture
d finishing and refinishing wood surfaces.
vers tools and supplies; types of wood;
eering; inlaying; repairing, restoring, and
pping; wood preparation; and much more.

oodworking and
binetmaking
RICHARD BOLLER

/2 x 8 1/4   Hardcover   360 pp.   455 Illus.
3N: 0-02-512800-0 $18.95

sential information on all aspects of work-
with wood. Step-by-step procedures for
odworking projects are accompanied by
tailed drawings and photographs.

MAINTENANCE AND
REPAIR

---

ilding Maintenance
econd Edition)
JLES ORAVETZ

/2 x 8 1/4   Paperback   384 pp.   210 Illus.
3N: 0-672-23278-2 $11.95

ofessional maintenance procedures used
office, educational, and commercial build-
js. Covers painting and decorating; plumb-
and pipe fitting; concrete and masonry;
d much more.

ardening, Landscaping and
rounds Maintenance
hird Edition)
JLES ORAVETZ

1/2 x 8 1/4   Hardcover   424 pp.   340 Illus.
3N: 0-672-23417-3 $15.95

aintaining lawns and gardens as well as
dustrial, municipal, and estate grounds.

ome Maintenance and Repair:
alls, Ceilings and Floors
ARY D. BRANSON

1/2 x 11   Paperback   80 pp.   80 Illus.
3N: 0-672-23281-2 $6.95

e do-it-yourselfer's guide to interior re-
odeling with professional results.

ainting and Decorating
EX MILLER and GLEN E. BAKER

1/2 x 8 1/4   Hardcover   464 pp.   325 Illus.
3N: 0-672-23405-x $18.95

practical guide for painters, decorators,
d homeowners to the most up-to-date ma-
rials and techniques in the field.

Tree Care (Second Edition)
JOHN M. HALLER

8 1/2 x 11   Paperback   224 pp.   305 Illus.
ISBN: 0-02-062870-6 $16.95

The standard in the field. A comprehensive
guide for growers, nursery owners, foresters,
landscapers, and homeowners to planting,
nurturing, and protecting trees.

Upholstering (Updated)
JAMES E. BRUMBAUGH

5 1/2 x 8 1/4 ~~~~~~~~~~~~~~~~~ *0 Illus.*

ully explained
the professional, the ap-
the hobbyist.

AUTOMOTIVE AND
ENGINES

Diesel Engine Manual
(Fourth Edition)
PERRY O. BLACK;
revised by WILLIAM E. SCAHILL

5 1/2 x 8 1/4   Hardcover   512 pp.   255 Illus.
ISBN: 0-672-23371-1 $15.95

The principles, design, operation, and maintenance of today's diesel engines. All aspects of typical two- and four-cycle engines
are thoroughly explained and illustrated by
photographs, line drawings, and charts and
tables.

Gas Engine Manual
(Third Edition)
EDWIN P. ANDERSON;
revised by CHARLES G. FACKLAM

5 1/2 x 8 1/4   Hardcover   424 pp.   225 Illus.
ISBN: 0-8161-1707-1 $12.95

How to operate, maintain, and repair gas engines of all types and sizes. All engine parts
and step-by-step procedures are illustrated
by photographs, diagrams, and troubleshooting charts.

Small Gasoline Engines
REX MILLER and
MARK RICHARD MILLER

5 1/2 x 8 1/4   Hardcover   640 pp.   525 Illus.
ISBN: 0-672-23414-9 $16.95

Practical information for those who repair,
maintain, and overhaul two- and four-cycle
engines—including lawn mowers, edgers,
grass sweepers, snowblowers, emergency

electrical generators, outboard motors, and other equipment with engines of up to ten horsepower.

Truck Guide Library (3 Vols.)
JAMES E. BRUMBAUGH

5 1/2 x 8 1/4 Hardcover 2,144 pp. 1,715 Illus.
ISBN: 0-672-23392-4 $50.95

This three-volume set provides the most comprehensive, profusely illustrated collection of information available on truck operation and maintenance.

Volume 1: Engines
JAMES E. BRUMBAUGH

5 1/2 x 8 1/4 Hardcover 416 pp. 290 Illus.
ISBN: 0-672-23356-8 $16.95

Volume 2: Engine Auxiliary Systems
JAMES E. BRUMBAUGH

5 1/2 x 8 1/4 Hardcover 704 pp. 520 Illus.
ISBN: 0-672-23357-6 $16.95

Volume 3: Transmissions, Steering, and Brakes
JAMES E. BRUMBAUGH

5 1/2 x 8 1/4 Hardcover 1,024 pp. 905 Illus.
ISBN: 0-672-23406-8 $16.95

DRAFTING

Industrial Drafting
JOHN D. BIES

5 1/2 x 8 1/4 Hardcover 544 pp. Illus.
ISBN: 0-02-510610-4 $24.95

Professional-level introductory guide for practicing drafters, engineers, managers, and technical workers in all industries who use or prepare working drawings.

Answers on Blueprint Reading
(Fourth Edition)
ROLAND PALMQUIST;
revised by THOMAS J. MORRISEY

5 1/2 x 8 1/4 Hardcover 320 pp. 275 Ill.
ISBN: 0-8161-1704-7 $12.95

Understanding blueprints of machines a tools, electrical systems, and architectu Question and answer format.

HOBBIES

Complete Course in Stained Glass
PEPE MENDEZ

8 1/2 x 11 Paperback 80 pp. 50 Ill.
ISBN: 0-672-23287-1 $8.95

The tools, materials, and techniques of art of working with stained glass.